50% OFF Online aPHR Prep Course.

Dear Customer,

We consider it an honor and a privilege that you chose our aPHR Study Guide. As a way of showing our appreciation and to help us better serve you, we have partnered with Mometrix Test Preparation to offer you **50% off their online aPHR Prep Course**. Many aPHR courses are needlessly expensive and don't deliver enough value. With their course, you get access to the best aPHR prep material, and **you only pay half price**.

Mometrix has structured their online course to perfectly complement your printed study guide. The aPHR Prep Course contains **in-depth lessons** that cover all the most important topics, over **1,050 practice questions** to ensure you feel prepared, and more than **400 digital flashcards**, so you can study while you're on the go.

Online aPHR Prep Course

Topics Included:

- Talent Acquisition
  - Identify Staffing Needs and Guide Talent Acquisition Efforts
- Learning and Development
  - Employee Orientation
- Compensation and Benefits
  - Benefits and Insurance Programs
- Employee Relations
  - Supporting Organizational Goals and Objectives
- Compliance and Risk Management
  - Laws and Regulations

Course Features:

- aPHR Study Guide
  - Get content that complements our best-selling study guide.
- Full-Length Practice Tests
  - With over 1,050 practice questions, you can test yourself again and again.
- Mobile Friendly
  - If you need to study on the go, the course is easily accessible from your mobile device.
- aPHR Flashcards
  - Our course includes a flashcard mode with over 400 content cards to help you study.

To receive this discount, visit them at mometrix.com/university/aphr or simply scan this QR code with your smartphone. At the checkout page, enter the discount code: **APHR50TPB**

If you have any questions or concerns, please contact them at support@mometrix.com.

Sincerely,

 in partnership with

FREE Test Taking Tips Video/DVD Offer

To better serve you, we created videos covering test taking tips that we want to give you for FREE. **These videos cover world-class tips that will help you succeed on your test.**

We just ask that you send us feedback about this product. Please let us know what you thought about it—whether good, bad, or indifferent.

To get your **FREE videos**, you can use the QR code below or email freevideos@studyguideteam.com with "Free Videos" in the subject line and the following information in the body of the email:

>   a. The title of your product

>   b. Your product rating on a scale of 1-5, with 5 being the highest

>   c. Your feedback about the product

If you have any questions or concerns, please don't hesitate to contact us at info@studyguideteam.com.

Thank you!

aPHR Study Guide 2025-2026

Practice Tests and aPHR Exam Prep Book for Certification
[4th Edition]

Joshua Rueda

Written and edited by TPB Publishing.

TPB Publishing is not associated with or endorsed by any official testing organization. TPB Publishing is a publisher of unofficial educational products. All test and organization names are trademarks of their respective owners. Content in this book is included for utilitarian purposes only and does not constitute an endorsement by TPB Publishing of any particular point of view.

Interested in buying more than 10 copies of our product? Contact us about bulk discounts:
bulkorders@studyguideteam.com

ISBN 13: 9781637757574
ISBN 10: 1637757573

Table of Contents

Quick Overview -- *1*

Test-Taking Strategies --------------------------------------- *2*

Bonus Content & Audiobook Access ----------------------- *6*

FREE Videos/DVD OFFER ---------------------------------- *7*

Introduction to the aPHR Exam --------------------------- *8*

Study Prep Plan for the aPHR Exam ----------------------- *10*

Talent Acquisition --- *12*

    Practice Questions 27

    Answer Explanations 28

Learning and Development ------------------------------ *29*

    Practice Questions 43

    Answer Explanations 44

Compensation and Benefits --------------------------- *45*

    Practice Questions 72

    Answer Explanations 73

Employee Relations ------------------------------------- *74*

    Practice Questions 116

    Answer Explanations 118

Compliance and Risk Management ---------------------*119*

    Practice Questions 156

    Answer Explanations 158

Practice Test #1 --*159*

Answer Explanations #1 ----------------------------------*174*

Practice Test #2 --**186**

Answer Explanations #2 ---**203**

Practice Test #3 --**215**

Answer Explanations #3 ---**233**

aPHR Practice Tests #4-#11 -------------------------------------**245**

Quick Overview

As you draw closer to taking your exam, effective preparation becomes more and more important. Thankfully, you have this study guide to help you get ready. Use this guide to help keep your studying on track and refer to it often.

This study guide contains several key sections that will help you be successful on your exam. The guide contains tips for what you should do the night before and the day of the test. Also included are test-taking tips. Knowing the right information is not always enough. Many well-prepared test takers struggle with exams. These tips will help equip you to accurately read, assess, and answer test questions.

A large part of the guide is devoted to showing you what content to expect on the exam and to helping you better understand that content. In this guide are practice test questions so that you can see how well you have grasped the content. Then, answer explanations are provided so that you can understand why you missed certain questions.

Don't try to cram the night before you take your exam. This is not a wise strategy for a few reasons. First, your retention of the information will be low. Your time would be better used by reviewing information you already know rather than trying to learn a lot of new information. Second, you will likely become stressed as you try to gain a large amount of knowledge in a short amount of time. Third, you will be depriving yourself of sleep. So be sure to go to bed at a reasonable time the night before. Being well-rested helps you focus and remain calm.

Be sure to eat a substantial breakfast the morning of the exam. If you are taking the exam in the afternoon, be sure to have a good lunch as well. Being hungry is distracting and can make it difficult to focus. You have hopefully spent lots of time preparing for the exam. Don't let an empty stomach get in the way of success!

When travelling to the testing center, leave earlier than needed. That way, you have a buffer in case you experience any delays. This will help you remain calm and will keep you from missing your appointment time at the testing center.

Be sure to pace yourself during the exam. Don't try to rush through the exam. There is no need to risk performing poorly on the exam just so you can leave the testing center early. Allow yourself to use all the allotted time if needed.

Remain positive while taking the exam even if you feel like you are performing poorly. Thinking about the content you should have mastered will not help you perform better on the exam.

Once the exam is complete, take some time to relax. Even if you feel that you need to take the exam again, you will be well served by some down time before you begin studying again. It's often easier to convince yourself to study if you know that it will come with a reward!

Test-Taking Strategies

1. Predicting the Answer

When you feel confident in your preparation for a multiple-choice test, try predicting the answer before reading the answer choices. This is especially useful on questions that test objective factual knowledge. By predicting the answer before reading the available choices, you eliminate the possibility that you will be distracted or led astray by an incorrect answer choice. You will feel more confident in your selection if you read the question, predict the answer, and then find your prediction among the answer choices. After using this strategy, be sure to still read all of the answer choices carefully and completely. If you feel unprepared, you should not attempt to predict the answers. This would be a waste of time and an opportunity for your mind to wander in the wrong direction.

2. Reading the Whole Question

Too often, test takers scan a multiple-choice question, recognize a few familiar words, and immediately jump to the answer choices. Test authors are aware of this common impatience, and they will sometimes prey upon it. For instance, a test author might subtly turn the question into a negative, or he or she might redirect the focus of the question right at the end. The only way to avoid falling into these traps is to read the entirety of the question carefully before reading the answer choices.

3. Looking for Wrong Answers

Long and complicated multiple-choice questions can be intimidating. One way to simplify a difficult multiple-choice question is to eliminate all of the answer choices that are clearly wrong. In most sets of answers, there will be at least one selection that can be dismissed right away. If the test is administered on paper, the test taker could draw a line through it to indicate that it may be ignored; otherwise, the test taker will have to perform this operation mentally or on scratch paper. In either case, once the obviously incorrect answers have been eliminated, the remaining choices may be considered. Sometimes identifying the clearly wrong answers will give the test taker some information about the correct answer. For instance, if one of the remaining answer choices is a direct opposite of one of the eliminated answer choices, it may well be the correct answer. The opposite of obviously wrong is obviously right! Of course, this is not always the case. Some answers are obviously incorrect simply because they are irrelevant to the question being asked. Still, identifying and eliminating some incorrect answer choices is a good way to simplify a multiple-choice question.

4. Don't Overanalyze

Anxious test takers often overanalyze questions. When you are nervous, your brain will often run wild, causing you to make associations and discover clues that don't exist. If you feel that this may be a problem for you, do whatever you can to slow down during the test. Try taking a deep breath or counting to ten. As you read and consider the question, restrict yourself to the particular words used by the author. Avoid thought tangents about what the author *really* meant, or what he or she was *trying* to say. The only things that matter on a multiple-choice test are the words that are actually in the question. You must avoid reading too much into a multiple-choice question, or supposing that the writer meant something other than what he or she wrote.

5. No Need for Panic

It is wise to learn as many strategies as possible before taking a multiple-choice test, but it is likely that you will come across a few questions for which you simply don't know the answer. In this situation, avoid panicking. Because most multiple-choice tests include dozens of questions, the relative value of a single wrong answer is small. As much as possible, you should compartmentalize each question on a multiple-choice test. In other words, you should not allow your feelings about one question to affect your success on the others. When you find a question that you either don't understand or don't know how to answer, just take a deep breath and do your best. Read the entire question slowly and carefully. Try rephrasing the question a couple of different ways. Then, read all of the answer choices carefully. After eliminating obviously wrong answers, make a selection and move on to the next question.

6. Confusing Answer Choices

When working on a difficult multiple-choice question, there may be a tendency to focus on the answer choices that are the easiest to understand. Many people, whether consciously or not, gravitate to the answer choices that require the least concentration, knowledge, and memory. This is a mistake. When you come across an answer choice that is confusing, you should give it extra attention. A question might be confusing because you do not know the subject matter to which it refers. If this is the case, don't eliminate the answer before you have affirmatively settled on another. When you come across an answer choice of this type, set it aside as you look at the remaining choices. If you can confidently assert that one of the other choices is correct, you can leave the confusing answer aside. Otherwise, you will need to take a moment to try to better understand the confusing answer choice. Rephrasing is one way to tease out the sense of a confusing answer choice.

7. Your First Instinct

Many people struggle with multiple-choice tests because they overthink the questions. If you have studied sufficiently for the test, you should be prepared to trust your first instinct once you have carefully and completely read the question and all of the answer choices. There is a great deal of research suggesting that the mind can come to the correct conclusion very quickly once it has obtained all of the relevant information. At times, it may seem to you as if your intuition is working faster even than your reasoning mind. This may in fact be true. The knowledge you obtain while studying may be retrieved from your subconscious before you have a chance to work out the associations that support it. Verify your instinct by working out the reasons that it should be trusted.

8. Key Words

Many test takers struggle with multiple-choice questions because they have poor reading comprehension skills. Quickly reading and understanding a multiple-choice question requires a mixture of skill and experience. To help with this, try jotting down a few key words and phrases on a piece of scrap paper. Doing this concentrates the process of reading and forces the mind to weigh the relative importance of the question's parts. In selecting words and phrases to write down, the test taker thinks about the question more deeply and carefully. This is especially true for multiple-choice questions that are preceded by a long prompt.

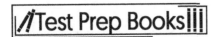
9. Subtle Negatives

One of the oldest tricks in the multiple-choice test writer's book is to subtly reverse the meaning of a question with a word like *not* or *except*. If you are not paying attention to each word in the question, you can easily be led astray by this trick. For instance, a common question format is, "Which of the following is…?" Obviously, if the question instead is, "Which of the following is not…?," then the answer will be quite different. Even worse, the test makers are aware of the potential for this mistake and will include one answer choice that would be correct if the question were not negated or reversed. A test taker who misses the reversal will find what he or she believes to be a correct answer and will be so confident that he or she will fail to reread the question and discover the original error. The only way to avoid this is to practice a wide variety of multiple-choice questions and to pay close attention to every word.

10. Reading Every Answer Choice

It may seem obvious, but you should always read every one of the answer choices! Too many test takers fall into the habit of scanning the question and assuming that they understand the question because they recognize a few key words. From there, they pick the first answer choice that answers the question they believe they have read. Test takers who read all of the answer choices might discover that one of the latter answer choices is actually *more* correct. Moreover, reading all of the answer choices can remind you of facts related to the question that can help you arrive at the correct answer. Sometimes, a misstatement or incorrect detail in one of the latter answer choices will trigger your memory of the subject and will enable you to find the right answer. Failing to read all of the answer choices is like not reading all of the items on a restaurant menu: you might miss out on the perfect choice.

11. Spot the Hedges

One of the keys to success on multiple-choice tests is paying close attention to every word. This is never truer than with words like almost, most, some, and sometimes. These words are called "hedges" because they indicate that a statement is not totally true or not true in every place and time. An absolute statement will contain no hedges, but in many subjects, the answers are not always straightforward or absolute. There are always exceptions to the rules in these subjects. For this reason, you should favor those multiple-choice questions that contain hedging language. The presence of qualifying words indicates that the author is taking special care with their words, which is certainly important when composing the right answer. After all, there are many ways to be wrong, but there is only one way to be right! For this reason, it is wise to avoid answers that are absolute when taking a multiple-choice test. An absolute answer is one that says things are either all one way or all another. They often include words like *every*, *always*, *best*, and *never*. If you are taking a multiple-choice test in a subject that doesn't lend itself to absolute answers, be on your guard if you see any of these words.

12. Long Answers

In many subject areas, the answers are not simple. As already mentioned, the right answer often requires hedges. Another common feature of the answers to a complex or subjective question are qualifying clauses, which are groups of words that subtly modify the meaning of the sentence. If the question or answer choice describes a rule to which there are exceptions or the subject matter is complicated, ambiguous, or confusing, the correct answer will require many words in order to be expressed clearly and accurately. In essence, you should not be deterred by answer choices that seem excessively long. Oftentimes, the author of the text will not be able to write the correct answer without

offering some qualifications and modifications. Your job is to read the answer choices thoroughly and completely and to select the one that most accurately and precisely answers the question.

13. Restating to Understand

Sometimes, a question on a multiple-choice test is difficult not because of what it asks but because of how it is written. If this is the case, restate the question or answer choice in different words. This process serves a couple of important purposes. First, it forces you to concentrate on the core of the question. In order to rephrase the question accurately, you have to understand it well. Rephrasing the question will concentrate your mind on the key words and ideas. Second, it will present the information to your mind in a fresh way. This process may trigger your memory and render some useful scrap of information picked up while studying.

14. True Statements

Sometimes an answer choice will be true in itself, but it does not answer the question. This is one of the main reasons why it is essential to read the question carefully and completely before proceeding to the answer choices. Too often, test takers skip ahead to the answer choices and look for true statements. Having found one of these, they are content to select it without reference to the question above. Obviously, this provides an easy way for test makers to play tricks. The savvy test taker will always read the entire question before turning to the answer choices. Then, having settled on a correct answer choice, he or she will refer to the original question and ensure that the selected answer is relevant. The mistake of choosing a correct-but-irrelevant answer choice is especially common on questions related to specific pieces of objective knowledge. A prepared test taker will have a wealth of factual knowledge at their disposal and should not be careless in its application.

15. No Patterns

One of the more dangerous ideas that circulates about multiple-choice tests is that the correct answers tend to fall into patterns. These erroneous ideas range from a belief that B and C are the most common right answers, to the idea that an unprepared test-taker should answer "A-B-A-C-A-D-A-B-A." It cannot be emphasized enough that pattern-seeking of this type is exactly the WRONG way to approach a multiple-choice test. To begin with, it is highly unlikely that the test maker will plot the correct answers according to some predetermined pattern. The questions are scrambled and delivered in a random order. Furthermore, even if the test maker was following a pattern in the assignation of correct answers, there is no reason why the test taker would know which pattern he or she was using. Any attempt to discern a pattern in the answer choices is a waste of time and a distraction from the real work of taking the test. A test taker would be much better served by extra preparation before the test than by reliance on a pattern in the answers.

Bonus Content & Audiobook Access

We host multiple bonus items online, including all 11 practice tests in digital format and this study guide in audiobook format. Scan the QR code or go to this link to access this content:

testprepbooks.com/bonus/aphr

The first time you access the tests, you will need to register as a "new user" and verify your email address.

If you have any issues, please email support@testprepbooks.com.

FREE Videos/DVD OFFER

Doing well on your exam requires both knowing the test content and understanding how to use that knowledge to do well on the test. We offer completely FREE test taking tip videos. **These videos cover world-class tips that you can use to succeed on your test.**

To get your **FREE videos**, you can use the QR code below or email freevideos@studyguideteam.com with "Free Videos" in the subject line and the following information in the body of the email:

- a. The title of your product

- b. Your product rating on a scale of 1-5, with 5 being the highest

- c. Your feedback about the product

If you have any questions or concerns, please don't hesitate to contact us at info@studyguideteam.com.

Thanks again!

Introduction to the aPHR Exam

Function of the Test

The Associate Professional in Human Resources (aPHR) is for professionals who are new to the HR career track and want to jumpstart their entrance into the HR profession. To be eligible to take the aPHR, one must have a high school diploma or the global equivalent to a high school diploma. The aPHR exam is a knowledge-based credential and is for those who wish to prove their knowledge of foundational Human Resources in a new career. As of January 31, 2018, 2,338 professionals hold the aPHR credential. There is an 85% pass rate for the aPHR.

Test Administration

Testing for the aPHR exam is offered year-round through computer-based testing at Pearson VUE testing centers. Before an exam appointment can be scheduled, test takers must complete a HRCI Application Process form at the Pearson VUE website. After the application is approved, 120 days are given to choose an exam date and location.

Those who wish to retest must wait 90 days, and they may take the exam no more than 3 times within a 365-day period. Testing accommodations are available to those who wish to make a request on the Pearson website.

Test Format

On testing day, candidates should arrive fifteen minutes early and bring a government-issued, non-expired, photo ID. All personal items will be placed in a locker, including mobile devices. There are no scheduled breaks while taking the HRCI exam, but test takers may take a break while the test is in process keeping in mind it will count against their allotted time.

The topics on the aPHR are Talent Acquisition; Learning and Development; Compensation and Benefits; Employee Relations; and Compliance and Risk Management. Below is a table with each topic and its percentage on the exam:

Topic	Percentage
Talent Acquisition	19%
Learning and Development	15%
Compensation and Benefits	17%
Employee Relations	24%
Compliance and Risk Management	25%

The aPHR is 2 hours and 15 minutes long with 100 scored multiple-choice questions and 25 pretest questions.

Scoring

Score reports are displayed at the testing center after the exam, and official score reports will be sent to test takers a couple days after the exam through the online platform. A "digital badge" is given by the HRCI as the official certificate, which can be displayed on social media or websites. Scores are reported as pass or fail, and a scaled score of at least 500 is needed in order to pass the aPHR.

Study Prep Plan for the aPHR Exam

1 **Schedule** - Use one of our study schedules below or come up with one of your own.

2 **Relax** - Test anxiety can hurt even the best students. There are many ways to reduce stress. Find the one that works best for you.

3 **Execute** - Once you have a good plan in place, be sure to stick to it.

One Week Study Schedule

Day 1	Talent Acquisition
Day 2	Training Formats and Delivery Techniques
Day 3	Employee Relations
Day 4	Compliance and Risk Management
Day 5	Practice Tests #1, #2, & #3
Day 6	Practice Tests #4, #5, & #6
Day 7	Take Your Exam!

Two Week Study Schedule

Day 1	Talent Acquisition	Day 8	Compliance and Risk Management
Day 2	Lifecycle of Hiring and Onboarding Applicants	Day 9	Laws Related to Compensation and Benefits
Day 3	Learning and Development	Day 10	Organizational Restructuring Initiatives
Day 4	Change Management Process	Day 11	Practice Tests #1 & #2
Day 5	Compensation and Benefits	Day 12	Practice Tests #3 & #4
Day 6	Employee Relations	Day 13	Practice Tests #4, #5, & #6
Day 7	Workforce Management	Day 14	Take Your Exam!

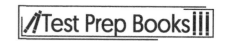

One Month Study Schedule					
Day 1	Talent Acquisition	Day 11	Employee Relations	Day 21	Laws Related to Workplace Health, Safety, Security, and Privacy
Day 2	Talent Sourcing Tools and Techniques	Day 12	Preparing HR-Related Documents	Day 22	Risk Assessment and Mitigation Techniques
Day 3	Lifecycle of Hiring and Onboarding Applicants	Day 13	Engaging Employees and Improving Employee Satisfaction	Day 23	Organizational Restructuring Initiatives
Day 4	Data Metrics	Day 14	Employee Complaints, Investigations, and Conflict Resolution	Day 24	Practice Test #1
Day 5	Learning and Development	Day 15	Diversity and Inclusion Initiatives	Day 25	Practice Test #2
Day 6	Training Formats and Delivery Techniques	Day 16	Unconscious Bias and Stereotypes	Day 26	Practice Test #3
Day 7	Change Management Process	Day 17	Compliance and Risk Management	Day 27	Practice Test #4
Day 8	Employee Development and Training	Day 18	DOL	Day 28	Practice Test #5
Day 9	Compensation and Benefits	Day 19	Laws Related to Employment in Union Environments	Day 29	Practice Test #6
Day 10	Supplemental Wellness and Fringe Benefit Programs	Day 20	Laws Related to Compensation and Benefits	Day 30	Take Your Exam!

Build your own prep plan by visiting:

testprepbooks.com/prep

Talent Acquisition

Forecasting

The two main **forecasting** methods used by companies to determine staffing needs are known as qualitative and quantitative forecasting.

Qualitative forecasting is based on the opinions and estimations of industry experts or managers. **Management forecasting** involves determining staffing needs from the managers of each department and making decisions by using their reports. **Expert forecasting** utilizes industry experts who can make decisions based on wider changes in the industry.

A specific example of expert forecasting is the **Delphi method**, where questionnaires are sent to a variety of experts, the results are shared, and then choices are updated. The objective of this method is to reach the most correct decision via consensus.

Quantitative forecasting is based on raw mathematical data and previous trends, such as employee productivity and output. Some common quantitative forecasting methods include ratio analyses, trend analyses, turnover analyses, and probability models. **Ratio analyses** compare current with past employment ratios to determine where staffing needs may change, such as the number of employees to the number of products made. **Trend analyses** compare single amounts instead of ratios, such as the number of employees. **Turnover analyses** compare the number of employees who leave the company over a certain time period with past data. Using this data, a company can utilize a **probability model** to predict future changes.

Companies need to determine whether their needs are short- or long-term when deciding which kind of method to use. Qualitative methods are usually more effective in the short term because they can manage changing staffing needs. Quantitative methods are usually more effective in the long term because staffing needs change at a steadier rate. Companies typically require both of these forecasting methods.

Job Analysis Methods and Job Descriptions

Conducting Job Analysis

A **job analysis** is a way of systematically gathering and analyzing information about the context, content, and human requirements of jobs within an organization. Typically, a member of Human Resources, an external consultant, or a manager conducts a job analysis. The following methods can be used to gather data during a job analysis to identify the knowledge, skills, and abilities that are needed to qualify an individual to perform a job effectively:

- Observations
- Interviews
- Highly structured questionnaires
- Open-ended questionnaires
- Work logs or work diaries

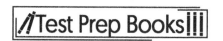
A job analysis is used to develop or create the following three items:

- **Job descriptions**: A detailed breakdown of specific tasks, skills, and knowledge required for a position. Job descriptions should communicate the type of work involved, the difficulty of the work, any unusual elements that may be required, and the frequency with which various tasks need to be performed. Job descriptions summarize the most important features of a job, include any duties that support exempt status, and also include the physical requirements of the job for consideration under the Americans with Disabilities Act (ADA).

- **Job competencies**: A detailed list of broad skills or traits needed for a position, such as leadership skills or attention to detail. Core competencies are those competencies that are aligned with key business objectives believed to contribute to organizational success.

- **Job specifications**: A detailed description of specific qualifications (i.e., professional licenses or certifications), experience, or education needed to perform the tasks. Job specifications can be included in a separate document or in a separate section of the job description, and they should reflect what is necessary for satisfactory performance in the role, instead of what specific skills the ideal candidate should possess.

Reviewing Essential Job Functions

While updating job descriptions, an employer must also be able to identify and update the essential functions for all positions.

Essential job functions are those tasks and responsibilities that are fundamental to a specific position. Each position is made up of both essential job functions and **marginal job functions** (duties that are ancillary or incidental to the nature or purpose of the job). For example, essential job functions for a hairstylist are coloring and cutting hair. A marginal job function for a hairstylist may involve answering the telephone to schedule appointments for clients.

There are three main considerations when determining if a job function is essential or marginal:

- How frequently the task is performed
- The percentage of time spent working on the task
- The importance of the task being completed

Under the Americans with Disabilities Act, for a disabled individual who is qualified, an employer may be asked to make reasonable accommodations to enable them to perform the essential (or core) job functions. Therefore, it is important for organizations to identify essential job functions in advance.

After a job analysis is performed, which results in job descriptions and job specifications, a job evaluation is conducted to determine the relative worth of each job position by creating a hierarchy. This ultimately leads to the establishment of a pay structure. There are two main job evaluation methods: non-quantitative and quantitative.

Non-Quantitative Job Evaluation Methods

Non-quantitative job evaluation methods are also known as **whole-job methods**. The three specific examples are job ranking, paired comparison, and job classification.

Job Ranking

Job ranking involves a job-to-job comparison by developing a hierarchy of jobs from the lowest to the highest, based on each job's overall importance to the organization. This is a quick, inexpensive way for small organizations to compare one job to another.

Paired Comparison

Paired comparison is a process of comparing each job to every other job for the purpose of ranking all jobs on a scale from high to low. This is also an effective, low-cost job evaluation method for small companies.

Job Classification

Job classification involves grouping jobs into a predetermined number of grades, each of which has a class description to use for job comparisons. Benchmark jobs that fall into each class can be defined as reference points. Another example of job classification put into practice is the Federal Government's use of the General Schedule classification system.

Quantitative Job Evaluation Methods

Quantitative job evaluation methods use a scaling system and provide a score that indicates how valuable one job is when compared to another job. The two specific examples are the point factor method and the factor comparison method.

Point Factor Method

The **point factor method** is less complex and most commonly used. This method uses specific, compensable factors, such as skill, responsibility, effort, working conditions, and the supervision of others, in order to evaluate the relative worth of each job. Each job receives a total point value, and then, the relative worth of all jobs within an organization can be compared.

Factor Comparison Method

The **factor comparison method** is more complex and rarely used. This method involves a ranking of each job by each selected compensable factor and then identifies dollar values for each level of each factor to develop a pay rate for an evaluated job. It is best to use this method when wages are not frequently changing, and the organization uses a flat rate of pay for each job. This method can sometimes be used as part of a labor contract.

Reporting Structure

There are many types of organizational structures, each with their own HR needs. One type is a functional structure, in which positions are grouped according to similar job roles (defined by skill, expertise, or resources) in a hierarchical chain. This type of structure separates distinct job tasks and creates a clear line of job advancement. Another example of this might be a retail store that has separate teams for sales and logistics; the sales team, for instance, is then further divided into sales associate, sales leader, and sales manager positions. Another type of organization structure is a divisional structure. This often applies to larger companies, and uses a department-based organizational style, where employees who work on similar projects are grouped together. The divisions may be separated by region, product type, or specific customer needs.

For example, an electronics company may have different divisions for producing televisions and cellphones, even though both divisions include similar jobs like electronic engineers, product marketers,

and sales representatives. A matrix structure combines elements of both functional and divisional structures. A flat structure seeks to eliminate much of the hierarchy and bureaucracy that exists in traditional companies, while a network structure outsources many key tasks to outside organizations.

Alternative Staffing Practices

Outsourcing

Outsourcing is the practice of delegating work responsibilities in a business to a separate third-party individual or organization not associated with the company.

There are three different types of outsourcing:

- Onshore: The vendor is located within the same country as the business
- Nearshore: The vendor is in a country adjacent to the business
- Offshore: The vendor is in a country far from the business

Frequently, a company will outsource when:

- The expertise needed for a specific task cannot be found within the business
- Cost-cutting is needed
- A greater focus on in-business operations is needed

Depending on an organization's needs, contracting with an external vendor to provide HR services may be necessary. Vendors can provide external support for recruitment, benefits, compensation and classification, employee relations, and systems management. Agencies may determine that external support is required only for specific needs such as recruiting for a high-level executive, conducting a point-in-time compensation review, or investigating an employee complaint. It may be necessary, though, for an agency to contract with an outside vendor to provide full cycle services that include all elements of a particular function, or even the entire HR department.

Recruitment firms can ensure that streamlined processes are established and fair practices are implemented across all hiring practices. Specialized subject matter experts in each field and position can be assigned to coordinate recruitment efforts instead of having an overall hiring specialist who has focused experience solely in recruiting. Many positions require specialized sourcing, niche marketing efforts, and even professional networking to engage prospective applicants for open employment opportunities. One such type of specialist is the benefits broker.

Some external HR providers focus on training. These providers enable an organization to determine the training needs of all employees, including all mandatory training, and then turn over the needs to the provider for a plan to implement and track. With mandatory training being established in some states, having accurate and updated information that shows employee training history is vital to ensure compliance if audited. Another example of this is in the state of California regarding sexual harassment training. All employees must attend an interactive one-hour training within six months of hire and afterward, every two years thereafter. All supervisory employees must attend an interactive two-hour training within six months of hire or promotion and afterward, every two years thereafter. Ensuring that the training meets the legal requirements and is delivered within the required timeframes is essential for an organization operating in the state of California. Contracting with a training company that specializes in this area could be a huge benefit for an organization.

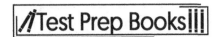

There are pros and cons to having an external provider service an organization. Costs, subject matter expertise, consistency, fair practices, and service are all elements that should be considered when reviewing this decision. Each element should be reviewed thoroughly to ensure that the best and most appropriate decision can be made. Outsourcing specific and specialized HR functions enables the department to focus on the core responsibilities that align with the organization's goals and strategies. Some projects require trained professionals that specialize in a certain program. It may be difficult to hire an HR professional with the specific experience and expertise for one specific task. It may therefore be in the best interest to contract with an external provider for this service.

Outsourcing work does have a disadvantage in that the company may find it difficult to monitor the third-party business's operations as opposed to its own employees. Additionally, there is a risk in entrusting business confidentiality to a third party not near the business at all—especially with elements such as financial information. It is also worth noting that the idea of outsourcing can decrease morale for onsite employees. They may become worried about their own job security, so it's important for employers to introduce the concept carefully.

Job Sharing

Job sharing involves two or more employees performing the tasks of a role normally performed by one person. Usually, the individuals are employed on a part-time basis. Job sharing has become more prevalent in recent times due to an evolving work culture and the development of alternative work arrangements.

Candidates looking for a work/life balance may see benefits in job sharing, even though the pay is lower and benefits are fewer. Consequently, overall productivity can increase for the business. However, it is essential for the individuals involved to have excellent communication with each other in order to succeed in a role normally designated for one person.

Phased Retirement

Phased retirement for older employees involves both the cutting back of working hours (or days of work) and the phasing in of retirement benefits such as Social Security funds. Phased retirement arrangements can take the form of part-time work, temporary or seasonal work, or job sharing.

Most commonly, these are informal agreements between an employer and an employee. A possible reason for the lack of formalized programs is the lack of legislation regarding regulations of benefits and salary coverage for potential retirees.

Phased retirement benefits employers by allowing more senior employees with years of workplace knowledge and experience to train their replacements over time.

Recruitment Sources and Methods

Recruiting refers to procedures and strategies designed to encourage and find potential, qualified candidates who seek employment. If the labor pool is unsuitable, then reaching these staffing goals is impossible, and so recruiting is essential for any organization's staffing plan.

An organization usually uses three types of recruiting: external, internal, and alternative. **External recruiting** seeks individuals from outside the organization for employment and usually emphasizes the advantages of employment with the organization, advertising benefits such as pay, insurance, leave, or employee discounts. **Internal recruiting** encourages individuals from within the organization to seek

transfers or promotions to fill vacant positions. **Alternative recruiting** seeks candidates from internships or temps to perform specific tasks for a limited period.

When a company seeks to recruit from within, some of the most common strategies to find potential candidates include internal announcements, which are made to employees before the general public; job bidding, which involves an employee expressing an interested in a position, whether it is available; and promotion plans, which detail an employee's skills and training and future positions for which they're qualified.

While most companies will recruit in the ways that are mentioned above, some may look elsewhere to find the required number of candidates. Some of these methods include:

- Passing out fliers
- Placing opportunities on online job boards
- Recruiting in professional organizations
- Finding employees through prison work programs
- Recruiting outgoing employees from a company's clients, vendors, or suppliers
- Offering sign-on bonuses to prospective employees
- Using online resume mining tools
- Participating in job fairs

The labor pool of available candidates can further be classified into three categories: active, semi-active, and passive.

Active candidates are those engaging in a search for new employment, whether they're already employed or unemployed. Most often these individuals are looking for new opportunities, concerned about their current employer's stability due to their employer's outsourcing, bankruptcy, etc. The most common method employers use to reach active candidates is through job postings. Using social media can aid in reaching the highest audience possible but can sometimes also attract many unqualified candidates. Another recruiting method involves active sourcing, which is made easier as these candidates are looking to be noticed. Again, using social media such as LinkedIn is an effective way in finding these jobseekers.

Semi-active candidates are not actively looking for work but are preparing themselves for new opportunities. These individuals most often do not have a resume prepared, and businesses looking to recruit them often allow submissions of alternatives, such as an online social media profile.

Passive candidates are employed but not looking for work. These individuals are sometimes still worth pursuing by employers, if candidates are willing to listen to a recruiter about a better career opportunity. Proactive searching is the most effective way of reaching this group, again, through avenues like social media.

A **candidate pipeline** is a set of candidates qualified to perform a certain job that have expressed interest in the company. Usually, these candidates have passed a preliminary screening, and the company maintains a positive relationship with them with regard to future employment. Candidate pipelines are an excellent recruitment tool because they ensure that there are several qualified candidates interested in filling a given position should a vacancy become available.

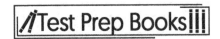

Organizational Branding

An organization communicates a unified message about its identity through **organizational branding**. Branding weaves together an organization's purpose, values, and strengths to give employees and customers a clear image of the organization's character. Effective branding is an essential part of marketing because it can build an organization's reputation and help it connect with its target market. When customers come to closely associate an organization with its unique character, organizational branding is succeeding.

Employee Referrals

Employee referrals can serve as a great tool when recruiting for positions requiring specialized skills that are difficult to fill via regular recruiting methods. Individuals who interview via employee referrals typically know what to expect regarding the work environment from their interactions with the employees who already work there, so there are fewer surprises. Employees who refer candidates usually benefit from a monetary incentive and can experience increased loyalty because they are having a "say" in the building of the workplace culture. It is important for a company not to rely solely on employee referrals to fill all open positions, to avoid creating cliques throughout the workplace. Such groups typically include individuals who are very similar to one another, which limits innovation.

Social Networking/Social Media

Social networking/media is a great tool for locating both passive and active candidates. LinkedIn, Facebook, and Twitter are the three most popular social media sites for professionals. However, other social media sites, such as Instagram and TikTok, are quickly gaining more attention. A company's social media recruiting strategy allows candidates to view job openings and gain a better understanding of the company's personality and culture. It is important for companies to designate an individual who will respond to candidates' questions and concerns in a timely manner. In addition, a company's social media efforts can be easily monitored (i.e., page likes, number of followers, etc.) to analyze what is truly working, and then adjust strategy accordingly.

Diversity Groups

Organizations are also working to recruit potential employees via various **diversity groups**, which also help to further promote their inclusion efforts. Examples include groups for African Americans, Asian Americans, Latino Americans, disability awareness, LGBTQIA (lesbian, gay, bisexual, transgender, questioning, intersex, and allies), former members of the military, multicultural professionals, and women.

Applicant Databases

An **applicant tracking system (ATS)** is a method used to make the selection process more effective by utilizing a software application to electronically process a company's recruitment needs. An applicant tracking system allows an organization to do this by sorting through large numbers of resumes that are submitted in order to find the candidates who are the best possible fit for a specific open position, based on a search for certain keywords. This allows employers to stay better organized, save time, and stay on top of the hiring process.

All institutions that receive federal contracts are required to track what is known as **applicant flow data**. This is information collected on the gender and race of all applicants who apply for open positions within an organization. The goal of collecting such data is to be able to perform an analysis of differences in selection rates among various groups for a specific position, to ensure a proper

demographic pool is being sourced for the role. This data can be collected using an Equal Employment Opportunity (EEO) information form. Employers must make a reasonable effort to obtain this information. It is important to note that any such type of information obtained is not to be used in hiring decisions. It is for Human Resources' eyes only and cannot be kept with an employee's application or personnel file. This is clearly disclosed in the application, so that the applicant is aware that the company is not basing their hiring decision on demographic information the applicant shares.

Human Resources Information Systems (HRIS)

Business technology, of which HRIS are a component, manage a great number of operations in organizations today. Business technology can refer to any software, online system, application, or other technological innovation that automates or simplifies jobs within an organization. Based on organization needs, HRIS can perform functions such as the following:

- Creating and managing online employee information systems
- Managing and updating job postings
- Updating candidate profiles over the course of the hiring process
- Managing and storing HR documents and reporting

HRIS can also store data related to the following:

- Employee productivity
- Performance
- Job satisfaction
- Benefit usage
- Historical data

This data can be analyzed through the HRIS to generate reports indicating internal trends, which can pinpoint organizational problems, needs, or successes. Due to the advent of HRIS, it is critical for business professionals to embrace new technologies and continuous learning on the job.

Skills Assessments

Skills Testing

A **skills audit** is performed for the purpose of identifying the current skills and knowledge within a company and the skills and knowledge the company will need in the future. A successful skills audit ultimately allows management to build a skills matrix that details the skills and competencies that employees need to fulfill each of their roles.

The skills audit begins by putting together a list of all the major roles within the organization, which is not necessarily every single position found on the organizational chart. Then both the technical and behavioral skills for each of these roles are listed. Surveys are created and distributed to the workforce. It is important to tell employees why they are being asked to participate in the surveys and to explain what will be done with the associated survey results. Depending on the size of the workforce, it may not make sense to survey every employee against every skill. The final steps are to compile the results (knowing what skills are required in each role and knowing what skills each employee has) and to analyze the survey data (identifying skill gaps in roles in the company, as well as determining needs for future skills).

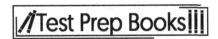
Skills Inventory

A **skills inventory** is a listing of a company's current employees' education, skills, and real-world experience, and is typically tracked in an internal database or a commercial software program. There should be a process in place to prompt employees to update their skills inventory so that it remains current, such as prior to annual review time. The skills inventory loses its value if it is not updated in a timely fashion. Managers use the skills inventory to identify gaps between the existing workforce's education, skills, and experience and what they know will be needed to meet present and future business needs. In addition, the skills inventory assists management with making decisions regarding hiring, staffing internal project teams; assigning employees to different areas; and identifying training and development opportunities for staff.

Workforce Demographic Analysis

Workforce demographics are the statistical characteristics, such as gender, income, and age that make up the human population at work. It is important for individuals working in human resource management to study and analyze trends in the labor force because this will help them recruit the specific types of talent that their organization needs. Current trends in workforce demographics include an aging population. In fact, the fastest growing employee population is those individuals in the age group of fifty-five and older. Many of these workers are interested in a phased retirement approach. This will affect organizations as they work to control the rising costs of benefits and healthcare, focus efforts to re-train older workers, and strive to attract, retain, and train younger employees.

Another current trend in workforce demographics is increased diversity in terms of gender, race, and ethnicity. In today's world, there are more women in the paid labor force than in the past, and employees that fall within the Asian and "other groups" categories are experiencing birthrates and immigration rates above the national average. This will affect organizations as they work to comply with the immigration laws and associated audits and paper trails. In addition, companies must strive to create cultures that value diversity and promote career development and advancement for women and minorities.

A third workforce demographics trend is increased skill deficiencies in the workplace. Many computers now perform routine tasks that employees used to do. Therefore, employers are looking for staff that, more often than not, hold college degrees and possess verbal, mathematical, technical, and interpersonal skills. Companies who are unable to find qualified candidates must agree to train employees on basic skills or partner with a community college or university that will offer basic courses for their staff.

Work Roles

Competent human resources (HR) personnel can do the following:

- Develop job postings that clearly and concisely explain the responsibilities required by the job
- Have the educational qualifications and knowledge skillsets that will support managing those responsibilities
- Acquire the soft skills that will ensure potential candidates will be a good fit for the role.

Not only must hired candidates be able to carry out the requirements of the job, their personal interests factor into their productivity and happiness over the long-term. HR professionals may utilize several personality assessment tools, such as the Big Five or Myers-Briggs personality assessments, to determine good fits between candidates and roles. Jobs within an organization are developed based on goals and objectives established by leadership to ensure that qualified employees perform duties that

contribute to the overall interest of the organization. Finally, HR personnel work with those in leadership roles to influence a company culture that sets the tone for how employees behave during work hours and how they interact with subordinates, lateral colleagues, and superiors.

Interviewing Techniques

An **interview** allows an employer to further evaluate a candidate's skills and knowledge while giving the candidate a chance to demonstrate their abilities.

The four most commonly used styles of interviewing are:

- Structured
- Semi-structured
- Unstructured
- Non-directive

A **structured interview** is controlled by the interviewer, who has a list of specific, job-related questions prepared prior to the start of the interview. The same questions are asked of all applicants in an effort to make comparisons between them easier. This can result in a better selection decision. A structured interview tends to be much more valid and reliable than other interview approaches.

Semi-structured interviews occur when interviewers have guided conversations with applicants that involve both broad questions and new questions that come about from the discussions that take place.

Unstructured interviews occur when interviewers improvise and ask applicants questions that were not prepared prior to the start of the interview. This can give the interviewer a chance to see how well the applicant thinks on their feet, and whether they can handle a lack of formalities or structure within a professional setting.

A **non-directive interview** utilizes open-ended questions that may be developed from an applicant's answers to previous questions. The interviewer must strive to keep the conversations job-related and to obtain comparable data from each applicant interviewing for the same position. This type of interviewing style is best used sparingly because comparing applicants is much more subjective than with the other styles.

Behavioral Interviews

The **behavioral interview** technique involves interviewers asking candidates to use specific examples to describe how they have handled a problem or performed a task in a past work situation. The thought behind this method is that past behavior is the best predictor of future job performance. Examples of behavioral-based interview questions are: "Can you tell me about a time when you had to go above and beyond the call of duty to get a job done?" and "Tell me about the last time you tackled a project that demanded a lot of initiative." Candidates can best answer these types of questions by using the STAR method, meaning they describe the past Situation or Task, explain the Action(s) they took, and describe the Results they achieved. It has been found that responses to questions about candidates' actual, past experiences tend to have high validity.

Situational Interviews

Situational interviews relate more to hypothetical situations that may take place in the future. For example, an employer may present a problem that could occur in the position for which the candidate is interviewing and ask the applicant how they might handle it. While this type of interview is useful in

determining the candidate's suitability for the position, situational interviews can neglect an applicant's past work experience.

Panel Interviews

Panel interviews are conducted by a group of individuals from the organization that may consist of managers, Human Resources representatives, and other future team members, in order to better evaluate whether a candidate is suitable. Panel interviews can help to reduce personal biases in the selection decision and are especially useful in work environments where teamwork is an important factor. This type of interview also gives candidates the opportunity to meet more people from the company and see how they interact with each other.

Diversity in Hiring

Diversity in hiring involves hiring employees with a variety of backgrounds, personalities, and working styles. Workplaces that are more diverse are associated with better financial gains and higher rates of employee retention, reported satisfaction, and performance. HR professionals can support an organizational culture that values diversity and promotes inclusion by actively recruiting talent with diverse, yet skilled, backgrounds that are otherwise underrepresented in the organization. If this talent pool is not available, HR initiatives can include internship, mentoring, or certification programs for candidates that are interested in careers offered within the organization. HR professionals must work to identify biases and be aware of how these biases affect their decision-making processes. Different metrics related to diversity (male to female, employees of color, age ranges) can be evaluated to see if an organization is incorporating diversity in hiring practices.

Reference and Background Checking

Reference checks are very important for companies during the hiring process. They can verify if an individual has the necessary skills, knowledge, and experience, based on prior job performance, while also validating an individual's application for employment.

Reference checks are also an important way for companies to protect themselves from lawsuits or damage to their reputation. For example, **negligent hiring** takes place when an employer hires an employee, and the employer either knew or should have known that the employee posed a risk to other employees or to customers. Another example of negligent hiring is when an employee who is hired as a controller at a financial institution is later charged with embezzlement. The employer (financial institution) can ultimately be found liable for failing to conduct a proper background check on the employee if this employee did have a past history of criminal activity at a previous employer.

Employers can prevent negligent hiring claims by conducting criminal background checks, verifying employment histories and college degrees, checking on past employment gaps, and reaching out to the references of potential employees. In some industries, employers can also perform drug screenings, require physicals, perform credit checks, and check driving records for specific jobs.

A **reference list** is usually provided upon request, meaning the individual provides the references after a prospective employer asks for them. There are two main types of reference checks a company would need to complete: education and employment.

Education references refer to any certifications, degrees, diplomas, licenses, or any professional documents that can validate an applicant's knowledge and education. Sometimes these reference checks provide employers with specific grades or indicators of performance, but they're mostly made to verify that education was completed.

Employment references refer to feedback from past employers, co-workers, customers, or clients who can verify the individual's professional experience. The main information sought from these reference checks are on-the-job performance feedback from previous employers, as well as the individual's position(s), wages, and duration with past companies.

Two less common reference checks are financial and driving history.

Financial reference checks relate to credit history and how an individual handles money. These are usually for positions where this would be important, such as in the banking industry, but also in the public services industry (positions in schools, hospitals, or government).

Driving history checks relate to an individual's driving record and verify that they are able to drive safely. This is necessary for positions where driving is required, including an employee's need to use rental vehicles while conducting company business.

Post-Offer Activities

Once a new employee is hired, several activities need to be completed for that individual to have a smooth transition into the organization. Some of the typical post-offer activities include:

- Perform any other necessary background checks
- Make copies of the offer letter (in some cases, this may be a counteroffer)
- Work with IT and other internal departments to prepare for the new employee's arrival (establish the workstation, create an email account, etc.)
- Prepare the new hire's packet of paperwork that they will need to complete on the first day
- Work to develop an on-boarding plan that includes a list of important people in the company that the new hire should meet
- Inform any internal applicants who were not selected for the position and provide them with feedback
- Notify any external applicants who were not selected for the role

Executing Employment Agreements

Employment-at-will is always presumed when a written employment agreement does not exist; it is a common-law doctrine that states employers have the right to hire, promote, demote, or fire whomever they choose, provided there is not a law or contract in place to the contrary. Under this doctrine, employees are also free to leave an employer whenever they choose to seek other employment.

There are two types of employment contracts (agreements): implied and express. **Implied contracts** are inferred from an employer's conduct or actions. Another example of an implied contract is when an employer promises an employee job security or hires an employee for an indefinite timeframe. An employee expectation is established, especially when the employer and the employee have enjoyed a long-term business relationship.

An **express contract** is based on an employer's written or oral words and is a formal agreement that outlines the details of the employment arrangement. In the past, these types of contracts were reserved for executive and senior management positions. Now they are also being used for technical and highly specialized employees who possess skills that are harder to come by. Finally, a **golden parachute clause**, is an agreement between an employer and an executive that guarantees the executive the right to certain benefits if their employment is terminated.

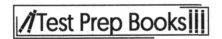
Completing I-9/E-Verify Process

Companies must be vigilant in their verification of new hires' right to work in the United States and their identities via the I-9 process within the first three days of employment. Because timeliness is of the essence, the Department of Homeland Security runs a government program to assist with this process; it is called E-Verify. At the current time, use of E-Verify is only mandatory for government contractors and subcontractors. For more information about I-9, please see the content under *Immigration Reform and Control Act (IRCA)* content of the *Compliance and Risk Management* section.

Coordinate Relocations

Many companies offer relocation benefits to assist new hires during a very stressful time in their lives. Such benefits can include any or all the following:

- Paying for temporary living expenses
- Reimbursing for moving fees
- Assisting a "trailing spouse" with their job search
- Allowing for the use of a company car
- Providing financial assistance with selling a home (or buying a new home)

Immigration

Organizations are held responsible for the verification of their new hires' credentials and identities. They must ensure that the documents presented to them (i.e., visas, passports, Social Security cards, etc.) are indeed official and are not fabricated in any way. At any time, the U.S. Immigration and Customs Enforcement (ICE) can audit a company's records to guarantee compliance with employment eligibility laws. If a company's Human Resources department is found with fraudulent documents, the company can be held liable. For more information about immigration, please see the *Immigration Reform and Control Act (IRCA)* content of the *Compliance and Risk Management* section.

On-Boarding

On-boarding, also known as **organizational socialization**, is the process by which new hires obtain the knowledge, skills, and behaviors they need in order to become valued, productive contributors to the company. The success of on-boarding programs is crucial because new employees decide whether to stay with an organization during their first six months of work. Therefore, it is important for companies to try to ensure that new employees feel supported and get adjusted to the social and performance aspects of their new roles quickly.

On-boarding can begin by having an employee's new managers and teammates reach out to them via email to welcome them even prior to their formal start date with the company. On the first day at work, the manager can introduce the new hire to the team member who will serve as their "buddy," to whom they can feel free to go to with any questions or concerns. Taking the new hire out of the office for a welcome lunch on the first day with a couple of staff members is always a nice gesture, as well as ensuring they have lunch partners for the first couple of weeks on the job.

Other aspects of successful on-boarding programs involve the new hire's manager scheduling meet-and-greet appointments to learn more about the roles that each teammate in the department plays and how the new hire will interact with them. These types of meetings can also be scheduled with individuals throughout the company who have key relationships with the department, such as members of IT, Marketing, Human Resources, etc. Additionally, providing the new hire with an on-boarding schedule that involves a variety of team members who will train on various processes and applications can be

helpful. It is also important for the manager to provide clear expectations by meeting with the new hire to discuss their performance and development plans for the first three months. Finally, to help a new hire build contacts throughout the company, it is imperative to get them involved in a cross-functional project.

There is no set time limit for on-boarding programs, but at some companies, these programs can last throughout an employee's first year.

HR Metrics

In order to understand its performance, evaluate which strategies are effective, and identify where improvement is needed, an organization must regularly analyze internal business information. Data is analyzed using **metrics** (sometimes known as key performance indicators). A metric is simply a method of measuring a particular set of data. Different metrics can be applied to different areas of an organization.

Attrition Rate
Worker attrition, or the number of workers who leave due to things like retirement or resignation, affects the workforce supply. The **attrition rate** measures employee turnover over time within an organization. This rate can indicate how well the HR team is retaining their employees. A high attrition rate usually means that employees are leaving often, and a low attrition rate shows that employees are staying longer.

Time to Hire
Time to hire refers to the amount of time between when a potential employee applies for a job and when they are hired. Knowing the current time-to-hire helps the company budget for how long it will take to recruit and onboard new employees based on the number of vacancies and available HR staff. Time to hire can be affected by the length of the hiring process, the availability of candidates both internally and externally, the type of role being fulfilled, and other related factors.

Time to Fill
Time to fill is a similar concept to time to hire but represents the time it takes for a job position to be filled. The starting point could be when an opening is advertised or when an open position is approved by HR or a manager. The number of days from the starting point to the point when someone is hired to fill that position is the time to fill.

Cost per Hire
The cost per hire is calculated by adding together the external and internal recruiting costs and dividing that amount by the total number of new hires during a specific time period. Examples of external recruiting costs include items such as: advertising the position on job boards, recruitment outsourcing, recruitment technology, background checks and drug testing, and pre-hire assessments. Examples of internal recruiting costs include such items as: in-house recruiting staff, payment of referral rewards, and internal recruiting systems.

Selection Ratios
There are several different selection ratios used to evaluate recruitment sources. For example, to find the percentage of qualified applicants, the number of qualified applicants is divided by the number of total applicants for a particular position. The percentage of minority applicants is calculated by taking the number of minority applicants divided by the total number of applicants for a position. Additionally,

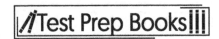

the percentage of offers accepted is the number of offers accepted divided by the number of offers that were extended.

Turnover Statistics

Turnover is typically calculated on either a monthly or an annual basis. Analyzing turnover is necessary to accurately forecast the number of new employees that are needed to replace individuals who have recently moved out of job positions. To calculate turnover, the number of separations per year is divided by the average number of individuals employed per month, multiplied by 100. For example, if fifty individuals separated during the year and there is an average of two hundred individuals employed per month, the turnover rate is:

$$\frac{50}{200} \times 100 = 25\%$$

Number of Grievances

Human resources (HR) often tracks the number and percentage of grievances received per employee. These numbers enable HR to establish a grievance rate and determine whether there are larger issues that need to be addressed. Grievance costs are also an important metric to monitor. For example, if a grievance is continually being filed because the incorrect individual is being selected to work overtime shifts, this could result in having to pay the employee(s) who should have been offered this opportunity. This could be a huge cost that the organization must absorb with nothing to show for it. In these cases, it is important to address the reason for the grievances and resolve the underlying issue.

A simple misunderstanding or inaccurate interpretation of the process may be causing the issue. Tracking the grievances based on subject matter is also important to address the root causes of problems and implement solutions that will make an impact and correct the concerns. Additionally, grievances should be tracked to show what the closing time is—when the grievance is filed and when the grievance is closed. Average close times vary, depending on the issue, and HR may want to implement target close times to improve performance. Tracking grievances can also indicate the health of the relationship between management and the labor union. Decreased grievances across the board can show there is a focus on employee relations.

Practice Questions

1. A truck driver kills a family's small child in an accident, and it is later uncovered that the truck driver lied on his employment application, had a history of unsafe driving, and had his license revoked twice. The employer was ultimately held responsible by the family's attorney for which of the following?
   a. Negligent retention
   b. Constructive discharge
   c. Negligent hiring
   d. Defamation

2. An HR team is developing a budget for a hiring campaign. The associated costs include marketing materials; a venue rental for a hiring fair; and the time, labor, and salaries of the staff who will work at the fair. What type of costs are these?
   a. Indirect costs
   b. Regulatory costs
   c. Direct costs
   d. Training costs

3. A detailed description of specific qualifications, experience, or education that is needed to perform tasks is known as which of the following?
   a. Job description
   b. Job specification
   c. Job competency
   d. Job analysis

4. A detailed list of broad skills or traits needed for a position is known as which of the following?
   a. Job analysis
   b. Job description
   c. Job competency
   d. Job specification

5. Tasks and responsibilities that are fundamental to a specific position are known as which of the following?
   a. Job competencies
   b. Marginal job functions
   c. Job specifications
   d. Essential job functions

Answer Explanations

1. C: In this example, the employer should have known that the employee posed a risk to other employees or to customers. If the employer had completed a thorough background check, they would have checked the employee's past driving record (since it was relevant to his position).

2. C: Direct costs refer to costs that are associated with a single project, its processes, and its outcomes.

3. B: Job specification is a detailed description of specific qualifications, experience, or education that is needed to perform tasks. Choice *A*, job description, is a detailed breakdown of specific tasks, skills, and knowledge required for a position. Job competency, Choice *C*, is a detailed list of broad skills or traits needed for a position. Finally, job analysis, Choice *D*, is a way of gathering and analyzing information systemically about the context, content, and human resource requirements of jobs within an organization.

4. C: Job analysis, Choice *A*, is a way of gathering and analyzing information systemically about the context, content, and human resource requirements of jobs within an organization. Job description, Choice *B*, is a detailed breakdown of specific tasks, skills, and knowledge required for a position. Finally, job specification, Choice *D*, is a detailed description of specific qualifications, experience, or education that is needed to perform tasks.

5. D: Job competencies, Choice *A*, are detailed lists of broad skills or traits needed for positions. Marginal job functions, Choice *B*, are duties that are ancillary or incidental to the nature or purpose of a job. Finally, job specifications, Choice *C*, are detailed descriptions of specific qualifications, experience, or education that is needed to perform tasks.

Learning and Development

Orientation

New employee orientation (NEO) is the first formal experience that an individual has as an employee with an organization. It is part of the administrative, transactional aspect of the overall on-boarding process, focused on having employees complete the following types of tasks within their first couple of days of employment:

- Have their photograph taken to create their corporate ID badge
- Take a tour of the building in which they will be working on a daily basis
- Complete I-9 verification
- Register for healthcare and other company benefits
- Participate in training on the company's time entry system
- Gain an understanding of the payroll process
- Review the company's history, vision, and mission, along with key policies and procedures
- Receive and sign off on a copy of their formal job description

During orientation, the organization should provide an overview of the corporate mission and vision, company history, executive management, and organizational structure. Employees should gain an understanding of where their position is located in the overall hierarchy of the organization. Additionally, separate locations should be identified and a complete directory provided.

Human resources basics should also be provided to new employees immediately upon hire. These basics include a complete tour of the corporate intranet. The **corporate intranet** is the internal website provided only to employees; it includes an employee portal for access to information such as medical information and summary plan descriptions, change forms for personal contact information and beneficiaries, policies and procedures, and important information. Some organizations incorporate the payroll portal into the corporate intranet; other organizations maintain a separate payroll portal.

During the NEO, employees should receive a full tutorial of the payroll system. This tutorial should provide training in how to submit a timecard, request leave time, and, if the employee is a supervisor, how to approve timecards and leave requests. Employees should receive an overview of the paycheck to explain compensation, deductions, and other information provided on the paystub. Employees should also know how to access leave accruals and request time off.

Employees should receive all paperwork necessary to enroll in benefits such as health insurance, life insurance, deferred compensation and retirement programs, and union membership, if needed. Employees should have a full understanding of the deadlines for returning these documents to ensure enrollments can be completed. Other items such as signing up for direct deposit, finalizing new hire paperwork such as the I-9, and taking a formal picture for the corporate directory should be conducted during the NEO.

Health and safety also constitute an area of focus that should be discussed at length to ensure that new employees are aware of and understand the organization's policies and procedures. Health and safety items such as the workers' compensation program, workplace injuries, personal medical leaves, and safety policies should be reviewed in depth. Employees should be made aware of procedures such as reporting a workplace injury, applying for a personal medical leave, understanding the safety protocols

specific to the organization and the position, and knowing evacuation plans for the location. Policies and procedures should be thoroughly reviewed, and a copy of the employee handbook should be provided. Many organizations request employees complete and sign an acknowledgement form to indicate that the handbook has been received, read, and understood. Policies and procedures such as sexual harassment, workplace violence, harassment, performance management, and other significant policies should be discussed at length during the NEO.

If the new employee is a supervisor or manager, additional time should be spent orienting the employee to this specific role. New supervisors should receive an informational report about the employees who they will be directly supervising. Standard information such as job title and duties, salary, and seniority can be provided as well. Approving timecards, leave requests, and running reports are standard job responsibilities for supervisors. Performance evaluations are also standard job responsibilities for new supervisors, as are providing an overview of the documents used, timeframes necessary for providing the evaluations, and resources available for performance management.

A new employee needs a lot of information. Therefore, an NEO best practice is to break up the information into blocks or sessions. This allows the employee to absorb the information in a more complete way and ensures a higher retention rate. The four main areas discussed above may be broken down into separate blocks, offered on multiple days or provided in one long session. It is important to note that the workspace for new hires is often set up in advance with the necessary office supplies and a welcome note or card to ensure as smooth of a transition as possible. Additionally, new employees should receive a tour of the workplace, including other locations if appropriate, introductions to the team and other employees, and a list of local resources such as local restaurants, coffee shops, post office, banks, gyms, and other amenities. If local businesses offer discounts, specials, or incentives to employees, this information should also be provided.

Some organizations provide a mentor or buddy to new employees during the NEO. The mentor is responsible for going to lunch with the new employee, meeting informally to discuss the organization and answer questions, and being a general resource and friendly face to the new employee. Depending on the working relationship between the new employee and mentor, it may be appropriate for the mentor to bring the new employee along to meetings or other events that would be helpful and informational. Depending on the size of the organization and resources available, multiple mentors may be assigned to allow for various viewpoints. Assigning a mentor from different departments such as payroll, information technology, human resources, customer service, and the hiring department can provide insight to the internal operations, lending to a more informed employee.

Finally, it is a best practice for human resources to schedule frequent NEO follow-up discussions with the new employee. Some organizations schedule these discussions for 30 days, 60 days, and 90 days following the start date. These discussions allow for specific questions that a new employee may realize were not addressed during the original NEO. New employees should be aware of the resources available through HR and the mentor assigned during NEO. If an employee has a specific question due to a certain life event or for other information, HR should be available to meet on an as-needed basis to ensure that employees have the necessary information at the time it is needed.

Instructional Design Principles and Processes

Needs Analysis
A **needs analysis** is the process in which an organization gathers information about the principal needs and requests of its members. This analysis studies the expectations and requirements of subjects who

are affected by workplace programs or regulations. Such individuals may include employers, teachers, administrators, donors, and family members of students. Needs analysis results may be used to clarify the objectives of an organization, or as a teaching tool in a classroom.

A needs analysis typically starts by gathering data. This process can be accomplished through a multitude of channels such as surveys, interviews, questionnaires, or polls. In a needs analysis, problems and inefficiencies are clearly identified. These issues are ultimately addressed by the organization through the implementation of improvements to maximize results. A needs analysis may serve as an efficient means of examining organizational procedures and techniques of training at minimal cost. Additionally, a needs analysis can be a helpful tool to develop occupational injury prevention programs within an organization.

If the needs analysis is conducted properly, the organization's next step is to implement the suggested changes in a way that promotes success. This endeavor requires the allocation of resources and personnel to the proposed plan. The proposed changes should meet the organization's productivity targets and fulfill the requirements of governmental agencies.

Process Flow Mapping

Instructional design requires analysis of the overall learning process. One way to visualize this is through process flow mapping (sometimes also called a process flowchart). **Process flow mapping** creates a visualization of the steps in a process, as well as how those steps are connected to each other, allowing planners to see the key decision areas. In instructional design, one of the most common process models is the **ADDIE model**: analysis, design, development, implementation, and evaluation. By mapping out these steps during the planning process, HR can ensure that educational programs are as effective and efficient as possible. In translating this model into a process flowchart, any individual step can be further broken into more detailed processes as needed (for example, the design stage might identify steps in research and consulting).

ADDIE Model

Each step in the multi-dimensional and adaptable ADDIE model is intended to bolster programs that bolster systems of personal development and training. The ADDIE model is not limited to strictly training programs and is widely accepted by educators, instructional designers, industry leaders, and the U.S. Armed Forces. ADDIE is noted for being highly applicable to any project and for its flexibility in practice.

The initial phase of ADDIE is **analysis** wherein the course and primary learning objectives are evaluated and determined. The trainees' potential and aptitude for the subject are assessed and determined, along with any significant learning limitations. The timeline for project completion is also determined during this initial phase.

The second phase in the ADDIE model is the **design** phase where the principal architecture of the training course is constructed. Aside from just learning objectives, relevant subject matter is gathered and determined while exercises are planned. After these are considered, a lesson plan must be carefully fashioned that synthesizes the objectives of the course and the specific abilities or constraints of the subject.

The third phase in the ADDIE model is the **development** phase. After the design of the course is constructed, its methodological efficacy needs to be tested. Creating the content that is drafted in the previous phase performs this test. Development encompasses creating and distributing tangible tools or

courseware for successfully engaging the program. For instance, graphics, handouts, or any other learning technologies would be circulated.

The fourth phase in the ADDIE model is the **implementation** phase. The implementation phase consists of establishing a procedure for training both facilitators and learners. Facilitators should continuously amend the course in order to maximize efficiency. After extensive analysis, the course should be amended and redesigned accordingly. For learners, this phase embodies preparation and gaining increasing familiarity with the course and content. In addition, learners should also develop an acute knowledge of the course materials and tools.

The fifth phase of the ADDIE model is the **evaluation** phase. Although the course is constantly being evaluated, this is a designated phase that empirically studies the efficiency and productivity of the course and material. Some of the questions that may be asked include: Were the course's primary objectives met? Were the learners' specified goals achieved? What (if any) were the most arduous aspects of the course or its materials, and how could any problems be appropriately addressed?

Training Program Facilitation, Techniques, and Delivery

There are two primary formats of training delivery: on-the-job training and off-the-job training. **On-the-job training** refers to training that is specifically done while observing or doing the actual job. This can include receiving instruction, shadowing, observing, and rotating with other employees to learn a wide variety of skills. **Off-the-job training** refers to training that occurs away from the job. This can include attending a classroom session or lecture, watching webinars or online tutorials, or attending a conference. Regardless of the format and delivery of the training, all training is important to the success of an employee achieving their individual goals and the organization achieving their strategic objectives. Regardless of the delivery format, training programs should always work to include multiple types of learning methods to ensure that employees are able to absorb, understand, and use the material provided.

In general, on-the-job training incorporates learning methods that relate directly to the work that an employee will be performing. Hands-on experience is sometimes the best training for an employee, depending on the work. On-the-job training can be used when job shadowing or cross-training employees to learn additional skills and operations.

Off-the-job training is just as important and provides learning opportunities in a different way for different topics. Learning how to function as a team, communicate better, and resolve conflicts are common topics that are best taught in a classroom setting. Additionally, training employees on policy, procedure, ethics, diversity, harassment, and other important subject matter is best taught in a focused classroom setting with a knowledgeable and interactive instructor.

When selecting the best method of training, employers should choose the method that enables employees to be completely focused on the subject they are learning. To teach an employee how to properly and safely use a drill press, on-the-job training is most likely the best option. If the training is to teach an employee how to report injuries, learn new communication techniques, or file a complaint regarding safety or harassment issues, off-the-job training is most likely the best option. In some cases, it may be beneficial to incorporate both training formats to ensure maximum success in learning the material. This type of hybrid training program may incorporate an hour of classroom training to review standards, protocols, safety procedures, and textbook operations before heading out to the field to

receive on-the-job training with the actual machinery at the worksite. Training delivery should always be selected based on the specific subject matter.

Learning Techniques

Organizations often employ several methods when attempting to teach new knowledge, capacities, or skills. A few of the principal methods instructors use to train subjects are lectures, group discussions, case studies, and demonstrations. A **lecture** is the act of an educator verbally articulating how to perform a task or a branch of knowledge. Educators plan a **group discussion** when they want students to work cooperatively. These permit students to engage collectively, verbalize key concepts, and improve aptitudes for listening and comprehension. **Case studies** give students the opportunity to situate themselves into real world, tangible scenarios. This brand of training allows students to think critically about how they would approach problem solving. A **demonstration** is a type of training that presents students with the opportunity to observe an educator in the act of performing a task.

Learning Styles

When considering a particular avenue of training, it is important to determine which will create an experience that will be conducive to learning. It is important to create in-class activities that will appeal to the various learning styles: visual, auditory, and kinesthetic. **Visual learners** prefer to associate information with images (e.g., watching videos or looking at PowerPoint slides) while **auditory learners** depend on hearing and speaking to learn (e.g., listening to lectures and participating in group discussions). **Kinesthetic learners** benefit most from participating in physical, hands-on activities (e.g., looking at the inside of an automobile or taking apart some type of model).

The most crucial objective for the educator is not to strictly possess understanding and expertise of the particular subject matter, but to also be able to articulate and impart those skills in an effective manner to others. A useful barometer for evaluating the efficacy of an instructor is to conduct a thorough evaluation of their students. If students demonstrate an aptitude for the particular knowledge, ability, or skill being taught, then one can safely assume that the faculties and techniques of the instructor can be considered proficient. Discussion, demonstration, and communication are all equally integral components of training.

Pilot Programs

For an organization to develop a large-scale project, it must launch a pilot program to test the feasibility of the intended project. Also called a feasibility study or an experimental trial, **pilot programs** are small-scale and should not be of significant cost. Before investing substantial time, financial, or human resources into a project, organizations need to determine its revenue-wielding potential, logistical considerations, and possible planning or structural deficiencies. Pilot programs are tests or trials that sample a small group of people and use empirical analyses to improve strategies.

Evaluating Training Programs

Training programs are a great way to enhance employee's knowledge, skills, and abilities related to their work efficiency and effectiveness. It is important though to ensure that the programs are evaluated to

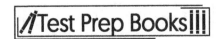

ensure they are effective, and employees are using the information and skills learned. The primary principles of training evaluations are to:

- Ensure training objectives and goals are clear and understood
- Provide specific areas for improvement, enhancement, or additional ideas for discussion
- Enable evaluation of the trainer and overall effectiveness in presenting the material
- Enable evaluation of the materials and resources provided
- Provide realistic target dates and follow up evaluations for the training information

There are numerous methods that can be used to determine the effectiveness of a training program, and each program or class should have an evaluation method that is appropriate to the training material. For example, training courses that are administered for mandatory education in topics such as corporate policy, sexual harassment legislation, or discriminatory practices may require a training evaluation that reviews employee's understanding of the material and recommendations for future courses. Training courses that teach employees how to be an effective supervisor and provide tools and resources to use in everyday situations should have evaluations that do the following:

- Assess the effectiveness of the training course immediately at the conclusion
- Assess the effectiveness of the new tools and resources 30 days after training
- Assess the effectiveness of the new tools and resources 6 months after training
- Determine which tools are being used and making a difference in the workplace

If the evaluations show that the participants are not really using the information presented in the training course, it may be useful to reassess how the participants are selected for the training program. Ensuring the participants are those who need and will use the information is vital to ensuring a successful training program. The best training programs will not be successful if the right employees are not identified to participate.

Training programs should be reviewed frequently to ensure that the material is the most recent, up-to-date information available. New learning methods are constantly being created and training courses should reflect various learning methods to ensure that all employees are engaged and involved in the learning opportunities. Individuals all learn in different ways, so it is important that instructors incorporate various learning techniques into the training programs. Asking employees to assess this during the evaluation can help determine whether the techniques were effective.

Assessing Training Program Effectiveness

A **training needs assessment** is conducted to determine whether a training program will be an adequate solution to correct a performance issue. A training program might be an appropriate solution when poor performance is due to an employee's lack of knowledge or skills, legislation requiring new knowledge or skills, higher performance standards, new technology, or placement in new jobs. On the flip side, the creation and implementation of a training program will not be effective in resolving poor performance that results from a recruiting, selection, or compensation issue, failure to provide proper coaching and feedback to an employee, problems with an employee's physical work environment, or a lack of employee motivation. These particular issues are best addressed through a non-training intervention, such as job redesign, improved communication and employee feedback, and goal-setting.

A thorough training needs assessment involves an organizational analysis, a task analysis, and a learner analysis. The **organizational analysis** is conducted to ensure that the company is on board with the

training initiative and will be supportive. The goal is to ensure that the training is aligned with the overall business strategy, supported by the necessary stakeholders, and that available resources are committed to the training program. Data is gathered for this analysis from holding focus groups of mid-level and senior-level managers, since they are the individuals who make decisions regarding training budget allocations and strategic planning. The organizational analysis is performed first, as there is no reason to move forward with the task and learner analyses if low interest or support for the training is found.

It is important to note that the task analysis and learner analysis can be completed simultaneously. The **task analysis** focuses on the specific tasks employees must complete to successfully perform their jobs. Data is gathered through interviews with or surveys of individuals, such as managers, top-performing employees, or subject matter experts (SMEs), who have direct knowledge of the work tasks and the associated, expected level of performance. The overall goal of a task analysis is to define what good performance looks like in the jobs that are chosen to be analyzed. A list of tasks that are performed in each of the jobs that are being analyzed is created. The individuals being interviewed/surveyed are asked to rate the frequency with which the tasks are completed, the importance each task has to the overall work, and the difficulty of each task. The results from this analysis are used to identify performance gaps in either desired or actual employee performance and to then decide if training can be used to address those gaps. If the decision is to move forward with a training program intervention, then the information from this analysis can also be used in the training design process.

The **learner analysis** identifies if the employees' performance issues are occurring due to a lack of knowledge, skills, and abilities, or due to some other issue, such as a lack of motivation or insufficient tools. During this analysis, it is important to determine if the learners are cognitively and physically able to complete their assigned tasks. Moreover, it is crucial to ascertain if the learners understand the level of performance that is expected of them and to determine if they are indeed receiving accurate and timely feedback regarding their performance. Additionally, the learner analysis identifies which employees need the training and determines their readiness for training. Data is gathered from managers, learners, and document reviews, such as personnel records and previous training records.

Data gathering methods that are used during a training needs assessment include: observation, questionnaires (surveys), interviews, focus groups, and document reviews. Each method has its pros and cons, and some methods may be more realistic to use than others considering time and resources constraints. It can also be helpful to collect data using multiple methods, such as using a questionnaire (survey) format that is followed by a one-on-one interview to clarify and expand upon responses.

Management personnel in some organizations do not want to take the time to conduct a formal training needs assessment. However, the information gathered during the training needs assessment will ultimately influence how a training program is designed, developed, implemented, and evaluated. Therefore, although there can be challenges associated with performing a training needs assessment, such as time constraints and lack of management support, when the proper information is not gathered, a training program may not be properly designed to address the true performance issue at hand.

Developing Organizational Learning Strategies

Change Management and Organization Development

Change management refers to an organization's ability to implement changes in a diligent and comprehensive manner. This concept of change is holistic and encompasses sweeping change of an organization. Equally important is how the changes made will affect pre-existing institutions (regulations, hierarchies). Similarly, **organization development** is a strategy of systematically planned

interventions that are employed by an organization. The primary purpose of organization development is to raise the infrastructural efficiency of bureaucracies by devising more operative processes. Change management and organization development are two concepts that focus on evaluation, implementation, and development strategies that are complementary and, in many ways, similar to one another.

How should an organization implement change? The classic 1961 text *The Planning of Change* by Warren G. Bennis tackles this question. The book outlines three strategies for managing change: the empirical-rational strategy, the normative-reductive strategy, and the power-coercive strategy.

The **empirical-rational strategy** assumes that people are rational and will naturally follow any course that's in their self-interest. Therefore, they are likelier to accept change when they think it will directly benefit them. To implement change in line with this strategy, an organization must either 1) demonstrate the benefit of the change or 2) demonstrate the harm of the status quo (or both). One way of accomplishing this is to incentivize change. For example, a growing company is gaining new employees, but it doesn't want to expand its available parking. The company decides to limit the number of parking spots and encourage public transportation use. Employees are reluctant to give up the freedom to drive, so the company holds an educational seminar about how to save money by using public transportation and also offers monthly reimbursement for employees who use public transportation.

The next approach proposed in *The Planning of Change* is the **normative-reductive strategy**. This strategy assumes that people will closely follow social norms and expectations. In order to implement change, it's necessary to first change one's idea of what is socially acceptable. This is the strategy that harnesses the power of advertising. For example, think of anti-tobacco advertising campaigns over the past few decades. Throughout most of the twentieth century, smoking was socially acceptable just about anywhere. However, especially in the 1990s and 2000s, aggressive anti-smoking advertisements attacked the tobacco industry and started anti-smoking education programs for students. The social norm turned *against* smoking in most public places, and now there are more anti-smoking laws than ever before.

Finally, the **power-coercive strategy** assumes that people are followers who will listen to authority and do as they are told. This approach to change is basically, "My way or the highway!" Where the empirical-rational strategy seeks to demonstrate how change will benefit employees, the power-coercive strategy argues that *not* following change will be *harmful* to employees, who might be punished or even fired for failure to comply. For example, a factory undergoes an intense safety inspection and decides to completely renovate its safety standards. Employees now have new dress code requirements. If they don't follow the dress code, they aren't allowed to work that day; after the third dress code violation, they will be fired.

Deciding which strategy to employ depends on the overall character of the organization as well as the importance and sensitivity of the change. For example, an otherwise friendly and collegial office might respond negatively to usage of the power-coercive strategy. The power-coercive strategy would be useful for changes with clear legal or financial liabilities, such as when an organization must follow new government regulations.

Organization Development Intervention

An **organization development intervention** outlines various strategies that an organization employs to effect a desired change. After identifying a problem, organizations target it by employing systematic and

designated institutional processes that endeavor to maximize productive potential. An organization development intervention is instrumental in analyzing, directing, and restructuring any underperforming phases in an organizational process. Within this process, there are three primary types of interventions: human process interventions, sociotechnical interventions, and techno-structural interventions.

Human process interventions are specific types of interruptions in an organization model through human interactions. Specific techniques used in human process interventions are coaching, large-group interventions, and training and development. **Coaching** typically involves working interpersonally (with a supervisor) to enhance techniques for self-management, strategy development, customizing strategies that are proximate to client needs, and meeting core objectives. **Third-party interventions** occur when an agent located outside of the organization mediates or manages disputing parties in problem solving. In order to sharpen educational capacities and skills, organizations develop **key training and development** programs. Another example is a program that will instruct employees on how to use a specific piece of machinery that is integral to performance.

A **sociotechnical intervention** is a process undertaken by organizations to maximize productivity by integrating machinery and technology into a pre-existing organizational structure. Since organizations are immensely affected by technological performance and change, it is imperative that strategies are designed to assimilate it, rather than cause institutional shock. Job rotation is one method organizations use to cope with technological change by ensuring that employees are equipped with the physical and cognitive capacities to perform a variety of disparate tasks. By delegating new tasks to meet expanding needs, job enrichment is a strategy that increases responsibilities and authority. Lastly, process improvement is an approach that investigates and alters the way a group performs specific tasks.

Techno-structural interventions represent a type of organization development intervention that focuses on how to most efficiently incorporate and use a piece of technology to maintain maximum productivity. These interventions describe a technique in which an organization redesigns and restructures by implementing more efficient methods. One of the most well-known examples of a techno-structural intervention is total quality management (TQM). **Total quality management** evaluates and changes an organization's dominant attitudes and culture if they are incongruent with the needs of customers. More precisely, styles of communication, leadership, ethical considerations, trust, training, and teamwork are examples of what total quality management reconsiders, if needed.

Maintaining Current Knowledge of PESTLE Factors

HR professionals often use the **PESTLE analysis** when working to provide recommendations to address concerns, updates, or new resolutions within an organization. When operating in a global environment, a PESTLE analysis is a vital tool that can be used to identify specific factors that can allow for a more effective and efficient organization. Comparing the information from two countries provided through the PESTLE tool can also provide insight into the gaps that an organization may have regarding policy and allow for recommendations that are supported by data. The PESTLE factors include the areas of political, economic, social, technological, legal, and environmental.

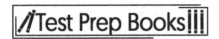

Below provides a list of example items that should be analyzed within the PESTLE tool when reviewing the global environment:

- Political: tax policy, tariffs, trade restrictions
- Economic: exchange rates, inflation rates
- Social: workforce demographics, career attitudes
- Technological: automation, research, development
- Legal: employment law, safety laws
- Environmental: climate change

Each topic above should have a policy directly related to it. Understanding how each country handles the above items and its relation to policies within an organization can help to identify necessary adjustments to policies and procedures. A gap analysis can be conducted by taking the information from two separate countries, reviewing the differences, and identifying recommended actions.

Facilitation Techniques, Instructional Methods, and Program Delivery Systems

William Edwards Deming

William Edwards Deming is one of the most discussed and influential proponents of quality control management. Deming developed fourteen core principles for improving efficiency and productivity of an organization. Among his principles, Deming emphasized a stringent dedication to constant improvement, firm and active leadership, establishing long-term relationships with suppliers and financial institutions, high levels of job security for employees in order to raise morale, and diminishing costs while increasing productive value. In addition, Deming prescribed that barriers between departments be minimal. For example, sales, production, and design must communicate without obstruction. Lastly, Deming felt it was important to encourage self-improvement, eliminate quotas, cultivate a unifying sense of pride throughout the organization, and ensure that all employees familiarize themselves with the fourteen core principles.

Joseph Moses Juran

Joseph Moses Juran was an engineer and a pioneer of quality control management. Similar to William Edwards Deming, Juran has been heralded for resuscitating Japanese industry after World War II. Juran is also responsible for applying the Pareto principle or Pareto analysis system, which is a statistical model used for decision-making in an organization, to quality management. It identifies the disproportionality between input and output. Also known as the 80-20 rule, the principle observes that 80% of output can be generated by 20 percent of the population.

For instance, if an employee managed their time effectively, 80% of their output could be produced by 20 percent of time spent actually working. In effect, 80% of the consequences are brought to fruition by 20 percent of the causes. The **Pareto analysis system** is a methodological process employed by business leaders to effectively determine their most revenue-raising technologies, workforce, and resources. After this evaluation, targeted and sustained investments will be made into the most valuable 20 percent. In order to satisfactorily identify factors that least and most heavily influence revenue, the Pareto analysis system is typically accompanied by a bar chart. Used for quality control issues, the bar chart is a thorough analysis of a company's net input and net output, used to find more efficient ways of employing scarce resources.

Juran Trilogy

According to Juran, there are three areas of quality management: quality planning, quality improvement, and quality control. These three principles are known as the **Juran Trilogy**. **Quality planning** is focused on the needs of customers—determining the customers, the principal needs of the customers, and figuring out how to develop a product that is congruent to the needs of the customers. **Quality improvement** is a process that revolves around designing a strategy that allows an organization to meet the needs of the customers. It involves creating an organizational infrastructure that serves the demands of customers. **Quality control** is the phase where the process is tested, ensuring that it can suit customer needs with minimal inspection. It is the phase that tests organizational efficiency. Intrinsic to Juran's philosophy is apt leadership, once stating, "It is most important that top management be quality-minded. In the absence of sincere manifestation of interest at the top, little will happen below."

Philip B. Crosby

In the field of quality management, **Philip B. Crosby** introduced several important ideas that remain highly consequential in organizations attempting to solve quality control issues. One of his principal ideas is "Zero Defects." **Zero Defects** is not just a program that is directed by an organization, but a philosophy of business and pedagogy. It requires one to assess the high cost of quality failures and then realize the relation to deflated revenues. If one is chronically wary of these damaging costs, they are more likely to advocate a Zero Defects philosophy, where errors are scrutinized as much as proficiencies. In conjunction with Zero Defects, Crosby advanced "doing it right the first time," or DRIFT.

DRIFT consists of four basic tenets:

- The need to conform to requirements
- The management system is responsible for preventing errors
- The standard of performance is zero defects
- The quality costs are the standard of measurement

An enduring emphasis throughout Crosby's thoughts focuses on powerful managerial operations. The four principles of DRIFT are contingent upon firm and authoritative management that establishes rules and standards. Throughout the production process, management is responsible for preventing costly glitches and backing a zero defects philosophy. Additionally, management bears responsibility for making the barometer of all decision-making subordinate to quality costs and the organizational conformation to firm requirements.

DRIFT is a system of managerial accounting that works closely with just-in-time production. **Just-in-time (JIT)** is a management technique where a business will only receive goods according to effective demand, rather than maintaining a stockpile inventory of unused supplies. For JIT to be a cost-saving program, DRIFT ensures that demand, inventory, and supply chains are congruent to business accounting expectations. If there is any error in JIT, it no longer becomes a cost-saving proposition, but rather it increases the costs of production. The stringent philosophy of DRIFT enables businesses to increase revenues, keep production costs low, and manufacture low-cost commodities.

Dr. Kaoru Ishikawa

Dr. Kaoru Ishikawa is a central figure in the rebuilding of the Japanese industrial base after the Second World War. He introduced several invaluable ideas, one of the most prominent is that production does not end after the commodity is purchased, but rather it continues to ensure maximum customer satisfaction. If a customer is not satisfied with the product, the organization must mobilize itself to

resolve the problem and create a better product. A forerunner in quality assessment, Ishikawa introduced numerous statistical analyses to improve productive processes, ranging from charts, graphs, diagrams, and algorithmic equations. Throughout his career, Ishikawa was a proponent of standardization in quality control. Standardization, according to Ishikawa, did not mean a set of rigid and unchangeable rules, but rather rules that are mutable and constantly subject to improvement.

Another one of Ishikawa's innovations is the **Fishbone**, or **Ishikawa Diagram**. The fundamental objective of the Ishikawa Diagram is to identify the principal causes of an effect of a particular problem to give an assessment of quality. Once there is a consensus on a problem (cause), a focus group can mobilize to identify all of its potential causes. These causes could range from employee performance, underperforming machinery, unsatisfactory calculations or methods, or responses to external stimuli. The Ishikawa Diagram is an efficient way of problem solving by isolating specific components and deconstructing positive or negative consequences through an investigatory lens. When a group employs an Ishikawa Diagram, it can be easily thought of as a brainstorming session, where each member offers contributions to amend and resolve current organizational processes.

Also used in quality assessment are histograms and stratification charts. Resembling a bar chart, a **histogram** incorporates bars and groups numbers into ranges. A histogram includes a horizontal distribution of data and is designed to give a visual representation of a certain distribution. For instance, if one were to calculate a histogram of the federal budget of the United States, the y-axis would measure the amount of money spent and the x-axis would parcel the different areas of spending (military, education, social programs, infrastructure, etc.). As histograms, stratification charts also use bars. However, the purpose of a stratification chart is to separate concentrated data to make identifiable patterns.

Six Sigma

Six Sigma is a methodological strategy that is used by organizations to devise more productive ways to organize processes. The principal reason for employing Six Sigma is to eliminate defects in organizational protocol that impede the ability to maximize profitability. In many instances, those people involved in the method must be highly trained in project management and statistics. The goal of organizations that incorporate Six Sigma into production is to maintain a rationally driven, scientific approach to output. As a preventive strategy, a key concept is to preclude wasteful, defective, and time-consuming policies by improving techniques.

DMAIC is the primary process that incorporates Six Sigma. An acronym, DMAIC stands for define, measure, analyze, improve, and control. The first step is to **define** problems, deficiencies, or areas of improvement. Second, **measure** means to simply measure the process performance. The third step instructs the group to **analyze** the process to ensure that it is the most effective strategy in solving the root cause of the problem. Fourth, the organization needs to **improve** process performance and gauge how successfully it targets and eliminates the root causes of defects. Finally, **control** requires that the most resourceful process be improved and salvaged for future use.

Career Development Practices

Career development encompasses six primary stages: assessment, investigation, preparation, commitment, retention, and transition. Career development is an important process when attempting to make a person attractive to prospective employers. During the assessment stage, a person begins to realize that he or she is unsure about their values, weaknesses, interests, and strengths. This stage requires a conscious effort on behalf of the person to begin an exploration process. In the investigation

phase, a person begins to search for opportunities that the world of work has to offer. After the investigation stage, a person has acquired knowledge about what best suits him or her and begins preparation. The commitment stage comes after a person recognizes their talents, prompting a commitment to a particular job or career. After a person feels most comfortable in their career, he or she begins to sharpen their skills and become acclimated with their industry—this is the retention stage. Lastly, the transition stage forces a person to assess their happiness and make connections to a new career (if necessary).

In addition to career development, there are other ways that enable a person to advance their career. Other methods include support programs, employee counseling, training workshops, and coaching programs. **Support programs**, which attempt to remedy personal and utility problems, create channels for employers to assist employees who are not maximizing their potential with training or counseling. Similarly, to support programs, employee counseling is an institutional program used by employers to maximize productivity within the organizational structure. Training workshops enable employers and employees to identify skills and ensure that they are placed in a position of maximum utility. Coaching workshops place workers under the supervision of a counselor in order to equip them with the tools to solve problems that may be inhibiting their work capacities.

In order to create an environment that allows all workers to maximize their potential in an organizational structure, employers offer programs that are designed to benefit the career development of employees. A few of these methods are evaluating, mentoring, counseling, and coaching. A proper evaluation of the deficiencies, skills, and psychological health of employees is important to identify their strengths and weaknesses, while determining their most efficient roles in the organization. Mentoring programs for employees is a critical component to making sure that they are under guardianship at a professional and emotional level. Counseling in the workplace permits employees to be given additional personal and professional support. Under the supervision of professional counselors, workshops that offer coaching to employees can bolster both organizational and personal health.

Over the course of their careers, individuals often use various methods to enrich their careers. Some of these methods include networking, pursuing supplementary formal education, and attending training workshops. Networking permits individuals to build beneficial connections with people who may be able to help them obtain employment. At networking events, an individual will attempt to speak to as many people as possible to establish relationships. When job searching, individuals may discover that many opportunities require more skills than they possess. To remedy this problem, many people pursue additional education to make them more marketable and attractive to prospective employers. Training workshops are events designated to let individuals discover their skills, allowing them to pursue careers that correspond to them.

Task Process Analysis

In order to design effective learning and development programs, HR must understand what knowledge, skills, and abilities it needs to foster, and for which essential job functions. This involves careful analysis of the task process associated with a particular position. This **task process analysis** is usually used to create detailed job descriptions, but it should be updated and audited regularly to ensure that it maintains accuracy and relevancy.

The first step is to involve current employees by having them complete a job analysis form and conducting a face-to-face interview in which they describe their essential duties and responsibilities. If they do not do so already, employees can then also fill out a log in which they account for the time spent on each task, as well as more detailed information about those tasks. Collect that information for

41

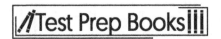

at least one week. In addition to gathering information directly from employees, directly observe employees throughout the day to see what tasks they are engaging in, and for how long. Interview supervisors, managers, and others who interact with the employee, included subordinates, team members, and customers and clients.

Based on the results of the analysis, a clearer picture of what an employee actually does in a day, what specific competencies are required, and how those tasks interact with other tasks within the organization can be formed. It is also possible to create a more detailed breakdown of individual tasks.

For example, an employee may be tasked with processing customer invoices. This involves receiving information from the sales team, calculating and recording sales information using accounting software, utilizing an invoice template to prepare documentation, sending the invoice to the customer, and filing appropriately. A task flowchart would show each individual step and decision point as well as indicate where input from others is needed. It can be used to evaluate the complexity of tasks (for example, this task involves knowledge of accounting, computer software, and customer communications) and therefore the overall complexity of a job position. It can also highlight the core competencies for a job and ensure that employees receive the training they need (for example, if the company were to adopt new accounting software, this task analysis flowchart would indicate that this employee is a high priority employee to receive new software training).

Coaching and Mentoring Techniques

To improve their leadership abilities and the performance of their companies, managers and executives may enlist a group of coaches. Different than trainers, **coaches** provide a level of self-improvement and teach leaders how to identify and solve problems. In addition, executive coaching also gives business leaders the occasion to receive crucial feedback that only outside coaches could provide. Having the opportunity to receive expert and unbiased analysis from trained professionals is advantageous to develop long-term strategies and thinking that will allow greater prosperity within a firm.

Mentoring is a specific process that involves influencing the way managers approach and think about solving problems. Specifically, it does not involve a rigid structure; it is long-term commitment on behalf of mentors and management. Mentoring is also vague and does not deal with specific accomplishments. Different kinds of problems that mentors deal with are preparing for a prospective promotion, personal growth, life transitions and adjustments, and developing an individual personally or professionally.

Creating Individual Development Plans (IDPs)

Individual Development Plans (IDPs) are a great way to engage employees directly in their career growth. IDPs enable employees to work with their supervisor and HR to discuss their current position and learning opportunities to increase their knowledge and skills specific to their current role. IDPs also enable employees to discuss future opportunities and the skills needed to achieve those opportunities and be successful. These assessments are known as **skills gap assessments**; they review the requirements for future positions and the skills and knowledge the employee lacks. These gaps can then be filled with training and learning opportunities, provided either in-house or outside.

Practice Questions

1. During new-hire orientation, Joe wants to illustrate the company culture to new employees. What are some things he could share with them to show the organization's culture?
    a. Share that employees can choose to work remotely one day per week, that leadership sits with employees in an open workspace, and that the last Friday of each month is used to celebrate an employee's personal heritage.
    b. Share that new equipment will be delivered at the end of the month, and that he will follow up with each employee on assignment.
    c. Share his personal career story, beginning from choosing a major in college.
    d. Enroll employees in a required CPR/AED course.

2. One of the six stages of career development is assessment. What occurs during this stage?
    a. The assessment stage demands that people assess their new occupation and begin working on assignments.
    b. The assessment stage requires that people begin looking for opportunities that reflect their interests and skills.
    c. The assessment stage occurs when people begin to feel a comfort and familiarity with their careers and become acclimated.
    d. Assessment is an introspective stage that requires that one be aware of their values, interests, and skills to discover a career that is most suitable.

3. Kinesthetic learning is accomplished most efficiently through which of the following?
    a. Kinesthetic learning is learning that is done by listening to lectures or group discussions.
    b. Also called spatial learning, kinesthetic learning is learning that is best done by watching videos, looking at maps, or copying notes from a blackboard.
    c. Kinesthetic learning is learning that takes place through physical touching or moving. Examples of kinesthetic learning are using building blocks or drawing.
    d. Kinesthetic learning is learning that is best done by reading text and writing down an alternate interpretation of that text.

4. What does a plateau learning curve indicate?
    a. A plateau learning curve represents initially slow learning but then a rapid acceleration.
    b. A plateau learning curve indicates quick initial learning followed by a stoppage.
    c. A plateau learning curve indicates sluggish learning, acceleration in learning activity, and then a deceleration.
    d. A plateau learning curve represents quick initial learning followed by a slowdown.

5. Which of the following statements is true regarding a learner analysis in the needs assessment process?
    a. Data is gathered from both mid-level and senior-level managers.
    b. It will ensure the company is on board with the training.
    c. It can be completed in conjunction with the task analysis.
    d. Data is gathered from individuals who have direct knowledge of the work.

Answer Explanations

1. A: These behaviors describe the attitudes, beliefs, and values that dictate the company's workdays. The other options are relevant to job duties or could be ways to connect with the employees but do not reflect the overall company culture.

2. D: Assessment is the first stage of career development. This stage asks that an individual do soul-searching. It demands that a person discover their values, interests, skills, and passions in order to find a career that is most suitable. It can be seen as a stage of self-affirmation that precedes the journey of job searching. During this stage, a person may ask: "What inspires me?" and "What is my purpose?" Assessment is unique to the other stages of career development because it is independent and exists outside of the workplace.

3. C: Kinesthetic learning can most easily be described as learning by doing. Whereas auditory learning occurs by listening, visual learning occurs through sight, and reading/writing learning occurs through interacting with text, kinesthetic learning occurs distinctly through touch and movement. Kinesthetic learners may grasp concepts more easily by physical activity, such as playing sports, laboratory exercises, drawing, charades, building, or role-play. To properly accommodate kinesthetic learners, one may use field trips, memory games, or flash cards. Studying while loud music is playing, poor penmanship and spelling, inability to sit still for long periods of time, and emphasis on breaks while studying are a few of the signs of a kinesthetic learner.

4. B: A learning curve is a graphical representation of a person's learning progress. A plateau learning curve indicates that learning takes place at an accelerated rate and then comes to a halt. Out of the four types of learning curves discussed, the plateau learning curve is unique. It is the only learning curve that indicates a stoppage in learning. A positively accelerating learning curve represents slow initial learning, but then a rapid increase. A negatively accelerating learning curve depicts an accelerated beginning followed by a slowdown. Lastly, an S-shaped learning curve denotes initial sluggishness, heightened learning activity, followed by a return to lethargy.

5. C: Data is gathered from both mid-level and senior-level managers during an organizational analysis, and the point of performing this type of analysis is to ensure that the company is on board with the training. Data is gathered from individuals who have direct knowledge of the work during a task analysis.

Compensation and Benefits

Pay Structures and Programs

Labor Market Trends

The supply pool from which employers attract new hires is called the **labor market**. Employers must identify the labor markets (i.e., geographic, global, industry-specific, educational, and technical) from which they can recruit candidates based on the jobs that need to be filled, especially for key positions.

An analysis of labor markets during workforce planning has several benefits that influence pay structures and programs, including:

- Gaining an understanding of the unemployment rate
- Identifying where employers are competing for labor
- Researching salaries paid for certain positions
- Identifying employment trends in a particular industry

The main federal institution that measures and collates nationwide employment data is the Bureau of Labor Statistics within the US Department of Labor. This department has separate state departments that also report state-specific data. Among the data collected are market activity, average salaries, basic job duties, and working conditions.

Base Pay

Base pay is fixed compensation that an employee receives in return for work that they have performed. An employee's base salary does not include any additional compensation, such as bonuses, and can be paid out in the form of an hourly wage or a salary, based on the nature of the job. Hourly wages are paid out per pay period, based on the number of hours an employee works; a salary is paid out the same amount of money each pay period, no matter how many hours an employee works.

Base pay is determined by a number of factors, such as the value of the job to the organization, an individual's knowledge, skills, and abilities, and the supply/demand of talent. An employee is often paid at a higher base pay if their job is perceived to have greater value as it has a greater impact and contribution towards an organization's strategic goals and objectives.

Additionally, an employee's base pay is often reflective of the essential duties and responsibilities associated with their position, along with the required knowledge, skills, educational background, and professional experience to perform in the role.

Finally, supply and demand of talent refers to the availability of individuals who are able to perform a specific role within the employer's geographic location. This determines how quickly the employer is able to fill an open position. For example, if an electric company is located within close proximity to a college with a reputable engineering program, then engineer talent will be readily available and will not need to be recruited at a premium base pay.

Differential and Performance-Based Pay (Merit Pay)

Even though it is not required by law under the Fair Labor Standards Act (FLSA), many employers elect to reward their employees in certain situations with compensation that is in addition to their base pay. Pay practices regarding these types of situations vary greatly among employers.

Differential pay programs are used to reward employees for performing work that is viewed as less than desirable. There are time-based and geographic differential pay programs.

- **Time-based differential pay** is allotted to employees based on when they work. For example, some employees receive additional pay, called **shift pay**, for working second or third shift or for being called in to work during an emergency, also known as **emergency shift pay**.

- **Premium pay** is sometimes paid to employees as a higher rate of overtime pay for working holidays or vacation days.

- Employees who work in a risky environment can be paid **hazard pay**.

- **Reporting pay** can be paid to employees who arrive at their place of employment and find that there is no available work for them to perform.

- **Geographic differential pay** is allotted to employees based on where they work. For example, sometimes employers have different pay structures for different locations and pay extra to attract workers to certain locales, such as remote, offshore oil rigs, and institute pay differentials for work in foreign countries.

Performance-based pay plans are used to motivate employees to perform their work at a higher level. Performance-based pay plans can be instituted at the individual, group, and organization-wide levels.

- Examples of **individual performance-based pay plans** are piece rates, commissions, and cash bonuses. These promote productivity (by 30 percent) but do not promote teamwork and may be difficult to measure.

- In **group performance-based pay plans**, an entire group is rewarded for exceeding performance standards and each person in the group receives the same amount of incentive as a percentage of their pay. Another example of a group performance-based pay plan is a gainsharing plan, where a portion of the gains an organization realizes from group effort is shared with the group. These promote teamwork but have a moderate impact on productivity (13 percent).

- **Organization-wide performance-based pay plans** are profit-sharing plans, performance-sharing plans, and stock ownership plans. These increase shareholder returns and company profits but generate only a 6 percent increase in productivity.

Pay Structure

Following the completion of job evaluations and the collection of data from salary surveys, a company works to establish an overall pay structure. A **pay structure** provides the overall framework for an organization to use to deliver its total rewards strategy. When creating a pay structure, companies establish pay grades by grouping jobs together that are found to have the same relative internal worth. Jobs within the same pay grade will pay the same rate or within the same pay range. When employers are setting pay ranges, they determine the minimum, midpoint, and maximum compensation for a pay grade and set some overlap between pay ranges.

Not every employee fits perfectly within the set pay ranges. For example, an employee who is paid a **red-circle rate** is paid at a rate above the range maximum. If this tends to be a common occurrence, it may mean that the organization's pay ranges lag the market and need to be re-examined. In contrast, an employee who is paid a **green-circle rate** is paid at a rate below the range minimum.

Broadbanding

Broadbanding occurs when employers decide to combine multiple pay levels into one, which results in only a handful of salary grades with much wider ranges. This type of pay structure is easier to administer and eliminates the green-circle and red-circle rates as described in the section above. Broadbanding also leads to a flatter organizational structure, which encourages employees' horizontal movement through skill acquisition versus the traditional vertical movement through promotions to new pay grades. Therefore, employees may feel that there are fewer promotion opportunities in a broadbanding pay structure.

Wage Compression

Wage Compression takes place when a new employee is paid at a higher wage than an individual who is currently employed in a similar position and with similar skills in an organization. Wage compression creates a pay inequity and should be avoided, if possible, as it can lead to existing employees becoming unmotivated.

Compa-ratio

A **compa-ratio** is computed by dividing the pay level of an employee by the midpoint of the salary range.

For example, in Company A, salaries in a certain position range from $12-$16 an hour, and an entry-level employee's salary is $12 an hour. The midpoint of the salary range is $14. The pay level of the employee ($12) is then divided by the midpoint of the salary range ($14), resulting in a compa-ratio of .86 or 86 percent.

Compa-ratios are used as indicators as to how wages match, lead, or lag the market. If a compa-ratio is below 100 percent, as with the example above, the employee is paid less than the midpoint of the salary range. This can be attributed to the fact that an employee is new to a job and/or an organization, is a low performer, or is working for a company that has adopted a lag-behind-the-market pay strategy.

If a compa-ratio is above 100 percent, the employee is paid more than the midpoint of the salary range. This can be attributed to the fact that an employee is long-tenured, a high performer, or is working for a company that has adopted a lead ahead of the market pay strategy.

Non-Cash Compensation

Non-monetary compensation is the category of employee benefits that do not carry tangible value. This includes flexible working schedules, company parties, a nice office, rewarding work, and a supportive work environment.

Benefit Programs

Using the EVP for Sourcing and Recruiting Applicants

Employee value proposition (EVP) refers to the overall brand that an organization provides to its workforce, both current and future. The EVP answers the question "what's in it for me?" and allows candidates and employees to have a full understanding of the total rewards that are available as an employee of the organization.

Five primary components make up the EVP:

- 1. Compensation
- 2. Benefits
- 3. Career
- 4. Work Environment
- 5. Culture

Compensation includes not only the current salary paid, but also future salary opportunities such as merit increases, bonuses, and promotions. Compensation should be managed with accuracy, timeliness, and fairness, and it should align with performance. **Benefits** include retirement programs and insurance such as medical, dental, vision, and life; however, benefits also includes paid time off, holidays, flexible work schedules, telecommuting options, educational reimbursement, and training opportunities. The **career** component refers to the ability for employees to move within the organization while progressing within their career. Career also includes stability, training, education, coaching, evaluation, and feedback. Employees should know where they stand with their supervisor and within the organization. Encouraging new opportunities to grow and develop, as well as to promote, is vital to supporting the EVP for employees. **Work environment** within the EVP includes recognizing and rewarding outstanding performance, balancing work life and home life, providing challenging and rewarding assignments, and encouraging engagement and involvement at all levels within the organization. Finally, the **culture** component of EVP encourages an understanding throughout the entire organization of the overarching goals and objectives. Culture includes the practice of values such as trust, support, teamwork, collaboration, and social responsibility.

A robust EVP will lead to a higher retention rate of current employees as well as maintain a higher employee satisfaction rate. Employees will trust the organization and its leadership while working hard to accomplish the goals established. A strong EVP will also attract highly talented candidates wanting to join the organization. This will lead to a higher number of qualified job applicants, increased candidate referrals from current employees, improved survey ratings that report the best places to work, fewer vacancies to fill, lower absenteeism rates, and ultimately, a lower cost per hire.

Employee benefits fall into two categories: discretionary and non-discretionary.

Mandatory Benefits

Mandatory benefits are those benefits that employers are mandated to provide based on certain statutes. These benefits include social security, Medicare, workers' compensation, unemployment insurance, unpaid family medical leave (based on FMLA), and continuation of healthcare coverage (based on COBRA).

Discretionary Benefits

Discretionary benefits are not mandated by law. Employers choose to provide these benefits in order to attract, motivate, and retain their workforce. Discretionary benefits fall into three main categories: health and wellness, deferred compensation, and work-life equity

- **Health and wellness benefits** include all aspects of healthcare coverage that employers offer, such as major medical plans, dental and vision plans, prescription drug coverage, addiction and substance abuse programs, employee assistance programs (EAPs), therapy resources, wellness programs, and disability/life insurance.

- **Deferred compensation** includes the various types of retirement plans that employers offer, where income is realized later as compensation for work that is performed at the present time.

- **Discretionary benefits** that fall under the category of work-life equity help employees to manage their work schedules with their personal commitments, paid time off for holidays, short-term illness, vacation, jury duty, and bereavement, along with flexible work schedules and telecommuting options. Some employers provide additional discretionary benefits that fall into this category, such as on-site childcare, tuition reimbursement, transportation stipends, and housing or relocation assistance.

Health and Welfare

Employers are moving towards consumer-directed healthcare to keep costs manageable. This simply means making employees responsible for how they spend their healthcare dollars, with the goal of smarter choices.

A direct outcome of this has been the evolution of high-deductible health plans. These plans do not pay for medical services until employees have first paid a very steep out-of-pocket amount, which can be close to a $4,150 deductible for an individual plan and a $8,300 deductible for a family plan. To help employees offset their costs, high-deductible health plans are often coupled with either a health savings account (HSA) or a health reimbursement arrangement.

- A **health savings account (HSA)** allows employees to pay for approved healthcare expenses pre-tax up to the contribution limits that are set by the IRS. Employers may also make contributions to these accounts, and any remaining balances roll over to the next calendar year, are portable, and can be used into retirement.

- A **health reimbursement arrangement (HRA)** is an employer-funded medical plan that reimburses employees only for eligible healthcare expenses. Each employee receives an employer-paid contribution that is treated as a benefit, not as compensation. Employees can roll over any unpaid funds into the next calendar year, but the funds are not portable.

Managed Care Plans

Managed care plans are healthcare plans that seek to ensure that the treatments an individual receives are medically necessary and performed in a cost-effective manner. There are several different types of managed care plans:

Health Maintenance Organization

A **health maintenance organization** (**HMO**) is structured to emphasize preventative care and cost containment. Under this plan, physicians are paid on a per-head basis, rather than for actual treatment. Employees covered under an HMO must seek treatment by physicians who are under the HMO contract.

Preferred Provider Organization

A **preferred provider organization** (**PPO**) is formed by an employer who negotiates discounted fees with networks of healthcare providers. In return, the employer guarantees a certain volume of patients. Individuals enrolled in a PPO can elect to receive treatment outside of the network, but they will pay higher copayments or deductibles for doing so.

Point-of-Service Organization

A **point-of-service organization** (**POS**) is a combination of a PPO & HMO that provides direct access to specialists.

Exclusive Provider Organization

An **exclusive provider organization** (**EPO**) is a plan in which the participants must use the providers who are in the network of coverage, or no payment will be made.

Flexible Benefit Plans

Flexible benefit plans—under section 125 of the Internal Revenue Code—allow employers and employees to save taxes on the money they pay toward their group-sponsored health and dental plans, as well as on out-of-pocket medical expenses.

Flexible Spending Accounts

Flexible spending accounts (**FSAs**) allow employees to use pretax dollars to pay for approved, out-of-pocket healthcare expenses that are not covered by insurance and dependent-care expenses. This increases employees' take-home pay while decreasing employer payroll taxes, since Social Security (FICA) payroll taxes are lowered.

Each employee determines the amount of pay to have deposited into their FSA account each month during the year. Unpaid funds cannot be rolled over into the next calendar year, so the money is commonly referred to as "use it or lose it." However, if the employee decides to leave their company prior to the end of the year before contributing the full dollar amount of a claim that was previously paid by the company, they cannot be held responsible for the remaining balance of the claim.

Full Cafeteria Plans

Full cafeteria plans—under section 125—allow employees to choose from a menu of eligible, qualified healthcare benefits and typically pay for them with pre-allocated benefit credits. Some plans permit employees to cash out any unused benefit credits or to buy additional benefits through pretax salary reductions. Full cafeteria plans allow employees to choose the benefits that are most important to them and their families.

Dental and Vision Insurance

Dental and vision insurance are additional health and wellness benefits frequently provided by employers. Dental and vision plans often stress preventive care, and it is common practice to have employees share in paying a portion of plan premiums.

Life Insurance

Life insurance is another health and wellness benefit typically provided by employers. In the event of an employee's death, the surviving family members will normally receive anywhere from one to two times the employee's annual salary as payment. Some companies allow their employees to purchase life insurance in addition to what they provide.

Disability Insurance

Disability insurance is provided by employers as a health and wellness benefit.

- **Short-term disability insurance** pays an employee a percentage of their salary—typically 50 percent to 70 percent—after a brief waiting period. This is if they are unable to work for a short period of time—normally between 10 and 26 weeks—following a non-work-related injury or illness.

- **Long-term disability insurance** takes over when an employee is still unable to return to work after being out on short-term disability. Long-term disability insurance pays an employee a percentage of their salary—typically 50 to 60 percent—until he or she can return to work or for the number of years listed in the company's policy.

Wellness

Corporate wellness programs are gaining in popularity and are used to maintain and improve employees' health before serious problems arise to offset the rising costs of healthcare. Often companies kick off these programs by having their employees participate in voluntary health risk assessments and biometric screenings, testing for such things as blood pressure, body mass index, and cholesterol/blood glucose levels.

Based on employees' individual scores, they can be referred to participate in various wellness workshops—e.g., cardiovascular disease prevention, diabetes prevention, healthy aging, nutritional counseling, or understanding back pain—and/or personalized coaching in order to bring about healthy changes. Additionally, employers may include gym memberships as part of a holistic wellness program. Employee participation in a wellness program is often tied to an incentive, such as a specific dollar amount taken off their healthcare premiums, in order to create a change in behavior. Employers directly benefit from employee participation in wellness programs through decreased absenteeism, improved productivity, and decreased spending on healthcare and workers' compensation.

Retirement

In **defined benefit plans**, employers agree to provide employees with a retirement benefit amount based on a formula. There are different approaches to this formula:

Flat-Dollar Approach

Plans using a **flat-dollar approach** pay a set dollar amount for each year of service under the plan. This is usually seen in plans covering hourly employees under a collective bargaining agreement.

Career Average

Plans utilizing a **career average** have two methods of computing their formula. In the first method, an employee earns a percentage of pay for each year they are a plan participant. In the second method, an employee's yearly earnings are totaled and then averaged over the number of years they are in the plan. At retirement, the benefit equals a percentage of the career average pay multiplied by the employee's years of service.

Final Pay Approach

Plans using a **final pay approach** base their benefits on the average earnings during a specified number of years—usually towards the end of an individual's employment.

Cash Balance Plans

Cash balance plans are a specific type of defined benefit plan. These plans express the promised benefit in terms of a hypothetical account balance. They are easily communicated to plan participants, and the accrued benefit is portable. Each year, a participant's account is credited with two types of credits:

- Pay credit: equates to a percentage of their compensation
- Interest credit: a fixed or variable rate linked to an index, such as US Treasury bills

Defined Benefit Plans

Some advantages of defined benefit plans are that the benefit is known to the employee, and the employer bears the burden of the financial risk. However, the cost is unknown. These plans tend to create higher rewards for longer-tenured employees.

Defined Contribution Plans

In **defined contribution plans**, employees and/or employers pay a specific amount into the plans for each participant. Employer contributions are often based upon a percentage of salary or a percentage of profits. Performance of the funds in these plans ultimately determines employees' benefits.

Examples of defined contribution plans are 401(k) plans, where the yearly amount employees can put into the plan is set by the IRS and adjusted annually for inflation. 403(b) plans are similar in nature and set aside for employees of certain tax-exempt organizations, such as K–12 public schools, colleges and universities, hospitals, libraries, churches, and philanthropic organizations. 457(b) plans are similar to 401(k) plans but are specifically for local and state government workers as well as employees of some nonprofit organizations. Additionally, profit-sharing plans are yet another example of this type of plan.

Some advantages of defined contribution plans are that they can provide valuable benefits to employees with less service and the cost is known. However, the benefit is unknown, and the employee bears the burden of the financial risk.

Here's a breakdown:

Characteristics Of Defined Benefit And Defined Contribution Plans Advantages		
	Defined Benefit Plan	**Defined Contribution Plan**
Employer Contributions and/or Matching Contributions	Employer funded. Federal rules set amounts that employers must contribute to plans in an effort to ensure that plans have enough money to pay benefits when due. There are penalties for failing to meet these requirements.	There is no requirement that the employer contribute, except in SIMPLE and safe harbor 401(k)s, money purchase plans, SIMPLE IRAs, and SEPs. The employer may have to contribute in certain automatic enrollment 401(k) plans. The employer may choose to match a portion of the employee's contributions or to contribute without employee contributions. In some plans, employer contributions may be in the form of employer stock.
Employee Contributions	Generally, employees do not contribute to these plans.	Many plans require the employee to contribute in order for an account to be established.
Managing the Investment	Plan officials manage the investment and the employer is responsible for ensuring that the amount it has put in the plan plus investment earnings will be enough to pay the promised benefit.	The employee often is responsible for managing the investment of his or her account, choosing from investment options offered by the plan. In some plans, plan officials are responsible for investing all the plan's assets.
Amount of Benefits Paid Upon Retirement	A promised benefit is based on a formula in the plan, often using a combination of the employee's age, years worked for the employer, and/or salary.	The benefit depends on contributions made by the employee and/or the employer, performance of the account's investments, and fees charged to the account.
Type of Retirement Benefit Payments	Traditionally, these plans pay the retiree monthly annuity payments that continue for life. Plans may offer other payment options.	The retiree may transfer the account balance into an individual retirement account (IRA) from which the retiree withdraws money, or may receive it as a lump sum payment. Some plans also offer monthly payments through an annuity.
Guarantee of Benefits	The Federal Government, through the Pension Benefit Guaranty Corporation (PBGC), guarantees some amount of benefits.	No Federal guarantee of benefits.
Leaving the Company Before Retirement Age	If an employee leaves after vesting in a benefit but before the plan's retirement age, the benefit generally stays with the plan until the employee files a claim for it at retirement. Some defined benefit plans offer early retirement options.	The employee may transfer the account balance to an individual retirement account (IRA) or, in some cases, another employer plan, where it can continue to grow based on investment earnings. The employee also may take the balance out of the plan, but will owe taxes and possibly penalties, thus reducing retirement income. Plans may cash out small accounts.

Catch-Up Contributions

Catch-up contributions are a type of annual retirement contribution for individuals 50 years of age or older at the end of a given calendar year. The purpose of catch-up contributions is to provide an opportunity for older investors to compensate for missed chances to save for retirement earlier in their careers. When elective deferrals exceed $19,500, the current limit, then they are treated as catch-up

contributions. Catch-up contributions are allowed for the following types of employer-sponsored retirement plans: 401(k), 403(b), SARSEP, and governmental 457(b). They are also permitted for Roth IRAs, which are individual retirement accounts not associated with an employer.

Any catch-up contributions made to an employer-sponsored plan must be deducted from payroll and completed before the end of the plan year. Employers are not required to match this type of contribution. According to the Internal Revenue Service (IRS), catch-up contributions can be made up to either the catch-up contribution limit or the excess of the individual's compensation over the elective deferral, whichever is less. If an employer allows catch-up contributions for one type of retirement account, then they must permit them for all types of retirement plans allowing elective deferrals that the company offers.

The amount permitted for catch-up contributions depends on the type of retirement account. A SIMPLE IRA or SIMPLE 401(k) account allows up to $3,000 in annual contributions. For 403(b) accounts, employees with at least fifteen years of service with the same eligible employer may also make catch-up contributions, even if they do not meet the age requirement. These employees can contribute the lesser of $3,000; $15,000 minus the amount of additional elective deferrals made in previous years; or $5,000 multiplied by the employee's number of years of service minus the total elective deferrals made in previous years. If an employee is 50 or older at the end of the qualifying year, then they can contribute up to $6,500 more than the elective deferral limit.

For a SARSEP, employees 50 or older may contribute up to $6,500. For 457(b) plans, special catch-up contributions must be the lesser of twice the annual limit or the basic annual limit added to the basic limit not used in earlier years. 457(b) plans also permit participation for individuals who have three years or fewer until the normal retirement age. Finally, for a Roth IRA, individuals 50 or older are allowed to contribute up to $1,000 by the tax return due date. All these amounts are subject to change because the IRS regulates retirement plan requirements based on annual cost of living adjustments.

Hardship Withdrawals

Hardship withdrawals are funds distributed from an individual's elective deferral account in the case of an immediate and heavy financial need. The amount for this type of withdrawal is limited to the amount required to fulfill the financial need and is taxed to the participant. The amount withdrawn reduces the employee's account balance permanently. Additionally, the individual must pay a 10% early withdrawal penalty if they are younger than 59 ½ years old at the time of withdrawal. Companies are not required to include hardship withdrawals in retirement plans. If they choose to do so, they must have appropriate recordkeeping systems and enough resources to gather the documentation necessary to judge hardship withdrawal requests.

The Internal Revenue Service (IRS) defines immediate and heavy financial need according to the plan criteria and relevant facts about the participant's situation. Examples of an immediate and heavy financial need include medical expenses, housing costs, educational expenses, funeral costs, or residential repairs. A circumstance may qualify as an immediate and heavy financial need even when the situation was foreseeable or knowingly taken on by the employee. However, generally, leisure purchases do not qualify. For a distribution to be considered necessary to fulfill an immediate and heavy financial need, the withdrawal must satisfy the following three IRS requirements:

- The withdrawal must not exceed the amount of the financial need, including the amount required to pay taxes on the withdrawn amount.

- The employee must have taken advantage of all other distributions available to them as well as nontaxable plan loans, including those available via other employer retirement plans.
- The employee must not be permitted to make elective deferrals to their retirement plan for six months minimum after taking the hardship withdrawal

There are often other resources available to employees to help them cover a financial need before resorting to a hardship withdrawal. These resources include but may not be limited to insurance or other reimbursements, liquidation of employee assets, employee pay, and qualified retirement plan loans. In most cases, employees must exhaust these resources before requesting a hardship withdrawal. However, they are not required to do so in cases where using the resource would increase the employee's overall need. Since the amount for a hardship withdrawal must be limited to the amount necessary to fulfill the participant's immediate and heavy financial need and it is often difficult to verify whether the employee can cover the need via other funding options, human resources professionals must accept the employee's written acknowledgement that they cannot meet the need through other sources.

Stock Purchase

Employee stock plans are another tool that companies can use to incentivize employees by making them think and behave as owners in the company. A stock option plan affords employees the opportunity to purchase a fixed number of shares of the company's stock at a fixed, or exercise price, during a certain period. Employees hope to buy the shares of the company's stock when those shares are trading at a price higher than the exercise price, which will lead to a profit.

An **employee stock ownership plan (ESOP)** is an example of a qualified defined contribution retirement plan that is a stock bonus program. ESOPs give employees significant stock ownership in their companies and allow them to benefit from any associated profitability and growth, which can motivate them to be more focused on the performance of their organizations. Although ESOPs can provide valuable benefits, the employees bear the burden of the financial risk.

Employee Assistance Programs (EAPs)

These are employer-sponsored benefit programs that are used to provide help for employees who are experiencing difficulties in the areas of anxiety, depression, marital or family relationship problems, legal issues, and financial concerns. These programs assist employees with identifying their problems with short-term interventions. For instance, employees may be referred to an expert for assistance with complex matters. Employees' use of EAPs is voluntary and confidential, and employers typically provide this service by contracting with a counseling agency.

Total Rewards Statements

Total rewards refer to the entire package that an employee receives when joining an organization. This package includes compensation, benefits, work-life programs, learning and development opportunities, and performance and recognition. Each of these components is extensive, unique, and important to the entire package. Compensation, or pay, indicates the salary that is paid for the work being performed. Compensation also includes merit increases, bonuses, cost of living adjustments, and promotion increases. Benefits include retirement programs such as deferred compensation plans known as 401(k) plans and defined contribution pension plans; insurance coverage including medical, dental, vision, and life; paid time off including vacation leave, holiday leave, and other types of leave such as maternity, paternity, and bereavement.

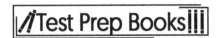

Work-life programs include items such as telecommuting options, alternate work schedules such as a 4x10 or 9x80 schedule, and wellness or employee assistance programs. Learning and development opportunities include internal training courses and educational reimbursement programs. Performance and recognition programs include service awards, contribution awards, and formal or informal recognition of achievements. Each of these components lends to the overall total rewards package that is offered to new employees. HR professionals should be fully aware of each of the elements and ensure that new employees have this information when offered a position.

Total rewards plans demand constant reevaluation to ensure that they are providing the most appropriate plan to employees—one that is in line with the organization's philosophy and comparable to those of competitor organizations. One way HR professionals can keep their total rewards plans current and competitive is by referencing total remuneration surveys, which provide market data on compensation and benefits plans from other organizations. HR professionals can use this data for benchmarking purposes when evaluating their own organization's total rewards plans, making adjustments as necessary. In addition to consulting remuneration surveys, HR professionals also need to consider the EVP, which refers to how employees perceive the value of the organization's total rewards plan and other intangible benefits from working for the organization. EVP can be assessed by conducting internal employee surveys. HR can also conduct stay interviews, or interviews with employees to determine which factors drive retention and how they can be improved. If employees know that their input is considered in the design of their total rewards plan, they may be more likely to support the project.

Total Reward Statement

In addition to more formal, organization-wide communications that may take place only a few times a year, ongoing, informal communications should be encouraged between managers and employees. To make these communications more personal, companies are distributing total reward statements to their employees to demonstrate that their pay is just one piece of the picture.

A **total reward statement** breaks down the rest of an employee's comprehensive benefits package to show them everything that goes into their total compensation, along with the company's contributions towards each of the items. The goal is to show employees an overall picture of the value and associated cost of their total compensation package.

Implementing Pay, Benefit, Incentive, Separation, and Severance Systems and Programs

Because total rewards plans represent a significant expense to any organization, they can be viewed from a return on investment (ROI) perspective—focusing on how to maximize the returns (employee satisfaction, retention, and value) from the investment (i.e., the rewards). HR professionals must ensure that plans are designed appropriately to meet the needs of employees by first assessing which benefits programs employees place the most value on as well as which benefits align with the organization's philosophy and business strategy. For example, in a sales division, annual bonuses might be aligned with employees' sales performances. Before implementing any performance-based rewards, though, the performance measures that will be appraised must first be clearly defined. In an organization that values internal advancement, an important benefit might be free employee training and educational opportunities. In designing and implementing monetary compensation rewards in particular, HR begins with a clear description of a job (its responsibilities, knowledge, and skills) and then determines the internal and external value of that position. Salary, raises, bonuses, separation, and severance pay should all be considered when designing a monetary compensation system.

External Service Providers

Benefits brokers can ensure that the best and most cost-effective benefits are offered to employees. Benefits, especially healthcare, has become an area of increased focus with specific attention to contain costs. Benefits brokers provide data and analysis to an organization that enables discussion regarding options and solutions to address the increasing costs of benefits. When an organization is considering options, such as becoming self-insured or aligning with other organizations to enhance the pool for calculating premium rates, benefits brokers can provide a different perspective.

Federal Laws and Regulations

A company's total rewards strategy is used to attract, motivate, engage, and retain employees through compensation packages made up of pay, incentives, and benefits. This rewards system should be aligned with the company's mission, strategy, and corporate culture, and it must comply with all applicable laws and regulations.

Davis Bacon Act (1931)

This piece of legislation applies to contractors and subcontractors working on federally funded or assisted contracts in excess of $2,000. The act requires employers to pay all laborers at construction sites—associated with such contracts—at least the prevailing wage and fringe benefits that individuals working in similar projects in the area are receiving. Employers who fail to comply with this act risk losing their federal contracts and the ability to receive new federal contracts for a period of up to three years.

Walsh-Healey Public Contracts Act (1936)

This federal law applies to contractors working on federally funded supply contracts in excess of $15,000. Under this act, employers associated with such contracts must pay employees at least the federal **minimum wage**—currently set at $7.25 per hour—and overtime pay. Overtime pay is calculated as one and one-half times an individual's regular rate of pay for any hours worked in excess of eight hours in a single workday or any hours worked in excess of forty hours in a single workweek.

The employment of youth under the age of sixteen and convicts is also prohibited under this legislation. Additionally, the act calls for job safety and sanitation protocols. Failure to comply with this law may result in the withholding of contract payments to reimburse any underpayment of wages or overtime pay due to employees. There is also a penalty of $32 per person per day for any employer who is found to be employing youth or convicts, along with possible additional legal action. Employers may ultimately face losing their federal contracts and the ability to receive new federal contracts for a period of up to three years for non-compliance.

Fair Labor Standards Act (1938)

The **Fair Labor Standards Act** (**FLSA**) is also known as the **Wage and Hour Law**, and it covers most governmental agencies and private-sector employers. This includes companies with employees involved in interstate commerce, employers with $500,000 or more in annual sales or business completed, and organizations caring for the physically and mentally ill, the aging population, and educational institutions. The act does not apply to employers working in industries who are covered under other labor standards that are specific to those industries. The law was put into effect to establish employee classification and to regulate minimum wage, overtime pay, on-call pay, associated recordkeeping, and child labor, as discussed in detail below.

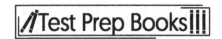

Minimum Wage

Under this act, employers must pay nonexempt employees at least the federal minimum wage. However, if the state in which an employee works pays a higher minimum wage than the current federal minimum wage, the employee will receive the higher state minimum wage. Additionally, employers must pay $2.13 per hour in direct wages to employees who receive tips as their form of salary. If the total of the employer's wage and the employee's tips is less than the minimum wage, the employer must make up the difference.

Overtime

Under this law, employers must pay nonexempt employees overtime pay at the rate of one and one-half times an individual's regular rate of pay for any hours worked in excess of forty hours of work in a single workweek. The act does not require that overtime be paid to employees for work performed on Saturdays, Sundays, or paid time-off days, such as sick days, vacation days, or holidays. Overtime pay that is earned in a specific workweek must be paid out in the pay period during which it was earned, instead of averaging overtime hours across multiple workweeks.

On-Call

Under this act, employers must pay nonexempt employees their regular rate of pay for **on-call time**—the time that they are required to remain at the employer's place of business while waiting to engage in work as required by their employer. Another example of this would be medical employees who are asked by their employer to wait to engage in work in an on-call room at a hospital. Since they are not free to leave the hospital and are expected to work if called upon, they must be compensated for their time spent on-call.

Record Keeping

Under this law, employers are required to keep specific records as defined by the Department of Labor. Regarding nonexempt employees, employers must specifically keep track of the following personal information for an employee:

- Name, address, occupation, gender, and date of birth, if employee is under the age of nineteen
- Day and time of the start of the workweek
- Total hours an employee worked during each workday and for the workweek as a whole
- Employee's daily and weekly straight-time earnings
- Employee's regular hourly rate of pay for weeks when any overtime is worked
- Total overtime pay for the workweek
- Any additions or deductions to an employee's wages
- Total wages paid to an employee during each pay period
- Date the employee received payment for work performed and the pay period that payment covered

Child Labor

This legislation also put provisions in place—commonly referred to as **child labor laws**—to ensure that working youth were guaranteed a safe workplace environment that did not pose a risk to their overall health and well-being or prevent them from pursuing additional educational opportunities.

Youth under the age of fourteen are only allowed to perform such functions as newspaper delivery, babysitting, acting, and assisting in their parents' business, if that business is non-hazardous in nature. They may also perform non-hazardous agricultural work on a farm that employs one of their parents.

Youth ages fourteen and fifteen are allowed to perform non-hazardous work, such as positions in retail, some yard work, and some kitchen and food service work. Youth in this age group are not allowed to work more than three hours a day or eighteen hours a week when school is in session. However, when school is not in session, these youth can work up to eight hours a day and up to forty hours a week.

Youth in this age group do have restricted work hours of 7:00 am to 7:00 pm during the school year. The evening time is extended to 9:00 pm during the period of June 1 through Labor Day. Youth ages sixteen and seventeen can work unlimited hours. However, youth in this age group are still prohibited from working on hazardous jobs, such as operating trash binders, shredders, or material-handling equipment.

Age	Legal Requirements
Under 14	• Children under fourteen years of age may not be employed in non-agricultural occupations covered by the FLSA, including food service establishments. Permissible employment for such children is limited to work that is exempt from the FLSA (such as delivering newspapers to the consumer and acting). Children may also perform work not covered by the FLSA such as completing minor chores around private homes or casual babysitting.
14 & 15	• 14 and 15-year-olds may be employed in restaurants and quick-service establishments outside school hours in a variety of jobs for limited periods of time and under specified conditions. Child Labor Regulations No. 3, 29 C.F.R. 570, Subpart C, limits both the time of day and number of hours this age group may be employed as well as the types of jobs they may perform. • Hours and times of day standards for the employment of 14- and 15-year-olds: • outside school hours; school hours are determined by the local public school in the area the minor is residing while employed; • no more than three hours on a school day, including Fridays; • no more than eight hours on a non-school day; • no more than eighteen hours during a week when school is in session; • no more than forty hours during a week when school is not in session; • between 7 a.m. and 7 p.m., except between June 1 and Labor Day when the evening hour is extended to 9 p.m. **Occupation standards for the employment of 14- and 15-year-olds:** • They may perform cashiering, shelf stocking, and the bagging and carrying out of customer orders. • They may perform clean-up work, including the use of vacuum cleaners and floor waxers. • They may perform limited cooking duties involving electric or gas grills that do not entail cooking over an open flame. They may also cook with deep fat fryers that are equipped with and utilize devices that automatically raise and lower

Age	Legal Requirements
	the "baskets" into and out of the hot grease of oil. They may not operate NEXCO broilers, rotisseries, pressure cookers, fryolaters, high-speed ovens, or rapid toasters.
	• They may not perform any baking activities.
	• They may not work in warehousing or load or unload goods to or from trucks or conveyors.
	• They may not operate, clean, set up, adjust, repair, or oil power driven machines including food slicers, grinders, processors, or mixers.
	• They may clean kitchen surfaces and non-power-driven equipment, and filter, transport, and dispose of cooking oil, but only when the temperature of the surface and oils do not exceed 100 degrees Fahrenheit.
	• They may not operate power-driven lawn mowers or cutters, or load or unload goods to or from trucks or conveyors.
	• They may not work in freezers or meat coolers, but they may occasionally enter a freezer momentarily to retrieve items.
	• They are prohibited from working in any of the Hazardous Orders.
16 & 17	• 16 and 17-year-olds may be employed for unlimited hours in any occupation other than those declared hazardous by the Secretary of Labor. Examples of equipment declared hazardous in food service establishments include:
	• **Power-Driven Meat and Poultry Processing Machines** (meat slicers, meat saws, patty forming machines, meat grinders, and meat choppers): commercial mixers and certain power-driven bakery machines. Employees under eighteen years of age are not permitted to operate, feed, set up, adjust, repair, or clean any of these machines or their disassembled parts.
	• **Balers and Compactors:** Minors under eighteen years of age may not load, operate, or unload balers or compactors. 16 and 17-year-olds may load, but not operate or unload, certain scrap paper balers and paper box compactors under certain specific circumstances.
	• **Motor Vehicles:** Generally, no employee under 18 years of age may drive on the job or serve as an outside helper on a motor vehicle on a public road, but seventeen-year-olds who meet certain specific requirements may drive automobiles and trucks that do not exceed 6,000 pounds gross vehicle weight for limited amounts of time as part of their job. Such minors are, however, prohibited from making time sensitive deliveries (such as pizza deliveries or other trips where time is of the essence) and from driving at night.

Age	Legal Requirements
18	• Once a youth reaches 18 years of age, he or she is no longer subject to the federal child labor provisions.

Employers who fail to comply with the FLSA may face lawsuits from both the Secretary of Labor and wronged employees for the repayment of backpay of proper minimum wages and/or overtime pay. If it is found that an employer willfully violated this law, the Department of Labor can also impose an $1,000 penalty per violation for repeated offenses.

Portal-to-Portal Act (1947)

This amendment to the Fair Labor Standards Act (FLSA) deals with the **preliminary tasks**—activities prior to the start of principal workday activities—and **postliminary tasks**—activities following the completion of principal workday activities.

- Examples of postliminary tasks include on-call or standby time, meals and breaks, travel time, and training time. The act requires employers to pay employees who are covered under the Fair Labor Standards Act for time spent traveling to perform job-related tasks if that travel is outside of the employees' regular work commute.

- Employers must also pay employees for any time they spend waiting to start work when requested to do so by their employer. Additionally, employees are to be paid for hours spent in job-related training that is outside of their normal workday.

Employers who fail to comply with this law may face consequences like those detailed above in the FLSA section.

Equal Pay Act (1963)

This law requires employers to pay equal wages to both men and women who perform equal jobs in the same establishment. The job titles need not be identical, but rather, the content of the jobs that must be equal in nature. Equivalent jobs are required to have equal skill, working conditions, effort, and responsibility defined as follows:

- Skill: The educational and professional background of the employee performing the job, combined with their ability and training

- Working conditions: The physical surroundings in which the work is performed, along with any associated hazards

- Effort: A measurement of the physical or mental exertion that an employee needs to have in order to perform their job

- Responsibility: The employee's degree of accountability in performing their job

The act does allow for pay differentials when based on other factors other than gender, such as seniority, merit, production quantities or quality, and geographic work differentials. If brought into question, the employer is faced with the burden to prove that these types of **affirmative defenses** do indeed apply.

If there is a need to correct a difference in pay, an employee cannot be penalized by having their pay reduced. Rather, the lower-paid employee's pay rate must be increased. Employers who fail to comply with this act may face up to $10,000 in fines and/or imprisonment up to six months.

Older Workers Benefit Protection Act (1990)

The **Older Workers Benefit Protection Act (OWBPA)** was passed as an amendment to the Age Discrimination in Employment Act (ADEA) of 1967. Under this act, it is illegal for employers to discriminate based on an employee's age in the provision of benefits, such as pension programs, retirement plans, or life insurance. The goal is for companies to offer equal benefits to all employees, regardless of age. However, when it can be justified by substantial cost considerations, an employer can reduce benefits to older workers.

The OWBPA also prevents older workers from waiving rights when it comes to the topic of severance agreements. An older worker is to be given twenty-one days for the purpose of consulting with an attorney and considering a severance agreement, which turns into forty-five days for group terminations. An older worker then has seven days after signing such an agreement in which they can revoke the agreement if they change their mind.

The releases associated with these agreements must reference ADEA age discrimination claims. This limits an employer's lawsuit exposure should an employee decide to challenge the criteria that was used to make decisions about which employees were retained and which employees were let go. Employers who fail to comply with this act may face both civil and criminal penalties.

Retirement Equity Act (1984)

This amendment to the Employee Retirement Income Security Act (ERISA) was passed to address concerns around the needs of divorced spouses, surviving spouses, and employees who left the workforce for some period to raise a family. Automatic survivor benefits were now required of qualified pension plans in the event of a plan participant's death, and the waiver of these benefits could only occur with the consent of both the plan participant and the participant's spouse.

Additionally, pension plans are now required to make benefit payments in accordance with a domestic relations court order to the former spouse of a plan participant. Under this act, plans were no longer allowed to consider maternity or paternity leave as a break in service for the purposes of plan participation or vesting. Employers who fail to comply with this act may face both civil and criminal penalties.

Consolidated Omnibus Budget Reconciliation Act (1986)

The Consolidated Omnibus Budget Reconciliation Act (COBRA) is an amendment to (ERISA) that allows for the continuation of healthcare coverage if such coverage would end due to certain situations, such as the termination of employment, a divorce, or the death of an employee. The act covers employers with twenty or more employees.

Under this law, employees can pay to continue group medical insurance coverage for a period of up to eighteen to thirty-six months, if they elect to do so in a timely manner and pay the full costs of coverage. They can also be charged a 2 percent administrative fee. Employers who fail to comply with this act may face both civil and criminal penalties.

Health Insurance Portability and Accountability Act (1996)

The Health Insurance Portability and Accountability Act (HIPAA) is an amendment (ERISA). It was passed to improve the continuity and portability of healthcare coverage. This act addresses pre-existing medical conditions or those for which an employee or a member of their immediate family received medical advice or treatment during the six-month period prior to their enrollment date into the employer's healthcare plan, such as a serious illness, injury, or pregnancy.

If an employee had creditable healthcare coverage—a group health plan, Medicare, or a military-sponsored healthcare plan—for a period of twelve months, with no lapse in coverage of sixty-three days or more, then an employer cannot refuse them coverage in a new group health plan due to a pre-existing medical condition and cannot charge them a higher rate for coverage. However, if an employee did not previously have creditable healthcare coverage, then an employer can exclude coverage for the treatment of a preexisting medical condition for a period of twelve months—with the exception of pregnancy—or for a period of up to eighteen months for late enrollees in the plan.

Additionally, this act only permits covered entities to use or disclose protected health information for treatment, payment, and healthcare operations. If protected health information is to be released for any other reason, written authorization is required from the patient.

Medical records related to the request for work-related accommodations under the Americans with Disabilities Act (ADA) and leaves of absences under the Family Medical Leave Act (FMLA) are not covered under this law. Employers must have a designated privacy officer who will oversee the organization's privacy policy, along with conducting all necessary training for employees. Employers who fail to comply with this act may face both civil and criminal penalties. Some criminal penalties can cost companies as much as $250,000 and up to ten years in prison.

Patient Protection and Affordable Care Act (2010)

This act—also known as Obamacare, after President Barack Obama—was phased in over a four-year period, making access to healthcare available to several million more Americans. If individuals do not have access to employer-sponsored healthcare coverage, Medicare, or Medicaid, they are now able to purchase healthcare from an insurance exchange and possibly receive a subsidy.

One of the goals of this act is to keep the overall cost of healthcare coverage down by having individuals take advantage of preventative care, such as blood pressure and cholesterol screenings, well-woman visits, and vision screening for all children. Additionally, under this act, children are now permitted to stay under the coverage of their parents' healthcare until the age of twenty-six, and individuals with preexisting medical conditions cannot be denied coverage.

Every American citizen was required to have health insurance each year or face paying an income tax surcharge, until the Trump Administration removed this surcharge in 2017. An employer mandate is still being enforced, which is a requirement that all companies employing fifty or more full-time employees provide at least 95 percent of those employees and their dependents with affordable health insurance or be subject to a per-employee fee, based on several factors.

Mental Health Parity Act (1996)

The **Mental Health Parity Act (MHPA)** was put into place to ensure that large group health plans provide coverage for mental healthcare in the same manner that they provide coverage for physical healthcare, such as surgical and medical benefits. For example, this act prevents an employer's group health plan

from placing a lower lifetime limit on mental health benefits than the plan's lifetime limit on surgical and medical benefits.

This act applies to employers with more than fifty employees, if compliance with the act will not increase the employer's cost by at least one percent. It is important to note that this act does not require large group health plans to include mental health coverage in the benefits that they offer. The law only applies to large group health plans that already include mental health benefits in their packages.

Family Medical Leave Act (1993)

The **Family Medical Leave Act (FMLA)** was passed to allow eligible employees to take up to twelve weeks of job-protected, unpaid leave during a twelve-month period for specific family and medical reasons. Employees are covered under this act if their employer has at least fifty employees—full- or part-time—working within 75 miles of a given workplace and if they have worked for their employer for at least twelve months and for a total of 1,250 hours over the past year.

FMLA covers leave for the following reasons:

- The birth of a child, adoption, or foster-care placement

- The serious health condition of a spouse, child, or parent

- The serious health condition of the employee, one requiring inpatient care or continuing treatment by a healthcare provider

- Qualifying exigency leave, or leave to address the most common issues that arise when an employee's spouse, child, or parent is on active duty or call to active-duty status—e.g., making financial and legal arrangements or arranging for alternative childcare

- Military caregiver leave or leave to care for a covered service member, such as the employee's spouse, child, parent, or their next of kin, with a serious injury or illness. Employees are to be granted up to twenty-six weeks of job-protected, unpaid leave during a twelve-month period to care for a covered service member.

Instead of taking all their leave at once, employees can choose to take FMLA leave intermittently or in blocks of time for specific, qualifying reasons as approved by their employer. One reason for doing so would be for an employee to attend medical appointments for their ongoing treatment and testing for a serious health condition.

Spouses who work for the same employer must share the amount of FMLA time they take for the birth of a child, adoption, or foster care placement or for the serious health condition of a child or parent. The total amount of leave taken by both spouses must add up to twelve weeks for the reasons stated above or twenty-six weeks for the care of a covered service member.

Employers also have the right to require employees to take unpaid FMLA leave concurrent with any relevant paid leave, such as sick time or vacation time, to which the employees are entitled under their current policies. In addition, a week containing a holiday still counts as a full week of FMLA, whether the holiday is considered to be paid time.

Employers are required to maintain an employee's group healthcare coverage while they are out on FMLA leave when the employee was covered under such a plan prior to leave. Once an employee's FMLA leave has ended, they are to be reinstated to their original job or to an equivalent job with equivalent conditions of employment, pay, and benefits.

Employers who fail to comply with the FMLA act may face both civil and criminal penalties. Also, if the Department of Labor finds that an employer did not post FMLA rights and responsibilities notices in the workplace, then a penalty of $211 can be assessed for willful failure to post.

Uniform Services Employment and Reemployment Rights Act (1994)

This law was passed to protect the employment, reemployment, and retention rights of civilian employees who serve in uniformed services, veterans, members of the reserve, and FEMA reservists deployed to major disaster sites. The act requires covered employees to provide their employers with at least thirty days' notice of their need for leave, if possible, and covers them for up to five years of unpaid leave.

Under the Fair Labor Standards Act, exempt employees must be paid their full salary while out on leave (see 29 C.F.R. §541.602), less any compensation that they receive for serving in the military (§541.603). Employees who are out on military leave are also expected to receive the same seniority-based benefits that they would have received had they not been out of work on leave, such as vacation time and 401(k) contributions.

Additionally, if an employee's military leave will be less than one month, an employer must continue healthcare coverage under the same terms as if the employee was still actively employed. After the first month of military leave, employers are not required to continue group healthcare coverage at their expense. Instead, employers can make healthcare coverage available at the employee's expense for a period of twenty-four months or the duration of their military service, whichever is less. Employers are also not allowed to count an employee's military leave as a break in service for pension plan purposes.

The act requires covered employees returning from leave to apply for reemployment within a specific timeframe following completion of their military service:

- If an employee has been out on leave less than thirty-one days, he or she must return to work on the first workday following completion of military service.

- If an employee has been out on leave between thirty-one and 180 days, he or she must apply for reemployment within fourteen days of completing military service.

- If an employee's leave has been in excess of 180 days, he or she must apply for reemployment within ninety days of completing military service.

An employee returning from military leave is to be reinstated to a position that he or she would have been in if not out of work on leave, which may require some retraining efforts on the part of the employer. If after some time and retraining efforts, the employee is found not to be qualified for the new position, the employee can return to the position that he or she held prior to military leave.

Under this act, employers are also encouraged to make reasonable efforts to accommodate disabled veterans returning from military leave. Such individuals have up to two years after completing their military service to apply for reemployment.

Employers who fail to comply with USERRA may face both civil and criminal penalties, ultimately repaying any wronged employees for backpay and lost benefits.

Old Age, Survivor, and Disability Insurance (OASDI) Program

The **Social Security Act (SSA)** of 1935 designed this program to ensure a continuation of income for individuals who are retired, spouses, and dependent children of employees who are deceased, and individuals who qualify for social security disability. This OASDI program is funded by contributions made by both employees and employers.

To be eligible for most programs, employees must work at least forty quarters or ten years to qualify for this program. The work requirements for disability benefits are based on the age at which the disability occurs. The maximum work required is 40 quarters, with the minimum being 6. A surviving spouse or dependent child's eligibility is determined by the length of time the spouse or parent has worked. The amount of benefits paid out to individuals who qualify is dependent upon the length of time the employee worked and the amount they paid into the program.

Most payments under this program are made in the category of Old-Age benefits. Individuals who qualify must be at least 62 years of age to receive partial benefits and between 65 and 67 years of age to receive full benefits, depending on the year they were born. In most cases, a non-working spouse can expect to receive half of the amount of benefits of the working spouse.

Individuals who qualify for Social Security disability and receive benefits under this program must prove that they are unable to perform profitable work because they are totally disabled.

Federal-State Unemployment Insurance Program

Unemployment Insurance was created under the Social Security Act (SSA) of 1935 to provide partial income replacement for a period of time to individuals who find themselves unemployed involuntarily. This benefit is funded primarily by employers—via a state unemployment tax—and administered by the individual states under national guidelines.

The number of weeks for which an employee can receive unemployment benefits can range from one to 39 weeks, with 26 weeks being the most common duration. During some periods of high unemployment, the period of 26 weeks can be extended up to an additional 13 weeks.

Eligibility in most states is contingent upon an employee having worked a minimum number of weeks, not being terminated for misconduct, not having left their job voluntarily, not finding him or herself unemployed due to a labor dispute, being available and actively seeking work, and not refusing suitable employment.

Medicare (1965)

This program is an amendment to the Social Security Act (SSA) of 1935 with the purpose of providing healthcare for individuals aged 65 and older, which are not dependent on their income or ability to pay. Some individuals under the age of 65 who are disabled, as well as those individuals suffering from end-stage renal disease, are also eligible for coverage under Medicare. The program is funded by employees and employers paying a percentage of salaries.

Medicare has four distinct parts:

- **Medicare Part A** is hospital insurance, which is considered mandatory, and most individuals do not have to pay for this coverage.

- **Medicare Part B** is medical insurance and covers such healthcare expenses as physicians' services and outpatient care. Medicare Part B is optional, and most individuals pay a monthly fee to have this coverage.

- **Medicare Part C** is referred to as Medicare Advantage Plans, such as HMOs or PPOs that are offered by private companies and approved by Medicare. The Medicare Advantage Plans are available to individuals who are entitled to Medicare Part A and enrolled in Medicare Part B. These plans provide participants with hospital and medical coverage, as well as with additional coverage, such as dental, vision, and hearing, and, in some cases, prescription drug coverage. Medicare Advantage Plans can provide substantial cost savings for individuals who are eligible to enroll in them once a year, during an open enrollment period.

- **Medicare Part D** is prescription drug coverage and is considered optional. Individuals who choose Part D pay a monthly fee to have this coverage. Part D is available to individuals who are entitled to Medicare Part A and enrolled in Medicare Part B.

Government-Mandated, Government-Provided, and Voluntary Benefit Approaches

Compensation and benefits can be an essential element in retaining employees and attracting new candidates. Retaining current employees avoids the additional time and costs associated with training a new candidate altogether, as well as the risk of losing any clients or customers the individual may take along when they exit the organization.

Competitive salary and wages can be important in recruiting and retaining staff. However, unless the difference in salary is significant, it is usually not a factor—especially if the overall compensation package value is comparable. A lower take-home pay paired with a wider selection of healthcare and retirement plans may allow a company to offer a better long-term financial plan to its workers. Bonuses are yet another technique for employers to compensate and reward worthy employees.

Benefits can also assist in retention while saving the company money. Voluntary benefits help employees save money by utilizing group discounts with no added cost to the business. Retention of employees is possible with benefits such as health insurance because many employees would not be able to afford having medical insurance if they exited their companies.

Payroll Processes

Payroll is responsible for numerous processes that occur on various schedules and at different times throughout the year. Running the standard paycheck cycle is a regular and frequent process that is done according to the organization's pay schedule. Whether weekly, bi-monthly, or monthly, payroll must ensure that time is tracked accurately and approved by the appropriate supervisor. Time off must be audited to ensure the appropriate leave is reported and any new accrued leave is added to the employee's balances.

If errors are made, it is important for payroll to review and audit the issue, make the necessary corrections, and establish a process to ensure the error does not occur in the future. Payroll may need to issue a check outside of the normal pay schedule and an established process should be followed in

these cases. When an employee resigns or is terminated, checks must be issued within specific timeframes to ensure compliance with state laws. Ensuring a process to issue these off-cycle is established and followed is important for any payroll function.

In addition to the standard pay schedule processing, payroll is also responsible for ensuring that annual W-2 tax forms are prepared, printed, and mailed to all employees who worked for any period in the previous year. This includes individuals that contracted with the organization as well as employees and can be a quite cumbersome process. The W-2 form must be sent to all individuals no later than January 31 of the following year (ex. 2017 W-2 forms must be sent by January 31, 2018) per federal IRS guidelines. Additionally, a 1095 schedule must be prepared to report the status of healthcare insurance of the employee and all dependents during the year to abide by the guidelines in the Affordable Care Act.

In addition to the above standard processes, Payroll is responsible for ensuring that employee's compensation is accurate. If back-pay is required, Payroll must calculate what is owed and ensure the employee receives this compensation as soon as possible. If a promotion is not entered in a timely manner, or a merit increase is delayed, Payroll is responsible for retroactively calculating this new rate for all the paychecks missed. Payroll is also responsible for working with auditors to ensure appropriate processes are established and followed, necessary checks and balances are put in place, and all general accounting practices are understood and incorporated into policy, practice, and procedure.

Taxation and Deductions

Human resources employees must have a thorough understanding of pay reporting as well as taxation and deduction information. All employees are required to pay federal income taxes based on the compensation received for their services. In some places, employees are also required to pay state or local taxes. Taxable income is a broad category containing all types of compensation that are deductible by the employer, extending to special circumstances like vacation pay, severance pay, back pay, disability pay, and golden parachute incentives. Federal income taxes can be taken directly from an employee's wages. To do so, employers are required to provide a **W-4 form**, or the Employee's Withholding Allowance Certificate, which is the paperwork that tells the company how much to take out an employee's paycheck for federal income taxes.

When an employer hires someone, they must provide a W-4 form for the individual to submit. The amount withheld from each paycheck is determined by factors relevant to the individual's circumstances, such as how many dependents the employee has and whether the employee is married. These factors are known as **withholding allowances**. The more withholding allowances an individual claims, the lower the amount of taxes withheld. Current tax rates, withholding amounts, and wage thresholds should be made available to all employees. Employees can update their W-4 forms annually or when their circumstances change. It is important to note that, according to the IRS, human resources may not guide employees on their W-4 responses. While employers should make information related to W-4 forms available, they should never advise employees on how to fill specific forms out nor complete them on behalf of employees.

A certain portion of employee deductions are designated for Social Security (Old Age, Survivors and Disability Insurance [OASDI]) and Medicare. The maximum amount of earnings subject to these taxes, or the taxable wage cap, changes based on the annual cost-of-living adjustment (COLA). However, the withholding rates for these deductions only change when a new tax law passes. Employers should keep track of current tax rates and limits on maximum earnings to ensure compliance with the IRS.

Currently, the rate for Social Security is 12.4% of payroll. However, the tax is divided in half, so a worker and employer will each pay 6.2% on a given paycheck. The Social Security tax is the only tax with a wage base limit, which is the maximum wage subject to the tax for that year. The Medicare tax rate is 2.9% split in half between the employer and employee. There is also an **Additional Medicare Tax** of 0.9% that applies to employees that receive pay exceeding $200,000 annually. Social Security and Medicare taxes, including the Additional Medicare Tax, are together known as the **Federal Insurance Contributions Act (FICA)**, or payroll taxes. These taxes must be paid during each payroll cycle since the taxes typically are withheld from each paycheck.

At the beginning of each year, employers must send W-2 forms to every employee. A **W-2 form,** or **Tax and Wage Statement,** is a record of any compensation the organization paid to the employee and any taxes withheld within the previous calendar year. Employers are required by law to send a W-2 form to every employee by January 31. The IRS may subject the organization to a financial penalty if statements are not sent by the deadline. Human resources departments should be prepared to answer any questions employees may have related to their W-2 statements since these forms are the basis for all employees' annual taxes. Many organizations set up Frequently Asked Questions or provide access to tax services to help employees navigate filing their taxes correctly.

Pre-tax deductions are funds taken from an employee's gross income for a designated benefit prior to local, state, or federal taxation. Essentially, pre-tax deductions are a way to offer benefits to an employee while lowering the employee's taxable wages. Employees must select the pre-tax benefits in which they would like to participate and choose the amount of their pre-tax contribution. There are many kinds of pre-tax deductions:

- **Retirement savings accounts** with pre-tax deductions include 401(k)s and traditional individual retirement accounts (IRAs). With these types of retirement plans, individuals can contribute a certain amount of their earnings to save for retirement and delay paying taxes on the money until they are ready to retire and withdraw the funds.
- **Health Savings Accounts (HSAs)** are health savings accounts linked with a company's **High Deductible Health Plan (HDHP)**. They allow employees to use pre-tax income to save money for a variety of health-related expenses including, but not limited to, copays, deductibles, vision care, dental care, and maternity services. However, since the money in these accounts rolls over annually, they can also serve as additional retirement accounts or be invested if the employee does not spend the funds. To be eligible for an HSA, an employee must be enrolled in the HDHP on the first day of the month, must not be part of another non-HDHP, and must not be a dependent on another individual's tax return.
- **Flexible Savings Accounts (FSAs)** are generally medical spending accounts not linked to any HDHP. However, there are some cases where an FSA may provide other non-medical benefits, such as transportation spending. Employees that choose to participate in an FSA program contribute a certain amount of pre-tax dollars to the account during each pay period. This money is then placed on a debit card to be used when paying for FSA-eligible services. It is important to note that the funds in an FSA do not roll over and must be used by the end of the year or forfeited.
- Group insurance plans are health-related pre-tax benefits in which pre-tax income can be used to pay for plan premiums. This type of pre-tax benefit can be advantageous for employees since the premiums for group insurance plans provided by employers tend to be lower than those in individual health plans.

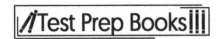

HR is responsible for understanding the details of pre-tax benefits and communicating that information to employees. Additionally, HR should communicate the benefits of available pre-tax deduction options and assist employees in signing up for these programs.

Wage Garnishments

Wage garnishments and levies are two ways government entities or private collections' agencies can withdraw funds to put toward a person's debt. A **wage garnishment** is when a creditor requires an employer to take a portion of an individual's wages to cover a portion of a debt. A **levy** is when a creditor freezes and takes money from a checking or savings account to cover a portion of a debt. In most cases, the collector must receive a court judgment to legally impose a wage garnishment or levy.

In IRS terms, a wage levy is interchangeable with a wage garnishment. When the IRS imposes a wage garnishment, an employer must send a portion of an employee's pay to cover taxes owed. The garnishment continues until the individual has paid their taxes, the IRS releases the levy, or the individual makes a different plan to pay their debt. Wage garnishments apply to all earnings the individual makes in exchange for their services as an employee. Wages may include money made outside of the individual's base pay such as commissions, holiday pay, bonuses, and workers' compensation payments. However, there are limitations to wage levies. The most important limitation is that the garnishment must be based on the individual's disposable income in accordance with the government's maximum garnishment laws.

Companies should have a protocol in place for handling wage garnishments. The employer usually receives notification of a garnishment or levy via a court order or IRS levy document. Companies receive paperwork that explains the process of fulfilling the garnishment request. Human resources departments must take care to send the correct payments to the right agencies to avoid any legal issues. When a garnishment or levy request is received, human resources should immediately inform the employee in writing, explaining the circumstances of the levy and specifying the amount to be taken from the individual's earnings.

Leave Reporting

Human resources departments should have clearly defined leave reporting policies and processes. Leave reporting includes systems for requesting and tracking vacation and sick time as well as other leave benefits an organization may elect to provide. Organizations may offer types of leave beyond vacation and sick time, such as sabbaticals, holidays, military leave, family leave, or medical leave. The Fair Labor Standards Act (FLSA) and Affordable Care Act (ACA) both require organizations to keep accurate records of all employee absences to ensure compliance with both laws. Human Resources Information Systems (HRIS) can be useful tools for tracking these records.

The human resources department has several responsibilities related to leave reporting. First, human resources should delineate the amount of leave available to employees at the time of hire, making sure to differentiate the circumstances under which each type of leave may be used. Employers should also have a reliable and verifiable timekeeping system, whether electronic or paper, to track employee work hours. Additionally, organizations should have a formal process in place for employees to request time off as well as a method for tracking approvals and actual leave taken. Employees should receive training on how to navigate these processes. Organizations should also provide employees with leave balance information each year. Finally, employers should maintain all records pertaining to leave for three years after the employee leaves the organization.

Salary and Benefits Surveys

A **salary and benefit survey** is an excellent tool that organizations can use to determine the appropriate salary for a job, benchmark wages against the market, and make decisions about benefits. Surveys should incorporate all compensation data, including salary, retirement benefits, healthcare benefits, time off, and any other form of compensation to ensure that a holistic view is available. Establishing the surveys can help provide insight regarding attrition, or why employees are leaving the organization, as well as recruitment difficulties, or why candidates are not wanting to join the organization. Various surveys are available for the private sector in specific geographic areas as well as specific to certain industries. Organizations can then compare the compensation and benefits offered against the market to determine if adjustments or corrections are necessary.

These are characteristics of an effective salary and benefits survey:

- Representative of the market and region
- Inclusive of multiple positions at various levels
- Low cost
- Convenient and easy to navigate
- Precise and accurate information

These are characteristics of an inadequate salary and benefit survey:

- Has inflexible design, reporting only statistics
- Does not address controversial issues
- May not reflect comparable industries

It is important to understand all the pros and cons when using a salary and benefits survey, specifically that the data may not hold all the answers. There may not be comparable positions or data points for every position in the organization, so various degrees of extrapolation may be necessary. This can be potentially contentious if an individual believes they are not paid a fair wage and is requesting an increase. Regardless, having the data is an important step in understanding how the organization compares with competitors and the marketplace. While a survey may not answer all an organization's questions, it can provide insight and when used properly, an effective tool.

Practice Questions

1. The federal minimum wage is currently set at $7.25/hour. However, in the state of Maryland, where Rachel's ice cream parlor resides, the minimum wage is currently set higher, at $12.50/hour. Which statement below accurately reflects the rate of pay that Rachel's new employees starting out at the minimum wage would receive?
   a. The new employees will receive $7.25/hour. When the federal minimum wage is set lower than a state's minimum wage, an employer can go with the lower rate of pay as its standard.
   b. The new employees will receive $12.50/hour. When a state's minimum wage is higher than the federal minimum wage, an employer must use the higher state minimum wage as its standard.
   c. The new employees will receive $9.88/hour, which is an average of the federal minimum wage and the state's minimum wage.
   d. Rachel's ice cream parlor does not have enough employees to fall under the guidelines of the Fair Labor Standards Act (FLSA), which governs minimum wage.

2. Which of the following is NOT one of the three categories that the IRS's twenty factors fall under for determining if an individual working at a company is an employee or an independent contractor?
   a. Financial control
   b. Reporting accountability
   c. Behavioral control
   d. Type of relationship

3. Which of the following items is NOT a covered provision under the Fair Labor Standards Act (FLSA)?
   a. Overtime pay
   b. Employee classification
   c. Child labor
   d. Hazard pay

4. Which piece of legislation requires employers to pay employees for preliminary and postliminary tasks, such as job-related travel time that is outside of an employee's regular work commute and time spent in job-related training?
   a. Equal Pay Act
   b. Portal-to-Portal Act
   c. Fair Labor Standards Act (FLSA)
   d. Davis-Bacon Act

5. Which of the following statements is true regarding differential pay?
   a. Differential pay is required by the Fair Labor Standards Act (FLSA).
   b. Differential pay programs are used to reward employees for performing work that is viewed as less than desirable.
   c. Pay practices regarding differential pay are standardized among employers.
   d. Differential pay programs are used to motivate employees to perform their work at a higher level.

Answer Explanations

1. B: When a state's minimum wage is set at a higher rate than the federal minimum wage, such as Maryland's minimum wage, an employer must use the higher state minimum wage as its standard when paying employees.

2. B: The three categories that the IRS's twenty factors fall under for determining if an individual working at a company is an employee or an independent contractor are Choice *A*, financial control, Choice *C*, behavioral control, and Choice *D*, type of relationship. Reporting ability is not one of the categories.

3. D: Hazard pay is not a covered provision. The Fair Labor Standards Act (FLSA) establishes guidelines around Choice *A*, overtime pay, Choice *B*, employee classification (exempt and non-exempt status), minimum wage, on-call pay, record keeping, and Choice *C*, child labor.

4. B: The Portal-to-Portal Act deals with the preliminary and postliminary tasks of employees. The act requires employers to pay employees who are covered under the FLSA for time spent traveling to perform job-related tasks if that travel is outside of the employees' regular work commute. Additionally, employees are to be paid for hours spent in job-related training that is outside of their normal workday.

5. B: Differential pay programs are used to reward employees for performing work that is viewed as less than desirable, and these programs vary greatly among employers. Differential pay is not required by the FLSA.

Employee Relations

HR Strategy

A company's strategic planning process is comprised of the following four steps:

1. **Strategy Formulation:** During this first step of the strategic planning process, a company focuses on the business it is in and develops its vision statement, mission statement, and values accordingly. Plans are also made for how best to communicate the company's mission and when it may be necessary to change the company's mission or adjust its strategy. This first step can be summed up by identifying where a company currently is and defining where it wants to be in the future and how it can arrive at that place.

2. **Strategy Development:** Environmental scanning and a SWOT (Strengths, Weaknesses, Opportunities, Threats) analysis are performed during this step of the strategic planning process (both of which will be described in greater detail). Additionally, long-range plans are established that will set the company's direction for the next three to five years. This second step can be summed up by collecting information that is both internal and external to the company, along with developing alternative strategies.

3. **Strategy Implementation:** During this step of the strategic planning process, short-range plans are created that will set the company's direction for the next six to twelve months. Additionally, there is a focus on motivating employees by developing action plans and allocating the necessary resources in order to achieve objectives (e.g., human, financial, and technological). This step can be summed up by implementing a plan for the strategy that is chosen.

4. **Strategy Evaluation:** During this last step of the strategic planning process, a company agrees to continue reviewing an implemented strategy at specific intervals by performing a SWOT analysis and taking note of any changes. In the event of changes, corrective action may be necessary. This step can be summed up by evaluating the success of the implemented strategy while continuing to monitor it and make any necessary tweaks.

Using Systems Thinking to Understand How the Organization Operates

Peter Senge was the founder of the Society of Organizational Learning and continues to serve as a senior lecturer at the MIT Sloan School of Management. He is a proponent of **systems thinking**, one of five disciplines he outlines to enable organizations to adapt to change; in systems thinking, managers spend more time focusing on the big picture than on individual actions, since actions and consequences are all correlated with each other. He also identifies shared vision, team learning, mental models, and personal mastery as the other four disciplines critical to adaptable organizations. In this same manner, Peter Senge believes organizations should seek out and embrace change versus waiting and responding to changes in crisis model. Essential to all five disciplines are communication, dialogue, team learning, and establishing common goals. Individuals must develop personal skills and mastery, but there remains an equal focus on the organization itself and how it integrates disparate elements that impact business functions.

Informing Business Decisions

Strategic planning is dependent on the knowledge and awareness of the goals and objectives for both the organization and the HR department. Ensuring alignment between the organization and HR is vital to

being successful at every level within an organization. Strategic alignment of goals and objectives sets up success for individual employees, teams, departments, and the organization. This strategy also allows for better decision-making for the business, which includes policy changes, practice updates, and possible reevaluation and redesign of the current state. Business decisions that are strategically implemented using this information will have a higher likelihood of being successful.

Developing and Implementing an Action Plan

In order for the HR department—or any department—to be successful in accomplishing their goals, objectives, and projects, HR leadership must develop an action plan. Action plans can be simple and high-level or complex and detailed. Regardless of the depth of detail included in an action plan, the items identified in the plan should be aligned with the SMART methodology to ensure that success can be accurately defined and described. The **SMART** methodology requires that all objectives be specific, measurable, achievable, realistic, and time-targeted. Without these elements, it is more difficult to know when an objective has been successfully achieved.

Additionally, it is more difficult to determine where improvements or course corrections are needed if the objective is not on track. Action plans are excellent tools that should be implemented at both the departmental and individual levels. Department action plans outline the course and path that will be taken by the entire department and all employees to achieve specific items. Individual action plans outline the course and path that will be taken by a single employee to achieve the specific items identified in the department action plan. Individual action plans can also be used to chart out an employee's growth, development, and potential career path for the future by identifying skills, gaps, and opportunities.

Using Benchmarks, Metrics, and Trends to Understand the Organization's Market Position

Achieving a competitive advantage can be done by identifying and analyzing factors that will allow an organization to distinguish their product or service from the competition. Human Resources should engage in this process regarding the employment experience and workforce planning in order to differentiate the organization from the competition. Strategically defining and maintaining the organization as an employer of choice allows for attracting and recruiting the best candidates, retaining top talent, and ensuring the success of the organization through the workforce. When assessing the competition from an HR perspective, it is important to have a holistic understanding of the organization. From the products and services offered to the total rewards provided, including compensation and benefits, HR should assess the competition and work to make enhancements as necessary to attract and maintain an exceptional workforce. This may include providing employees with a better retirement system, increasing compensation, or allowing for telecommuting and alternate work schedules. Each employee will value something different. Human Resources can truly make an impact by being aware of and understanding what motivates employees. In doing so, the organization will be seen as a leader in the market.

Informing HR Leadership of Opportunities to Align HR's Strategy with the Organization's

Organizations often employ practices to solicit feedback and ideas from employees. Being engaged with the workforce, while allowing opportunities to provide insight into new programs or practices, is vital to the evolution of the organization. From suggestion boxes to employee surveys, the Human Resources department is in a unique position to have insights into what employees want, need, or value. When new ideas for programs or practices are discovered, it is important to communicate them to leadership for further discussion, if necessary, and the idea should be fully investigated for possible

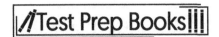

implementation. This same philosophy should apply to previously considered ideas or even ideas that were previously implemented but found to be unsuccessful. Timing is vital to the success of a new initiative, as is leadership commitment and communication. It is important to communicate effectively when presenting these new ideas to leadership for consideration. Effective communication can be accomplished by following the 7 C's:

- Clear
- Concise
- Correct
- Complete
- Considerate
- Concrete
- Courteous

Communications are most effective when they are simple, specific, accurate, thorough, thoughtful, tangible, and respectful. When new ideas are presented to leadership with these elements in mind, there is a much higher likelihood of approval than when information is incomplete or vague.

Providing HR Leadership Information

Timeliness and accuracy are two of the most important factors when presenting information that will be used for making decisions. Data that is outdated and inaccurate can result in decisions that are not the best or most appropriate given the reality of the current circumstances. Decisions could be made that do not adequately resolve issues or may even create more issues. It is equally important to ensure that information is regularly updated when new insights are gained. This will allow for adjustments to projects or decisions that accurately reflect the new circumstances. Wyatt Earp, a deputy marshal in the early 1900s, stated "fast is fine, but accuracy is everything." This quote holds true when HR professionals are delivering data and information to leadership when making decisions.

Organizational Strategy

Quality leadership skills are essential to any organization, and thus leadership training is typically provided to mid and upper management professionals. Effective leadership skills include strategic thinking, solving problems as they come, and managing time in the most financially responsible manner. While these skills are essential, there are also more human characteristics that must be mentioned. A successful leader must have the ability to build confidence within their organization, obtain the trust of others, inspire others, and engender a sense of pride and purpose within their company.

Vision

For any organization to be successful, it must have a clear idea of what it's doing and where it's going. Mission and vision statements are two ways for an organization to express its objectives. A **mission statement** focuses on the work of the organization on a day-to-day basis and answers the following questions:

- What do we do now?
- Why are we doing it?
- What makes us different from other companies?

A **vision statement** focuses on the organization's future goals and answers the following questions:

- What do we want to accomplish?
- Where do we aim to be in the future?

A successful mission statement should be clear and direct. In short, it states *why* the organization exists, and in turn guides its values, standards, and other organizing principles. For example, an organic restaurant might have the following mission statement: "To serve customers healthy meals made from the freshest, locally sourced organic ingredients." With this mission statement, the restaurant could decide to focus its efforts on building relationships with local farmers or staying up to date on health food trends.

A vision statement focuses on specific future goals, and in turn guides the steps that the organization will take to achieve them. The same restaurant might decide on the following vision statement: "To become a top-rated restaurant in the city." The restaurant can then design a plan accordingly, perhaps by focusing on marketing campaigns or inviting influential reviewers to dine at the restaurant.

Navigating the Organization

Successful Implementation of HR Initiatives

An organization's processes, systems, and policies will vary depending on the overall goals and function of an organization, but most HR initiatives focus on several key categories that intend to most effectively utilize the personnel within the organization. These include, but are not limited to, the following:

- Finding, hiring, and retaining qualified candidates
- Employee compensation and benefits (such as hourly pay, salary, health insurance, paid leave, disability benefits, pension, and other perks based on employee interests)
- Organizational and employee development activities (such as professional trainings)
- Termination and retirement tasks
- Risk management, such as drug screening employees and providing safety courses relevant to job functions

The details and successful implementation of these initiatives are largely subjective, beginning with understanding an organization's mission. This is often defined by an established mission statement or company vision. All HR initiatives should contribute to the advancement of the organization's mission.

Political Environment and Culture

How employees think and feel about a company is critical to an employer. If members of an organization have negative associations with their workplace, it can be difficult to motivate them. The overall "mood" of an organization is known as its climate, and organizational climate cannot be directly controlled. However, climate is closely affected by work environment, company standards, interactions, and a general sense of "how things are done around here." Together, these factors add up to what is called organizational culture. So, if an employer wants to improve the company's climate, they need to make changes to the company culture.

Managing HR Initiatives

Project Requirements

Senior leadership plays a role in dictating project timelines and end goals for an organization, and HR initiatives can support the processes that bring forth outcomes through high-level project management. In the planning stage of projects, HR professionals will need to consider the skills that are needed for

projects to be completed. Additionally, they will need to consider factors like timeline development, establishing mini-goals and deliverables, the resources needed and associated costs (such as labor, time required, materials needed, and so on), risks that may need to be mitigated, and analyses that determine returns on investment (ROI) of resources. These are often intrapersonal activities that may require the input and cooperation of stakeholders from various departments across the organization. Therefore, to move project processes forward in the most productive manner, HR professionals should anticipate selecting the appropriate stakeholders and fostering positive communication between them.

Project Goals and Progress Milestones

Project goals are steppingstones toward organizational goals, and projects are comprised of milestones that indicate outcome success. Milestones are progressive in nature and influence the general timeline of the project. In order to be useful, both goals and milestones should exhibit SMART qualities. SMART is a commonly used acronym in goal and milestone setting that states an effective end point should be specific, measurable, achievable, relevant, and timely. This ensures the goal or milestone is detailed, can produce data to show evidence of its effectiveness, can feasibly be attained, is relevant to the organizational goal at hand, and occurs at appropriate and useful intervals that benefit the project. When developing project goals, HR personnel should be able to address each of the five SMART aspects. Often, these values are documented before the project begins.

Project Budgets and Resources

A project can require a wide array of resources depending on its scope. Beyond the number of personnel needed and their individual compensation packages, resource costs also include time spent, materials, potential trainings needed, long-term sustaining actions, and so on. Costs can be categorized into direct costs, which impact one project specifically (such as labor and materials), and indirect costs, which may affect specific projects but also serve the organization as a whole (such as leadership salary and permanent office furniture). These costs can be fixed, or they can vary over time. Developing a budget includes reviewing a project proposal fully and anticipating all projected costs over the completion of the project. These may be divided into chronological milestones (such as monthly, quarterly, or annually) or by outcome benchmarks (such as when a department is fully staffed or when a component of a product is developed). Budgets and resources should remain flexible and be updated as needed.

Overcoming Project Obstacles

No project is likely to be without obstacles. Anticipating potential obstacles and preparing for them can help the project remain on track for completion. Start-up plans should be reviewed and revised throughout the course of the project to account for any unexpected changes. Most importantly, these revisions must be communicated to project members. Most often, obstacles arise when team members do not have the skillset or resources to contribute to their role, when the content and timeline of deliverables are not clear or documented, and when communication from relevant leadership and between colleagues is lacking. Beginning the project with SMART attributes and allowing for communication with project staff and key stakeholders can reduce any obstacles that should arise. While some obstacles may be out of the organization's control (such as a sudden loss of external funding), internal obstacles can often be mitigated with appropriate contingency planning.

Necessary Resources

Once a project outcome has been identified, finding the resources needed to see the project to fruition is key. Allocating resources is a balancing act. Utilizing too many resources will lead to waste, but utilizing too few resources can result in delays, errors, or other obstacles. Skilled HR personnel will know

how to produce the best value from the least resources—a concept based on "Lean leadership" relies on respect, which was once used primarily in manufacturing. HR personnel can examine internal data from similar projects to anticipate what resources other initiatives might need. Tools from the Six Sigma approach, such as process mapping and value stream mapping, can also help objectively determine the resources needed at each step of the project and the actual value-add associated with them.

Resource Allocation

Milestones can serve as an indicator of when resources are inconsistent with project needs. If deliverables are not fulfilled by an established milestone, HR personnel may choose to examine the role of the resources that are in use. A gap analysis, a root cause analysis, or a cause-and-effect diagram, which pinpoint why an expected outcome was not met, can review discrepancies between expected and actual performances. Often, these indicate that there is a constraint in one or more resources, such as lack of material, lack of qualified employees, or lack of time. Once the resource in question has been addressed, implementing a test of change may show if shifting resources allow established milestones to be met. If not, this may indicate that components of the timeline for the project are not reasonable. Milestones, outcomes, or the construction of the timeline itself may require revision.

Project Adaptability

Project requirements, goals, and constraints are developed and anticipated during the planning stage. They are, however, subject to changes that may or may not be in the team's control. Changes in funding, personnel, and regulation, are examples of items that often cannot be fully accounted for during the project planning stage. HR project managers may benefit from managing their own expectations during the project planning stage and accepting that all baseline plans are fluid. Project plans should be continuously reviewed, and they should be revised when unexpected changes arise. Developing contingency processes during the project planning stage, cross-training team members, and developing the ability to critically and creatively think about new solutions are ways to mitigate unanticipated changes. Becoming aware of the professional strengths and weaknesses of team members and drawing on this knowledge during times of change can also help to fill gaps. These techniques allow the entire team to cohesively demonstrate agility and adaptability when needed.

Influence
HR Expert

There are numerous ways to build credibility as an HR expert, like having a formal educational background in industrial organization and related fields, such as psychology, project management, business, and communication. Continuing education after formal schooling, such as earning certifications through nationally recognized credentialing bodies, is another way to further develop one's theoretical skillset. Staying abreast of literature pertaining to topics relevant to human resources is yet another avenue to illustrate professional expertise. From a practical standpoint, using one's knowledge to offer solutions to personnel issues within the organization is a way to showcase credibility. Sharing success stories with colleagues in the field can build professional credibility outside of one's organization.

Promoting Buy-In

The most effective way to promote buy-in among organizational stakeholders for HR initiatives is to show the added value of an initiative to the stakeholders, employees, and organization. Added value will need to be large enough that it is worth the associated costs of implementing the initiative. To this end, HR personnel who are proposing initiatives have the responsibility of understanding what outcomes each of their stakeholders perceives as valuable. An initiative that the HR team finds valuable may not

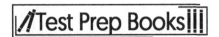

have meaning for stakeholders. Often, stakeholders consist of leadership personnel whose buy-in is necessary for the initiative to be approved. Leadership buy-in is also crucial in order to successfully implement change (known as top-down change), otherwise gaining subordinate approval proves extremely challenging. Finally, determining what is of value may vary across departments. Therefore, finding umbrella goals or interest overlaps can be useful.

Motivating HR Staff

An effective leader understands that team motivation is influenced by several factors, and that some fall outside the leader's locus of influence. The first step in motivating HR staff is ensuring that candidates who are passionate about the field, the organization, and the organization's interests are hired as staff. Candidates who are not a good professional or cultural fit for the team may be difficult to motivate, may be unhappy on the job, and may not find success within the organization. Ensuring that qualified employees remain motivated may include providing opportunities for professional growth, recognizing and rewarding professional excellence, promoting work-life satisfaction, and creating an open, encouraging, and positive work environment. Motivating other stakeholders to support HR's visions and goals is most likely to include continuous highlights of the value that the department provides to both the stakeholder as an individual, and to the organization as a whole. This may be expressed in program evaluations, reports, presentations, graphs, anecdotal evidence, or employee testimonials.

Advocacy

HR personnel are responsible for managing the productivity and welfare of an organization's employees but also for ensuring that employees can safely perform their jobs in a way that advances the organization's interests. It can be a balancing act to manage employee needs with business needs, especially during times when one side needs more than the other (such as if an essential employee must take an extended medical leave, or if a valued business customer needs a complex product on short notice). It is also important that employees do not take advantage of the organization, and vice versa. HR personnel are often in charge of developing guidelines that help to regulate these dual needs; these are often documented in a company handbook that is accessible to all employees. Guidelines may be established for instances such as leaves of absence, overtime, meal breaks, harassment, and other contexts specific to the industry.

Establishing Relationships: Outside Organizations

As much as organizations must understand and analyze their internal operations, they must also look outward and engage with the industry. This is equally true of HR relationships, which should be fostered both within and outside of the organization. By building external relationships, HR professionals can stay abreast of industry developments, develop innovative solutions, and be active (or even proactive) members of their field.

Competitive Advantage

A **competitive advantage** is anything that gives an organization an edge over its competitors. In order to determine its competitive advantage, an organization must have a clear understanding of its direct competitors, its products and services, and its target market. For example, a budget clothing company might be successful based on offering lower prices than other stores. Its competitive advantage is its prices. On the other hand, a luxury designer clothing brand could have the opposite competitive advantage—because its product is high quality and expensive, its name-brand reputation makes it successful with customers in a wealthier target market.

Corporate Social Responsibility (CSR)

Corporate Social Responsibility (CSR) refers to an organization's sense of responsibility for its impact on the environment and community. CSR can be evaluated based on the three Ps of the "triple bottom line": people, planet, and profit. *People* refers to fair employment practices as well as the organization's impact on members of the community; *planet* refers to the organization's environmental impact (such as pollution, consumption of natural resources, etc.); and *profit* refers to the organization's overall contribution to economic growth. Having a CSR program encourages an organization to operate within legal, moral, and ethical boundaries. From an HR perspective, an organization's CSR program can also affect employee recruiting because the program demonstrates the organization's commitment to fair working conditions.

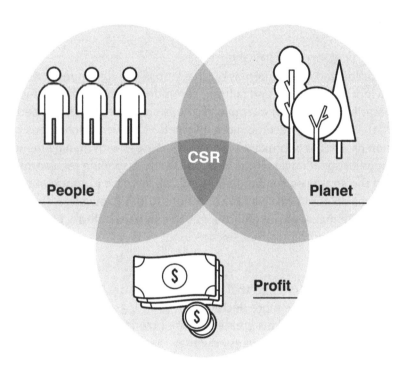

Community Partnership

In addition to financial capital, organizations also rely on **social capital**, the community's relationship with, and attitude toward, the organization. An organization can boost its social capital by engaging community partners from schools to social or volunteer groups to other organizations. These partnerships demonstrate an organization's commitment to the community in which it operates and offer an opportunity for community members to develop a closer relationship with the organization. For example, a computer networking company might partner with the local public school system to offer a free summer camp program for high school students interested in computers.

Organizational Culture

A team-oriented organizational culture is one that actively views professional efforts as a group accomplishment. Individualistic terms (such as "I achieved this" versus "We achieved this") are rarely used. Knowing each team member's strengths and leveraging those when establishing project

responsibilities promotes effective use of resources. However, implementing cross-training sessions to address weaknesses also helps to establish a strong team unit by allowing members to feel as though they can support one another in times of need. All members should feel accountable for their work in the team. This can be achieved through documenting expectations for each member and discussing how individual objectives integrate to create results. Finally, resources that support team culture (such as physical space in the organization to accommodate groups) should be available.

How employees think and feel about a company is critical to an employer. If members of an organization have negative associations with their workplace, it can be difficult to motivate them. The overall "mood" of an organization is known as its climate, and organizational climate cannot be directly controlled. However, climate is closely affected by work environment, company standards, interactions, and a general sense of "how things are done around here." Together, these factors add up to what is called organizational culture. So, if an employer wants to improve the company's climate, they need to make changes to the company culture.

Encouraging Communication and Involvement

Encouraging communication and involvement is often a step in the right direction toward changing company culture. And much like climate and culture, communication and involvement are closely related, but not necessarily identical. For example, if John's boss gives him increased responsibility over an aspect of his work, then John has become more involved. However, if John does not have input from his boss on the decision process or a formal way to share his ideas with management, then the boss has not encouraged communication. Conversely, if John's boss starts sending regular memos detailing company activities and the strategies behind them, this is an increase in communication. However, if John and other employees do not have a way to contribute to this knowledge, then the boss has not encouraged involvement. To make meaningful changes to company culture, both communication and involvement should be addressed.

Involvement Strategies

There are numerous involvement strategies that companies can use. For example, the act of delegating authority allows an employee to make more decisions. By granting a staff member more responsibility, an employer can encourage them to take a greater sense of ownership over a company's successes. An **employee survey** can be used to ask employees how they feel about the company. Surveys can be formal (written or online) or informal (casual conversation), and can address topics such as concerns, suggestions for improvement, and priorities. It should be noted that, even in an anonymous survey, employees may feel hesitant to share their true feelings if the workplace culture is viewed as unfriendly.

In addition to surveys, a **suggestion program**, via an idea box or an online submission form, allows employees to recommend ways to address company problems. Unlike a survey, a suggestion program is an ongoing part of company involvement. Employees can also work together in a formal capacity as part of a committee to address company concerns. Committees may be temporary or ongoing, and employees' service on a committee may also be for a specific term or a permanent appointment.

Moreover, an **employee-management committee** is a specific kind of committee where employees work alongside management to address company concerns. Sometimes known as employee participation groups, these committees also can be temporary or ongoing, depending on the needs of the organization. Finally, employees can also serve on a task force, which is like a committee but focused on a specific problem and is usually temporary in nature. Employees on a task force work to determine the cause of a problem and develop a solution.

Organizational Structure

Organizational structure is used to help companies achieve their goals by defining the hierarchy of employees and allocating resources through decisions surrounding the following factors:

- **Chain of command**: This clarifies to whom employees report. It is the continuous line of authority from senior-level managers to employees at the lowest levels of the company.

- **Centralization**: A company where lower-level employees carry out the decisions made by senior-level managers is highly centralized. The opposite of this is **decentralization** or employee empowerment.

- **Span of control**: This refers to the number of employees a manager can effectively supervise. This can be affected by such things as a manager's skills, the physical proximity of the employees, the employees' characteristics, and the complexity of the work being performed. If a manager directly supervises seven employees, the span of control for that manager is seven.

- **Formalization**: An organization with standardized jobs, allowing for little discretion over what is to be done because the work is guided by rules, has a high degree of formalization. The opposite of this is low formalization, where employees have more freedom to decide how they can complete their tasks.

- **Work specialization**: This is also known as division of labor and refers to the degree to which a company divides tasks into separate jobs that are completed by different employees. This allows employees to become very proficient in a specialized area, such as painting or framing.

- **Departmentalization**: This comes into play when a company divides up its work by the specialization of its departments. Companies are known to departmentalize by function, product, geography, or division.

Functional Structure

This is the most common type of organizational structure in which jobs are according to function, such as finance, IT, sales, purchasing, and HR. Efficiencies are gained from grouping together individuals with common knowledge and skills. This type of organizational structure is good for a company that has one product line that can benefit from specialization. However, employees can have a limited view of the company's goals, and there can be poor communication across the various functional areas.

Product Structure

This is a type of organizational structure where jobs are grouped by product line. For example, a product organizational structure for a transportation company might be grouped by rail products, mass transit products, and recreational and utility vehicle products. Organizing by product allows managers to become experts in their industry and for specialization in certain products and services. However, employees can have a limited view of the company's goals, and there is a duplication of functions within each product line.

Geographic Structure

This is a type of organizational structure where jobs are grouped according to geographic location. For example, a company's sales directors for various regions (Eastern, Western, Midwestern, and Southern) may each be responsible for the business functions in their areas and report to the company's vice

president of sales. This type of structure is the best way to serve the unique needs and issues that may arise in different geographic markets. Since most decisions are made at the location level, decision-making is decentralized. However, employees may feel isolated from other organizational areas, and there is a duplication of functions within each geographic region.

Division Structure

This is a type of organizational structure where jobs are grouped by industry or market. A divisional organizational structure also experiences decentralized decision making and is similar in nature to the geographic structure.

Matrix Structure

Employees report to two managers in this type of organizational structure. Typically, one manager has functional responsibility, and the other manager has a product line responsibility. Employees have a primary manager they report to and a second manager they also work for on specified projects. In order for a matrix structure to be successful, there must be a high degree of trust and communication among the employees involved. This type of structure is a good way to share resources across functions.

Business Functions

In order to understand its performance, evaluate which strategies are effective, and identify where improvement is needed, an organization must regularly analyze internal business information. Data is analyzed using **metrics** (sometimes known as key performance indicators). A metric is simply a method of measuring a particular set of data. Different metrics can be applied to different areas of an organization.

For accounting and finance, metrics are essential for evaluating an organization's financial status.

Cash flow metrics are concerned with analyzing money coming in and going out. One straightforward cash flow metric is net cash flow, which measures the difference between incoming and outgoing cash over a fixed period (e.g., monthly, annually). Net cash flow can provide an immediate answer to the question, "Are we gaining or losing money over this period of time?" By reviewing this metric, an organization can determine if any strategic planning changes are necessary, particularly if the organization is losing more money than expected.

Another cash flow metric is **return on investment**, or **ROI**. ROI is generally expressed as a ratio or percentage comparing the gains of a particular investment with its initial investment price. In other words, ROI measures the ratio between an investment's profit and its cost. ROI is particularly useful in helping an organization evaluate the overall value of a given investment. For example, one investment may yield a high return, but perhaps the initial investment is costly as well. Another investment with a much lower yield also has a far lower initial cost—so the cheaper investment might have a higher ROI than the high-return investment. This metric can help an organization to devote its financial resources to investments with the highest ROI.

Shareholders might be especially concerned with an organization's **return on equity**, or **ROE**. Like ROI, ROE is also expressed as a ratio or percentage. This ratio can be found by dividing a company's fiscal year net income by the total shareholder equity. The purpose of this metric is to demonstrate how efficiently a company uses investments to generate profit by measuring the company's rate of return on its shareholders' equity. It can give shareholders confidence that their investment is being well-used—or it can tell them to invest their money elsewhere. In order to evaluate its competitiveness, a company

can compare its ROE with that of other companies in its field. If the comparison is unfavorable, then it's time to make some strategic planning adjustments.

For marketing and sales, metrics can indicate if a particular marketing strategy is succeeding or if it must be reevaluated. As with financial metrics, there's a wide range of marketing and sales metrics. Let's focus on a few of the most useful categories.

First, many sales and marketing metrics focus on leads. A **lead** is any person or group who interacts with the organization and might become a customer or client. For example, an online shopping mall might consider anyone who registers an account or joins their mailing list to be a lead. Some helpful metrics consider lead volume (the total number of leads at any given time) or leads generated (the total number of new leads gained during a fixed period, useful for evaluating whether a new marketing strategy is drawing more leads). Sales are like a funnel: the lead volume is wide at the top and then slowly narrows as the sales team nurtures leads into profitable customers. So, another leads-related metric includes lead-to-customer percentage (also known as a lead conversion), or the ratio of lead volume to new customers. This allows an organization to gauge the effectiveness of its sales team.

Another important metric is **average transaction value** *(ATV)*. This metric measures the average amount that one customer spends on one transaction. To return to the example of the online shopping mall, perhaps their ATV is $45—on average, each customer spends $45 when they place an order. This metric allows the online shop to predict its revenue by multiplying the ATV by the anticipated number of customers during a set period. Analyzing this metric also presents different marketing options to increase revenue—the organization can choose to focus on drawing more customers or on increasing the ATV of current customers. Some strategies to increase ATV are to offer rewards programs or special sales to established customers.

Finally, many helpful metrics relate to sales cost. How much money is spent on sales? Is a sales strategy cost-effective? The gross profit margin for a period can be found by subtracting the cost of sales from the total revenue and then dividing that number by the total revenue. This metric shows if a current sales strategy is effective and profitable. Another metric is the customer acquisition cost, or the amount spent getting a new customer. Analyzing the ratio between a customer's lifetime value (LTV) and the customer acquisition cost (CAC) can reveal whether current sales strategies are too costly compared to the overall value of a particular customer.

Operations and Business Development

There are also many important metrics related to operations and business development. Three important ones highlighted here are the number of activities, the opportunity success rate, and the innovation rate.

When measuring the **number of activities**, an activity is any task currently undertaken by the organization. This metric can show whether an organization is properly investing its resources in profitable work or if it's overextending its resources into too many tasks. Multi-tasking and diversifying are important in developing a business but taking on too many activities can hinder an organization's performance.

The **opportunity success rate** overlaps somewhat with the sales and marketing metrics described above. In this sense, an opportunity is a halfway point between a lead and a customer—the lead has been contacted by the sales team but isn't yet a customer. The opportunity success rate measures how many opportunities are closed by sales. This metric can help marketing and sales strategies as well as the

overall business development plan. If the opportunity success rate is high, the organization can easily bring in new customers and develop its business. If the opportunity success rate is low, the organization might focus on developing current customers rather than spending resources on new ones.

A third metric to keep in mind is the **innovation rate**. Innovation includes any new or improved products and services. To find the innovation rate, divide the revenue generated by new products and services by the total revenue from all products and services over a given period. This allows the organization to see how much of an impact innovation has on its overall operations, and whether more resources must be devoted to developing innovative ideas that will give the organization an edge over its competition.

Impact of Technology on HR

Technology Solutions

Nowadays, organizations rely on information technology to carry out essential business functions. Some conduct the entirety of their business via the internet. These metrics can help organizations get the most out of their IT departments.

One important category analyzes the functionality of an organization's IT resources. That is, how well are IT services working? This can be measured by looking at the number of software bugs over a given period, or the average number of hours required to resolve IT issues. If there's a large volume of IT problems, or if it takes too long to fix critical IT issues, the organization must devote more resources to improving its IT functionality.

IT metrics can also consider online business activities that examine an organization's online sales presence. If a business has a website, one important metric is the number of page views. This measures the organization's reach—how many potential customers is the organization reaching through its online marketing? How many page views lead to actual purchases? How many visitors are registered on the site or subscribed to a newsletter? If the organization isn't satisfied with this number, it's time to try new online marketing strategies. The business can also look at the ratio of online sales to sales from non-internet business (for example, over the phone or in person) in order to determine where it should focus sales and marketing efforts.

Finally, as with any department, organizations must consider the cost of IT. This metric helps the organization see what portion of its financial resources is devoted to IT services, and whether this investment adds value to the organization. For example, an organization may invest on new project management software, but this software increases productivity and helps managers keep project costs low—so the cost of the software is offset by the savings it creates.

HRIS

As organizations become increasingly dependent on technology management, it is incumbent on HR professionals to identify and implement technologies that are most beneficial to their work. Human resource information systems (HRIS) are tools for managing relevant HR data, including employee information and benefits administration. It may also include an ATS that aids with recruitment by managing resumes, applicant information, open positions, etc. In the past, such information tended to be stored in discrete databases, making it difficult to integrate data and leading to frequent duplication of information. However, as the rising trend of big data analysis continues, organizations and HR departments can obtain a wealth of information from data that is properly stored and organized. Therefore, in choosing and implementing HRIS, HR professionals should consider what information is being stored at the organization, what information HR needs to know based on that data, and how data

could be integrated for easier access and analysis. There is no one-size-fits-all HRIS; rather, HR professionals should consider the unique needs of their organization.

Electronic Media and Hardware Policies and Procedures

If a firm wishes to maintain competitiveness and maximize its capabilities, management should develop policies that streamline communication. These policies will allow for the freer flow of ideas and dialogue. Furthermore, the integration of electronic media will increase a firm's ability to reach out to consumers and market the company's products. Harnessing this technology can increase market share and make innovation easier.

Electronic mail, or email, is communication that occurs by exchanging digital messages. Email was developed in the early 1990s and came into widespread use by 1993. Email has become a common means of communication, particularly within a corporate environment. This mode of communication allows an individual to send messages to one or more recipients at once. Email has been enormously successful in streamlining the communication process while reducing the cost of using paper.

Many organizations currently integrate the use of social media into corporate strategies. Social media is online applications that allow users to share content. These sites have become so advantageous in marketing that companies hire designated employees to increase social media presence. Many firms presently require their employees to have social media skills, knowledge, and familiarity. Programs such as Twitter™, Facebook™, and Instagram™ have proven to be tremendously successful marketing tools used by companies to reach a broader audience. In addition, social media has revolutionized advertising by placing a growing emphasis on Internet marketing instead of traditional television ads.

As technology has increased the use of the internet, the necessity of a company website and the demand for website accessibility has grown. In order to promote equal access to websites, companies should attempt to accommodate those with cognitive, neurological, physical, visual, or auditory disabilities. In addition to disabled persons, elderly people who lack familiarity should be able to understand and navigate websites. Because the internet is an integral resource for participating in commercial activity, gaining employment, accessing healthcare, and finding recreational activities, equal opportunity and access to website navigation is also crucial.

Data sharing is the practice of making information accessible through public or private networks. Individuals within the network have access to the information, while those not in the network require consent for access. Data sharing usually involves varying levels of access and is generally regulated by administrators in the system.

A password is a code that is required to access restricted information. A complex password provides more security to the user and better protects sensitive information. Typically, passwords consist of letters, numbers, and symbols. This unique combination affords better protection to the user. Password sharing should be limited to those individuals who may be trusted with confidential information.

Social engineering is the act of manipulating people for the purpose of revealing sensitive information. Typically, an attacker will employ deceptive tactics to convince the target to provide information such as bank numbers, passwords, and Social Security numbers. Social engineers take advantage of a target's natural tendencies of trust. Social engineers may gain access to information by infiltrating computer systems and installing malware. Organizations should educate employees on security and the identification of untrustworthy individuals. Employees should be able to assess suspicious situations and clearly recognize red flags.

Social media is a platform where people can freely express ideas, exchange information, market goods, and advertise. Social media establishes important individual connections and can even result in locating employment. While a helpful and useful tool in many circumstances, social media may also carry unintended consequences. For example, employers often use social media to obtain personal information about a potential or current employee. Questionable social media content can influence an employer's decision to hire an individual.

Monitoring software, also known as computer surveillance software, regulates the activity performed on a certain network. If this software detects anything that may threaten the safety and security of the network, it reports the activity to an administrator. This type of software may be employed in individual or corporate networks. Typically, monitoring software checks all information flow of network traffic on the internet. Computer surveillance software is sophisticated enough to easily detect any abnormal or suspicious action in a multitude of network information.

In the field of computer security, biometrics refers to an authentication process that requires physiological proof to validate a user. Once the measure of the user's physiology is authenticated, they will be granted access to appropriate information. Biometric identification ranges from fingerprints, facial recognition, voice recognition, hand patterns, or eye patterns. The individual's biometric information is uploaded and stored in a security system that must recognize these physical characteristics to provide information access.

Managing Vendors

One of the primary benefits of a well-designed and -managed HRIS is its ability to use data to develop evidence-based solutions. Traditionally, many solutions and recommendations have been based on experience, common business practices, or long-standing assumptions that may not actually be founded on objective facts. HRIS can provide HR professionals with the analytical tools necessary to answer questions that influence policy decisions. For example, by pulling data related to employee pay, retention, and future performance, HR can formulate a more compelling case for increasing an organization's standard raise structure with recommendations that are based on concrete results from the data analysis. When there is a difficult problem, data can provide something humans sometimes cannot—an unbiased perspective. For example, an organization may be committed to diversity in its upper management, and yet it still finds that it is unable to meet diversity goals in promoting employees. Conscious and unconscious biases may be influencing who managers recommend for advancement. Standardized performance metrics that are evaluated by employee management software could produce a fair and representative list of who is qualified for a particular promotion.

Using Technology that Analyzes Data

In selecting HR technology solutions, HR professionals need to coordinate with vendors. Because salespeople are obviously not the best source for unbiased product recommendations, it is important for HR professionals to understand their organization's technology needs and do their due diligence on industry standards. Although it is important for an organization's technology capabilities to stay current, innovation can be balanced with realistic day-to-day operational needs. The time, cost, and training needed to implement a new HRIS should be weighed against the benefits it will bring to the organization. Also, cybersecurity is of vital importance in an organization's technology plan, especially when it comes to employees' sensitive personal data. While it is impossible for any vendor to guarantee absolute security, vendors should still provide security protections that are at or above industry standard, as well as provide a response plan for how to handle any software failures.

Tools to Compile Data

Organizations often implement systems or software specific to HR functions. These tools can allow easier access to and downloading of data. HR can then use the downloaded data to review it for various purposes. Excel spreadsheets can be a vital tool for HR. From analyzing average or median compensation data for salary surveys, to determining which employees are eligible to retire for succession planning purposes, to running a mail merge with Microsoft Word of mailing addresses to send out a newsletter, spreadsheets can be an extremely useful and effective tool. Human resources management systems (HRMS) provide many services to an organization in one platform; they can handle employee information such as personal data, payroll functions such as issues with paychecks, training schedules and rosters to ensure compliance with mandated training, and compensation data to evaluate an employee's salary. HRMS platforms often have a custom report program as well. These platforms usually allow users to download the data from the system to an Excel spreadsheet for further analysis and review. Reports can be run that show many different topics and status, including:

- Types of employees (full-time, part-time, limited-term)
- Employee demographics (male/female, over/under 40, years of service, retirement eligible)
- Compensation Information (last increase, annual wage)
- Training Records (mandated training, voluntary training)
- Open positions (recruitment needs)

This information can be vital when:

- Preparing budget and headcount reports and analysis
- Preparing company overview information for prospective applicants
- Initiating voluntary retirement programs
- Preparing succession plans
- Planning service awards and recognizing milestone anniversaries
- Analyzing compensation for salary surveys and reviews
- Ensuring compliance with mandated training as well as required training for certain positions
- Determining recruitment strategies

By having accurate information available quickly, HR can properly assess multiple areas to ensure effective strategies are implemented to address them.

Methods to Collect Data

Data Advocate

Using Data to Inform Business Decisions

Data that is collected from reliable, relevant, and unbiased sources can provide a tremendous amount of objective information from which evidence-based, logical decisions can be made. Therefore, good data can provide several benefits to business and non-profit organizations. Data can provide information about consumer trends, customer preferences, client engagement, and advertising techniques. Internally, data can provide information about employees, including productivity trends and influencers, job satisfaction, the effects of specific performance rewards and benefits, turnover rates, and so forth. This information can then be further explored to develop and implement process changes that affect how business operations take place; how employees are recruited, trained, and rewarded; and how the organization impacts its surrounding environment. A number of data collection, management, and

analytical tools that convert raw data into clear trends are available for use. This allows even individuals who have limited background experience using statistical methods to learn how to best leverage information available within the organization.

Evidence-Based Decision-Making

Evidence-based decision-making is a concept that utilizes information grounded in statistically significant data, peer-reviewed scholarly research, the reported values and preferences of stakeholders, and reputable anecdotes of industry experts to drive industrial, organizational, or scientific efforts. When HR professionals make decisions based on evidence, they provide credibility and logical support to their endeavors as they can show that such decisions have had consistent prior success. Published evidence also provides transparency—a vital component of communication that builds trust—as to why certain decisions are made; it can be easily communicated to and shared with employees who are interested. Utilizing established, proven information to drive decisions is also associated with outcomes that are of higher quality and less prone to failures or errors. Finally, evidence-based decision-making allows the process to be a collaboration between leadership personnel, individuals who are affected by the decision, and other stakeholders, as necessary. This can be an empowering practice for all parties involved.

Validating HR Programs, Practices, and Policies

Validation as it relates to HR programs, practices, and policies refers to monitoring their step-by-step processes from start to finish to ensure that the same, desired output occurs every time. They should be regularly audited for strict operating parameters, controlled processes, and clearly defined outcomes within each of these categories. Validation ensures that a program, practice, or policy delivers results in a consistent and predictable manner. Each of these aspects of HR should be reviewed at periodic intervals to ensure that they are still valid, as variable circumstances such as employee changes, regulatory reforms, customer preferences, and environmental factors are inputs which can influence process validity. When process validation is compromised and products or services are not produced in a consistent manner with expected specifications, there is an increased risk to product or service quality. In turn, this can translate to poor customer or stakeholder experiences, failure to meet expected deliverables or metrics, and an overall waste of resources.

Decision Points Informed by Data and Evidence

Decision points for which large sets of clean, relevant data exist should always draw upon analytics of the data to drive decision-making. Analytics software can analyze large data sets for trends that show how certain decisions have played out historically. Additionally, external studies conducted by universities or other research groups may have published manuscripts that provide relevant evidence to guide a decision. When HR professionals finds themselves at a point where an organizational decision needs to be made, they should first examine if any data or published research exists that could indicate best practices relevant for the decision at hand. If absolutely no data or published research on the topic exists, HR professionals have a responsibility to make an educated hypothesis to drive decision-making, implement a test of change, and gather relevant data along the course of the initiative that can be later analyzed. Outcomes should be shared with colleagues.

Data Gathering

Data Collection, Research Methods, Benchmarks, and HR Metrics

Data collection should procure information that is relevant to the process or outcome of interest. Quality assurance is the process of establishing a relevant, unbiased system of data collection. HR professionals must define data to be collected (i.e., qualitative, quantitative, anecdotal), standardize

collection processes and instruments, and train data collectors. Data collection should be free from bias, confounders, unethical practices, and any other influences that skew the reliability and validity of the data. When possible, data collection should be random, objective, and standardized to the greatest extent. HR professionals will need to understand basics of different research design methods (i.e., experimental, observational) in order to select the most appropriate one for the context. Benchmarks and HR metrics should guide the type of research design and data collection utilized. For example, a metric focused on employee satisfaction will collect data differently than a metric focused on employee absenteeism.

Ensuring that Documents and Systems Reflect Workforce Activities

Human Resources handles many key documents and paperwork that must be stored appropriately, securely, confidentially, and accurately. This documentation should also be readily accessible and easy to locate. Files should be handled in the same way to eliminate wasting time to locate specific documents. It is also important to have a centralized location for all files to ensure that all of the information is accessible and available when needed. HR professionals should not have to look in multiple places for documentation. A good example of this is personnel files. HR should be responsible for maintaining the master personnel file which includes all new hire paperwork, status change information, benefits selections, training records, disciplinary records, performance evaluations, and more. While many departments like to maintain a separate file of documentation for their employees for easier access, it is vital to ensure that HR has the master records on each employee so that there are no missing documents. This could be a cause for concern if the department is not maintaining a secure and confidential filing system or adhering to the strict retention laws about maintaining certain documents for required time periods.

Solving Organizational Problems and Answering Questions

When using data to solve organizational problems and answer questions, HR professionals can expect to come across less than ideal sources. These sources of data may be factually inaccurate, collected with poor research design methods, irrelevant to the interest at hand, biased, or otherwise ineffectual. HR professionals should turn to high quality, reputable sources of data and data synthesis before reviewing it and relevant studies. This can include internal sources, such as a data information or statistics team within the organization whose sole purpose it is to collect and analyze data, or external sources, such as academic journals or industry renowned publications. HR professionals should ensure that data and studies are recent (ideally collected or published within the past three years). Meaningful data should be statistically significant, answer questions of interest, and come from a controlled collection mechanism. All sources should be cited and dated to provide complete context.

Data Gathering

Data collection methods will vary based on the type of solution or review process that is needed. Surveys can be used to gather individual feedback from a wide demographic. They can be conducted in person, online, or over the telephone; however, they are subject to interviewer bias, voluntary completion, and low completion rates. Focus groups utilize the services of a skilled facilitator who solicits feedback and opinions about a specific topic from identified stakeholders. Focus groups run the risk of low engagement or facilitator bias. Observational data collection utilizes one data collector to observe a specific context and take notes; however, this is highly subject to bias if the data collector is visible. Other types of data collection can be quantitative, such as records of sales, customer satisfaction scores, number of process failures, or returning clients. If an organization maintains diligent data management practices, these can usually serve as easily accessible sources of information. Permission to use personal information is normally required.

Relevant Data in External Sources

Scanning external sources for data relevant to the organization can include reputable news sources, highly regarded digital and paper publications, keynote speakers and workshops at industry-specific conferences, discussions at high-level networking events, and data disseminated by successful competitors or colleagues. HR professionals should note any threats or opportunities that may present from competing organizations, demographic changes in the organization's geographic region, new relevant federal or state regulations, consumer trends relevant to their organization's products or services, changes in technology or innovation that could impact the organization's operations and output, potential environmental factors that could affect the organization's productivity, shifts in political climate and social culture, and so on. This type of information can be organized into a PESTLE chart or SWOT analysis to best review the potential impact to the organization. HR professionals should always ensure that external sources are credible and legitimate before utilizing information in any capacity.

HR-Related Threats and Liabilities

HR-related threats and liabilities refer to events that could produce a negative impact on the organization's ability to recruit, retain, reward, and manage skilled employees who fit with the company's culture and with its professional needs. HR-related threats and liabilities can come internally, such as from high turnover rates, or they can come externally, such as from a lack of qualified applicants in an area. SWOT analyses are comprehensive tools that help to identify both internal and external threats and opportunities. In addition, they can also be used to identify strengths and weaknesses, which can then be utilized to address the more challenging aspects of established threats and opportunities. The SWOT matrix is a flexible tool that can be used to analyze small HR-related issues at the individual or departmental level, or larger issues that impact the entire organization.

SWOT Analysis

	Helpful	Harmful
Internal origin	**S** Strengths	**W** Weaknesses
External origin	**O** Opportunities	**T** Threats

Benchmarks HR Initiatives and Outcomes Against the Organization's Competition

Benchmarking, or comparing one's initiatives and outcomes against competition, industry established standards, and industry established goals, is one way for HR professionals to determine the efficacy and

value of their endeavors. It allows the organization to understand if they are creating, pricing, and delivering products or services appropriately for their targeted consumer base. Benchmarking involves developing internal metrics for key variables that can be translated to provide a comparable review against other top players in the industry. HR professionals should ensure that their benchmarking practices are relevant and comprehensive. For example, if they are trying to compare average compensation for a certain department against a competitor's, they may need to look beyond annual salary to include benefits such as 401(k) matching rates, time off, flexible work culture, and other aspects that employees could view as benefits in order to draw a true comparison between organizations.

Reporting Techniques

Data Analysis
Statistics and Measurement Concepts
While several software and online applications exist to make statistical methods and measurement concepts easier to use, HR professionals should maintain a basic working knowledge of these fields in order to create functional research designs and collect clean data that can be interpreted with an end goal in mind. In addition, this knowledge allows HR professionals to understand, accurately communicate, and productively apply trends derived from data sets. HR professionals should feel comfortable inputting data into software and running appropriate analyses to find the information they want. HR professionals should have a basic understanding of concepts such as means, hypothesis testing, regression analysis, and variance analysis in order to compare tests of change from baseline levels. This provides evidence that implemented initiatives are effective and can also provide insight toward certain factors which may be more effective than others.

Identifying Misleading Data
Working knowledge of statistics, measurement concepts, and other aspects of data allows the HR professional to understand when data are flawed, misleading, or should otherwise be avoided. When reviewing scholarly literature or articles in which statistics are cited, it is important to read beyond the conclusion drawn by the author. HR professionals should review sampling and methodology text within manuscripts to ensure that the sample of data collected was large enough to be statistically significant, that all influencing bias or confounders were controlled for, and that inappropriate correlations were not drawn from the data. Visual representations of data can also misconstrue the true meaning and should always be examined further. For example, if a bar chart shows a large pay gap between two sets of employees in the same department, it may appear that the organization has an unjust compensation system. However, further investigation could show that one set of employees is entry-level in experience while the other is senior.

Conducting Analyses
HR professionals must be able to apply research of best practices to practical application within their workplace and test these applications to ensure efficacy. In order to determine which research findings are critical and could make an impact within their organization, HR professionals need to examine the context in which best practices were determined. For example, a case study may correlate the implementation of a worksite wellness program with a reduction in employee health insurance claims. However, if this case study took place in an organization with 100 employees, it may not produce the same correlation in an organization with 1,000 employees. Therefore, HR professionals may need to tailor the methodology for their specific organization if this is an initiative they hope to pursue successfully. Additionally, they will need to establish a basic framework for evaluating new initiatives.

Finally, HR professionals should be eager to solicit verbal or written anecdotal feedback from key stakeholders.

Objective Data Interpretation

Once data is collected, it can be challenging to maintain objectivity when interpreting it, especially if personal responsibility, time investment, or interest is at stake. Data collection is always subject to confirmation bias by the researcher, which can skew results. Additionally, data analysis does not always reflect trends that an organization hopes to see, and these findings can be indicative of ineffective processes or performance. It can be difficult to maintain an objective, rather than emotional, stance when this occurs. Additionally, negative qualitative data, especially data that come from interviews with personal opinions of stakeholders, can be difficult for interpreters to not view as a personal attack. However, it is vital to treat these contexts as learning opportunities and to reflect upon setbacks that may have occurred to cause such outcomes with nonjudgmental clarity. From there, rational and effective process and performance improvements can take place.

Communication Techniques

Two-Way Communication

HR professionals can develop effective and satisfactory working relationships with supervisors and HR leaders by engaging in two-way communication about project expectations, deadlines, needs, and goals. These aspects should be discussed and documented when a work assignment is first received and should take priority during the planning aspect of the project. HR professionals should expect superiors to dedicate time to this planning period. In return, HR professionals should utilize this time to ask questions about the project and bring up any questions to best respect the time that leadership is providing. Developing a written project proposal with leadership that outlines the timeline, milestones, resources needed, and concrete dates for deliverables can be a useful method to ensure that both HR staff members and leadership have the same expectations. Once expectations are communicated, HR professionals should make every reasonable effort to deliver results autonomously, without the need for constant leadership follow-up.

Communication Among Team Members

As an HR professional, high levels of human interaction are inherent to the nature of the work. Beyond serving employees within an organization, HR professionals can expect to work in a team within and outside of their department. Team members may be assigned by project rather than personally chosen; therefore, it is important to develop wide-ranging engagement skills that promote positive interactions. HR professionals can build their intrapersonal skills by examining their own strengths and weaknesses through analytical personality tests, and actively working to improve areas of weakness. This can be achieved by utilizing pockets of time to practice intrapersonal skills with colleagues, such as over lunch or during a meeting. Developing emotional intelligence (EI) skills also helps one recognize others' feelings and communication styles, and this information can be used to build better relationships. Maintaining a positive attitude, showing appreciation for support and tasks done well, and avoiding negative talk and behaviors also fosters team cohesiveness.

Communication Among Stakeholders and Team Members

It is also important to create teams that have members with similar professional interests and goals, in order to minimize resistance as the project progresses. However, open communication may be the most crucial component of fostering collaboration among a team. While cultivating open communication lines is a team effort, those who choose to actively model behaviors that lend to open communication are

likely to become leaders within the team. Team leaders should promote an encouraging environment that allows all members and stakeholders to voice their opinions and concerns without fearing retribution. This may involve speaking with team members individually, especially if they are quieter or prefer speaking one-on-one. Finally, building relationships outside of the work setting, such as over creative social events, allows team members to get to know one another better. This can allow team members to feel more open and collaborative during the work setting.

Ways of Communication

Town hall meetings, formal gatherings for the entire company that are commonly referred to as "all-hands meetings," tend to focus on sharing information "from the top down" concerning the overall organization, and thus are not usually designed to allow feedback from employees about smaller detail issues. An **open-door policy** is used to establish a relationship where employees feel comfortable speaking directly with management about problems and suggestions. In essence, an open-door policy enables a supervisor or manager to be a "human suggestion box." There are several potential roadblocks to a successful open-door policy. In certain situations, it can be difficult to create an environment where employees feel comfortable discussing problems in person with management. In addition, depending on the problem reported, it may not be possible to maintain confidentiality. However, in the right situation, an open-door policy can help companies identify problems quickly, almost in real-time, without having to wait for a formal meeting to address an ongoing issue.

Management by Walking Around (MBWA), as the name suggests, involves having managers and supervisors physically get out of their offices and interact with employees in person. MBWA allows management to check on employee progress, inquire about potential issues, and gain feedback without relying on employees to "make the first move" through an open-door policy or online suggestion form. This strategy also helps prevent management from becoming isolated behind a desk and seeming distant and disinterested in employee problems.

Email makes it easy to get information to a lot of people very quickly. However, this communication method can result in employees suffering from "information overload" from too many emails, making it more likely that important information is overlooked. Also, there is a danger that confidential information may be accidentally communicated to the wrong people.

The **intranet** (internal website and computer network) has the benefit of eliminated risk of important information being accessed by someone outside the organization. Intranets can be very effective at communicating important ongoing information about the company, such as policies and procedures. In addition, companies often store necessary workplace documentation, such as HR-related forms, on an intranet. This allows employees to access that information when necessary. However, if outside parties need information on the intranet, they cannot access it. In addition, intranet communication is often "top-down" and does not allow for feedback from employees. It is also important to note that some intranet systems are not user-friendly, causing employees to be discouraged from using them.

Newsletters can provide a variety of information and have the potential to do so in an engaging, welcoming manner. However, newsletters can be labor-intensive. Since they are relatively infrequent, newsletters are not always useful for communicating urgent or immediate information. In addition, newsletters do not allow for formal two-way communication from employees, although this can be remedied by involving employees in the creation of the newsletter.

Finally, **word-of-mouth** communication can quickly spread information throughout a group of people. However, as in the children's game "Telephone," information can become muddled, misinterpreted, and

downright unrecognizable as it is passed from person to person. A manager or supervisor has no control over misinterpretations and misunderstandings that can result from word-of-mouth communication.

Exchanging Organizational Information

Communicating HR Programs, Practices, and Policies to Both HR and Non-HR Employees

Organizational communication must be appropriately delivered by the sender and received by the intended recipient in order to be effective. Communicating within the HR department may be an easier task for the HR professional than communicating with outside departments, as the HR department is likely to house similar values, interests, goals, and methods of communication. The HR department, however, establishes many crucial programs, practices, and policies that affect the operations and culture of the entire organizations. Entities such as employee benefits, ethical handbooks, and company-wide events often originate in the HR department and must be shared across all departments. Effective communication strategies often employ the influence of top leadership, a reliable mode of dissemination that is favored by most recipients, and evaluation practices that focus on utilizing recipient feedback to analyze the overall efficacy of the communication channel. When communicating, HR professionals should also account for informal avenues, such as break room conversation.

Helping Non-HR Managers Communicate HR Issues

Managers are excellent vectors of communication and leveraging the relationships and influence managers have with their team members can be a method of communicating organizational HR issues. In order to effectively utilize this resource, HR professionals should network with managers to build rapport and credibility. This also helps HR professionals understand what values are important to the manager; consequently, HR professionals can illustrate how HR issues impact the manager and their team. HR professionals should keep in mind that managers may welcome or resist serving as their team's communication channel for HR topics. It is important to make this process easy for the manager to implement, rather than seem like an additional burdensome responsibility. Finally, once this practice is established, HR professionals should remain an open and reliable liaison for the manager to return to should any HR-related questions or concerns arise.

Voicing Support for HR and Organizational Initiatives in Communications with Stakeholders

HR professionals serve as a champion for their department. Their interactions with stakeholders should reflect pride, value, and confidence in the department's work in order to maintain positive engagement from the stakeholders. Stakeholders are more likely to remain resistant if HR personnel display neutral or negative stances about their own department's initiatives. Additionally, previously engaged stakeholders may begin to lose interest or feel a loss of value. If an instance occurs where the HR professional feels they cannot support an initiative in communications with stakeholders, leadership should be notified in order to find a resolution. This may involve changing a component of the initiative, altering the communication process between the department and the stakeholder, or shifting job responsibilities in order to achieve a better fit.

Communicating with Senior HR Leaders

Effective communication with senior HR leaders allows both leadership and subordinate personnel to openly share information related to the organization's HR needs. It allows both groups to communicate in a timely manner. HR personnel should be mindful of leadership's time and commitments. This means limiting unnecessary interaction. Communication should remain concise, professional, and on topic. This

can be achieved by specifically addressing why the communication is being made, what is needed from the leader, and if there is a time constraint associated with any of the needs. It can also be beneficial to recognize leadership's preferred method of communication. Finally, HR staff members should take initiative to communicate expected correspondence, such as monthly department reports or deliverables.

Listening

Listening Actively and Empathetically

Active listening pushes the listener into an engaged position. Beyond using their sense of hearing, active listeners also use their sense of sight to notice the speaker's body language. Both auditory and visual information are consciously synthesized to perceive what the speaker is trying to communicate. In addition, the listener verbally reflects the information provided by the speaker, and then asks for confirmation that the information was perceived in the way the speaker intended. Only then does the listener formulate a response. Empathetic listening includes placing oneself in the perspective of the speaker and formulating a response based on how the speaker will accept it. HR personnel often face emotionally charged conversations dealing with an employee's job or family. Utilizing active and empathetic listening skills conveys concerns for the employee and helps diffuse tense situations.

Competing Points of View

Competing points of view, when expressed respectfully, are healthy components of communication that often lead to new perspectives, collaboration, innovation, opportunities, and improvements. HR professionals should always remain open to hearing dissenting opinions and actively seek to understand the reasoning behind them. Rather than perceiving dissenting opinions as a personal attack, competing points of view should be welcomed as part of the inherent business process. They should be treated with logic and objective reasoning in order to come to a resolution. While it is impossible to satisfy every employee's opinion, HR initiatives and decisions should be made with trying to achieve the highest percentage of employee satisfaction and the best processes for company productivity in mind.

Seeking Further Information

Ambiguity can cause conflict, affect business processes, and cause distress to employees. Unfortunately, ambiguity is not always preventable due to factors that are often outside of the organization's control. In situations that are within the control of the HR professional, active listening practices are an important component of clear communication. The listener may need to directly state that they are confused and ask specific questions that result in a clear "Yes" or "No" answer. The listener may also need to observe the speaker's body language to determine whether the content is purposely being presented with ambiguity. However, speculation is never a good route to take to determine answers. When possible, directly asking the speaker to clarify is most likely to result in a positive result.

Addressing Stakeholder Communications

Stakeholders are considered as such because they are directly impacted by the actions of the HR department. Therefore, they are highly valuable to the efficacy of HR initiatives. Comments from them should be prioritized. Stakeholder communications can take place in person, in meetings as a group, through email, or through social media. There may not always be time to respond to stakeholder questions, especially if they are unanticipated and come up in person. In these instances, it is important for HR professionals to clearly indicate that they will need to source more information and follow up with the stakeholders. Additionally, it is important to always have the best method of contact information for each stakeholder on hand.

Received Communications

When HR professionals receive communication, they should be able to accurately identify the reason behind it. While motives for a message may not be directly stated, HR professionals can use contextual understanding. However, HR professionals should form this understanding based on objective logic, without making assumptions that are not rooted in fact. When motives for a message cannot be objectively determined, the HR professional should feel confident responding in a way that asks clarifying questions and dispels any ambiguity. Otherwise, assumptions about intention within a message can cause muddled decision-making that can have widespread ramifications.

Soliciting Feedback from Senior Leaders

Soliciting feedback is a crucial component of program evaluation, guiding and sustaining initiatives, and providing valuable customer service. HR professionals serve all units of an organization. Therefore, they should solicit feedback from leadership in all areas, keeping in mind that different leaders may have various needs and values. Learning organizational needs through the lens of each department can increase employee engagement, provide the value that leadership are asking for, and propel operations. HR professionals can solicit feedback from leadership through online evaluation surveys, in-person meetings, and group meetings. They should ask leadership what initiatives are going well and why, and what areas need more support. HR professionals should always leave open communication channels for leadership to propose new projects and ideas. These endeavors highlight the value of a company's HR department.

Employee Relations Programs

Employee Recognition

Employee recognition has been proven to be the most effective method of improving motivation and engaging employees. Regardless of the program, formality, award, or method, recognition is key to ensuring a high level of employee satisfaction and morale in an organization. Informal recognition programs can include the following:

- Recognizing a team or individual for a particular job well done in an employee newsletter
- Extending recognition during standing department meetings
- Saying thank you when an employee goes above and beyond
- Making sure employees feel appreciated in general

Formal recognition programs generally have a policy written to ensure that elements such as funding and budget, resources, and other specifics are identified. These programs can include the following:

- Service awards: 5 years, 10 years, 15 years
- Milestone service awards: 20 years, 25 years, 30 years
- Employee of the year
- Manager of the year

These awards may be given during a formal lunch, recognizing everyone and the contributions made to the organization. Gifts may be provided as well to truly convey a message of gratitude for the employee's hard work, dedication, and loyalty to the organization.

Employee Recognition Vendors

Due to a lack of staff resources, time, or in-house expertise, companies may choose to outsource their employee rewards program to a trusted recognition vendor. Since a vendor can, ultimately, determine

the success or failure of a company's rewards program, there are several items that an employer should evaluate when entering this type of relationship.

An exceptional recognition vendor will take the time to learn about a company's culture, business goals, employee rewards needs, and program budget. The recognition vendor should have an offering of high-quality awards and be able to accommodate rush orders and unique awards, if needed.

Additionally, world-class customer service is the key to employees receiving timely reward fulfillment and recognition for their efforts and achievements. An employer should be assured that the company will receive correct invoices and accurate reporting from the vendor. The ultimate goal for both the employer and the recognition vendor is to ensure that employees feel valued and remain loyal.

Special Events

Companies can use **special events** to engage employees and promote a positive organizational culture. These events can involve managers serving lunch to employees during customer service appreciation week, organizing monthly employee events such as an ice cream social on a random Friday afternoon or an after-work happy hour, or planning an annual holiday party or company picnic for employees to enjoy with their co-workers and their families at a local amusement park. Additionally, these events can incorporate an element of community service, such as employees getting together to assist a local organization (an animal shelter or a food bank) during a "day of caring" event. Employee wellness can also be factored into these special events by scheduling yoga classes onsite for employees to participate in, or by providing monthly chair massages in a conference room at a reduced price for staff.

Diversity and Inclusion

Diversity comes in many forms. In its simplest definition, workplace diversity refers to differences in employees' characteristics. While many people may think of diversity in terms of race and gender, diversity also includes a plethora of other characteristics like age, nationality, sexuality, personality, education, family background, and socioeconomic status. While diversity refers to bringing together a team of people with different characteristics, inclusion refers to valuing, listening to, and using the products of those differences. In this way, diversity can be thought of as bringing different people to the table, while inclusion is giving them a chance to contribute to and lead the discussion.

Providing Training on Cultural Differences

For employees from the younger generation, D&I involves a more proactive mixture of diverse ideas, strategies, and backgrounds to lead an organization to innovation and modernization. From this perspective, D&I involves not only a commitment to equality, but also programs that harness the skills of a diverse workforce. One way for HR professionals to foster this is by building opportunities for mentoring and coaching between employees. For example, if an organization wants to retain and promote female employees, it might implement a mentoring program that pairs new employees with more experienced women in the company who can share their advice and insights about achieving professional success. Cross-cultural training can also be useful in creating opportunities for employees to hear about and benefit from diverse ideas. Many organizations also have employee resource groups (ERGs), which are groups created by employees who share some demographic factor(s) based on things like race, gender, or age. ERGs help diverse employees to feel represented within the organization while also helping leaders to gain insight into the needs of diverse customers and other stakeholders.

Distinguishing Between Performance Issues and Cultural Differences

While HR should work with employees at all levels, there are also specific concerns for D&I policies with managers. For example, managers may need additional training and guidance on distinguishing between performance issues and cultural differences. Culture refers to a shared set of beliefs, behaviors, attitudes, and values. Every organization has its own culture, but, particularly in organizations that have not yet developed a great deal of diversity in upper management, it can be easy to conflate the organization's culture with its leaders' demographic culture. Behaviors and customs that are assumed to be universal may not be present in every demographic, leading to conflict when a more diverse workforce is recruited. Managers may perceive their employees as "not fitting in" or "not having the right attitude" simply because they come from a different background with different expectations; this in turn can lead to conscious and unconscious biases in employee evaluations and promotions. HR professionals can anticipate and counteract this effect by providing cultural training for managers. They can also help managers to define clear, reasonable, and appropriate guidelines for clarifying performance measures.

Diversity and Inclusion (D&I) Current Trends

In addition to developing an organization's relationship with external stakeholders, a well-managed D&I program should also build employee relations and satisfaction within an organization. First, it's important to understand how employees view diversity in the workplace. For many older generation employees, diversity means equality and fairness for all workers regardless of their individual characteristics. In this view, less attention is made to what those differences actually are. Rather, employees look for policies that are defined and applied with fairness. This applies to organizational structures in particular. If it becomes evident that management- and executive-level positions are not being filled in a way that adheres to an organization's D&I principles, it is up to HR to investigate and resolve why this is happening. For example, HR may need to craft policies that remove demographic barriers to success or avoid nepotism or cronyism.

Valuing D&I Policies

Research shows that organizations with robust D&I policies are more profitable. Beyond the financial benefits, though, D&I makes sense for organizations operating in increasingly diverse environments. Many organizations say that it just makes sense to have a workforce whose makeup reflects that of the population they serve. In this way, then, an organization's commitment to diversity should be communicated to external stakeholders, helping the organization to build its relationship with clients and customers in the community. This can be accomplished by partnering with external diversity-focused programs and initiatives as well as by incorporating D&I accomplishments into marketing materials.

Fairness of Policies to All Employees

Fundamentally, an organization's D&I program needs to be all-encompassing and top-to-bottom. The commitment to and accountability for D&I need to begin with executive-level leadership and spread through leaders of all areas of the organization. However, leaders often defer to HR professionals when it comes to planning and executing D&I policies and programs.

HR professionals can also develop training programs to communicate D&I policies and model desired behavior. Again, these programs and policies should target employees from all levels of an organization, because lower-level managers will look to upper-level managers as a model for their diversity practices. Topics to cover can include things like cultural awareness, unconscious bias, generational differences,

and communication styles. Research shows that employees consider things like creativity and innovation to be closely linked to diversity, so these topics can also be included in training programs.

Workplace Accommodations

Workplace accommodations fall within the scope of D&I, too. This generally relates to the Americans with Disabilities Act (ADA), which requires employers to offer reasonable accommodation to any employee with a medical condition that prevents them from performing all the functions of a job as described. Generally, it is up to the employee to request the accommodation rather than the employer to offer it first. Also, "reasonable" means that the accommodation will not place undue burden on the employer or fundamentally change the nature of its business. Examples of reasonable accommodations include installing ramps to make areas in the workplace wheelchair accessible or providing employees with additional break time. Of course, what constitutes a "reasonable" accommodation and "undue" employer burden must be evaluated on a case-by-case basis.

Also, accommodations do not only apply to physical disabilities and medical conditions. Employees might also request accommodations based on religious beliefs, for example, such as requiring time off during religious observations or refusing to perform job activities that violate their religious beliefs. Because reasonable accommodations still require employees to perform the essential function of their position and contribute to the overall purpose of the organization, HR professionals are responsible for reviewing job descriptions and determining whether the employees' requests can be accommodated.

Work-Life Balance

Work-life balance is a goal for everyone. Organizations that promote flexibility and balance generally have happy, engaged, and motivated employees. Organizations should constantly look for new ways to incorporate flexible practices in the workplace. Employees appreciate and are grateful for the opportunity to balance life and work by incorporating these practices into their lives. Some common best practices for work-life balance are:

- Flexible work schedules (4 x 10 or 9 x 80 workweek)
- Telecommuting or work-at-home options
- Reduced work schedules such as part-time work
- Reduced overtime
- Onsite child care and child-friendly policies
- Relaxed dress code policies and programs
- Approving extended leaves of absences to accomplish outside goals

It is important to understand that what one employee values may not be important to another employee. Having a variety of programs available can help to ensure that there is something for everyone. It is also important to understand that work-life balance does not mean an equal balance. Depending on the position, operations, customer needs, and organizational requirements, flexibility may not be available at certain times. Flexibility in work schedules may be available only at certain times of the year, depending on the industry and the needs of the company.

Additionally, as an employee's personal situation changes, their needs may also change. Single employees with no children will have a different definition of work-life balance than a married employee with five children. While it is impossible to provide a program that satisfies every single employee, it is possible to have various programs that align with the business and potential needs of individuals. A best practice to incorporate into an organization is to establish employee surveys and focus groups to hear

directly from many employees what programs would increase work-life balance. There may be possible solutions and recommendations that can be researched and implemented. Not only is a new program available, but employees will be more engaged and motivated because they were involved in the process.

When employees have a healthy work-life balance, employers see an increase in focus, motivation, and job satisfaction. Additionally, employers see higher productivity levels and less negativity and stress in the work environment. Employees are generally healthier and less stressed, and they accomplish their work goals. Additionally, employees have healthier relationships outside of work. The work culture is one of engagement, motivation, and high morale. Employees know they are valued, supported, and important to the success of the organization.

Alternative Work Locations

Technological increases have created viable scenarios for employers to offer alternative work locations, which provide another opportunity to improve work-life balance for employees. If a corporation offers alternative work locations, employees are allowed to work from home or another off-site location rather than a traditional office space. Communication between organizations and its remote employees generally takes place through the Internet and phone calls. Alternative work locations can also be helpful in disaster recovery because organizational data is decentralized and more difficult to corrupt entirely.

Performance Management and Appraisal

Performance appraisal is a process that is integral to maintaining standards that are essential to consistent productivity in an organization. An intricate process, performance appraisal measures and evaluates the quality of work that is performed by employees. It is a barometer by which employees must exceed pre-established benchmarks and simultaneously uphold organizational protocol. Moreover, managers and administrators compare performance appraisal results with other employees and expectations while making rational decisions regarding efficacy and value. From the process, management crafts a compilation of results and data with the intention of performing a cost-benefit analysis. After these analytical methodologies are conducted, management and administrators will enact appropriate changes for improvement.

After a performance appraisal, management will affect these improvements through incentivizing programs. Increasing salaries or rewarding promotions are typically two strategies that are used to reinforce desired behavior. For employees who are found to be less efficient or productive, training or counseling programs are a means of providing underperforming individuals with the tools to improve. In some instances, management will pursue punitive responses to underperformance: demotions, reductions in pay, or termination of employment. Essential to performance appraisal is the establishment of firm standards and procedures for an organization in which underperformance will be quickly rectified. An inflexible organizational infrastructure forces employees to conform to the institution, rather than institutional codes being disregarded and ignored.

Communicational development is a crucial advantage of performance appraisal. A channel of communication is clearly delineated through two principal means: organizational rules and regulations, and explicit managerial examinations. Organizational policies offer nonverbal guidance to employees by consistently challenging them to assimilate to protocol while sustaining maximal productive capacities. After performance appraisals are conducted, managerial expectations can be developed, and solutions to remedy underperformance can be pursued. Any disputes between labor and management can

quickly be softened by maintaining stringent channels of communication, where both sides have assigned responsibilities and coordinate to meet shared goals.

Goal Setting

A robust system of planning can be incorporated into an organization's agenda to set expectations and devise strategies to meet them. Monitoring performance levels enables organizations to ensure that operations harmonize with expectations. If specific goals are not met, this indicates an error in planning or execution. Identifying any unmet goals makes organizations more likely to become more productive by constantly improving.

Benchmarking

Employers use salary surveys to assist them when working to establish the pay structures for their organizations. These surveys collect information from multiple employers regarding salary and benefits, such as employees' starting salaries, merit increases, bonus amounts, and work hours. In order to be comparable, salary surveys are conducted by focusing on a specific geographic region or industry.

Employers can make use of free government salary surveys and inexpensive industry-specific salary surveys, such as those for civil engineering and construction. Employer associations, like the **Society for Human Resource Management (SHRM)**, also conduct salary surveys and provide the results to their members at no charge. Additionally, companies can elect to outsource a salary survey to a survey vendor, which can be quite pricey.

It is important to note that salary survey data contains time-sensitive data that can become outdated rather quickly. Salary data may also need to be aged and/or leveled. **Aging** is the process of adjusting salary data to keep pace with market movement. **Leveling** can be used if a job included on the salary survey is similar—but not identical—to a position within the organization. The data for that job can be weighted or leveled to create a better match.

Instruments

Some types of performance appraisals are the 360-degree feedback, general appraisal, employee self-assessment appraisal, and the technological/administrative performance appraisal. The 360-degree feedback method is a way for employees to receive feedback about their performance in an anonymous manner from individuals they frequently work in close contact with, such as their managers, peers, direct reports, customers, and suppliers. The employee self-assessment appraisal forces employees to examine their own work, while management conducts a concurrent appraisal. After these are completed, the two are jointly compared. The technological/administrative performance appraisal concentrates on employees who perform technical jobs. The type of work they do, productivity levels, output, and other important tasks are barometers by which employers measure.

Ranking/Rating Scales

A system for rating employees is the **behaviorally anchored rating scales**, or **BARS**. BARS is a unique system because it specifically focuses on behaviors that are necessary for performing a task successfully, rather than evaluating more analytical employee habits. Instead of appraising general behaviors that are required to be present in all employees, BARS examines precise behaviors that are unique to a certain job or task. After an investigation has taken place, management will employ a designated rating scale that appropriately locates an employee based on performance. On the rating scale, a "1" designates unsatisfactory performance, a "2" designates marginal performance (troublesome employees), a "3" designates fully competent performance, a "4" designates excellent performance, and a "5" designates exceptional performance.

The 1–5 rating scale method demonstrated above is just one of the numerous varieties. In addition to the 1–5 rating scale, they can also express a 1–3 model, 1–4 model, 1–5 model, or 1–10 model. These models are known as rating scale methods. Moreover, another prominent method of appraisal is the checklist method. The **checklist method** features a series of questions that determine a specific level of performance, with the participant placing a check next to applicable statements.

Relationship to Compensation

Rating is a tactic that employers use to incentivize employees to efficiently fulfill tasks in a timely manner. In addition, rating is a way that employers can measure and identify their productive, talented, and best workers. After employees are rated, the highest-performing individuals will be rewarded. Similarly to rating, rewarding is a mechanism used to incentivize and reinforce positive behavior. In all successful organizations, employers have discovered the most efficient means of regulating, monitoring, and sculpting maximal performance strategies.

Training for Evaluators

One key reason why performance appraisals tend to be ineffective is that most individuals who evaluate employee performance have received little or no training on how to do so, and they are not adequately supported throughout the performance appraisal process.

Therefore, many types of performance appraisal errors may result. Evaluators make the similar-to-me error when they rate employees more favorably who are like themselves. Contrast errors come into play when an evaluator focuses on a particular stereotype, such as age or race, instead of on performance when rating employees, or when an evaluator compares two employees who have similar performance records and rates one of the employees higher than the other due to their likeability. Excessive leniency or excessive strictness occurs when performance appraisals are written to be too accommodating or too harsh and tend to be more about the evaluator's temperament than about the employee's job performance. The halo effect takes place when an employee receives a glowing performance appraisal (is rated highly in all areas regardless of actual job performance), after the evaluator notices that he or she is really very good at performing one aspect of their job (perhaps something that the evaluator values personally).

The opposite of halo effect is what is known as the horn effect. The horn effect takes place when an employee receives a negative performance appraisal (is rated poorly in all areas regardless of actual job performance), after the evaluator notices that he or she is poor at performing one aspect of their job (perhaps something that the evaluator values personally). In addition, central tendency error takes place when the evaluator gives all employees a middle of the range performance appraisal score (i.e., a 6 out of 10), so he or she cannot be perceived as "the bad guy" if the truth about employees' job performance is told. The recency effect takes place when an evaluator bases an employee's performance appraisal solely on a recent event (good or bad) instead of on the employee's entire performance history during the established rating period. The opposite of this is what is known as the primacy error. This error takes place when an evaluator bases an employee's performance appraisal solely on their initial impression of the employee (good or bad) instead of on the employee's performance history during the established rating period.

Evaluators should receive the necessary training to ensure that employees' performance appraisals are free from all bias and discrimination. This involves training on how to use the performance tool, training on the various types of performance appraisal errors listed above and how to avoid them, along with how to manage difficult conversations with employees. Performance appraisals should be based on formal evaluation criteria that has been previously set and on evaluators' personal interactions with the

employees. Evaluators should accurately describe employees' behavior by citing specific examples using objective criteria and to document situations as they occur. Additionally, equitable treatment should be provided to all employees during the performance appraisal process.

Outcomes of Performance Management Programs

There are several outcomes of the performance management process, including:

- Disciplinary actions that can be taken for underperforming employees
- Pay increases and incentive rewards
- Opportunities for employee advancement and promotions
- Employee development plans
- Career/succession planning

Performance management gives organizations the opportunity to identify the most suitable jobs for the most qualified people. After analyzing the results of goal setting, if certain individuals possess skill sets that indicate that they would be more productive in other areas of the business, this phase allows those transitions, or transfer assignments, to occur. Furthermore, promotions can be used to reinforce positive behavior. Another strategic use of promotions is to maximize each individual's utility by encouraging them to take positions that they may not have otherwise been interested in. These types of employment moves should be properly documented through the employees' performance appraisals to ensure that the organization is protected should any legal concerns arise.

Collecting Employee Feedback

Employee Attitude Surveys

Employee surveys are a tool that management can use to determine how HR programs are being received by staff, to uncover problem areas in the organization, and to reveal employee preferences or needs. These surveys can be distributed as attitude surveys with the goal of measuring employees' job satisfaction or as opinion surveys with the goal of gathering data on specific issues. It is important that employees know they will be guaranteed anonymity in return for their participation in the survey so they will, in turn, be as honest as possible on how they view their jobs, supervisors, coworkers, organizational policies, etc. This type of employee input provides management with data on the "retention climate" in the company. Collecting this data is extremely important to an organization's retention measurement efforts. It is important for management to share the results of the survey with employees, even if the feedback is negative. By continuing to administer employee surveys annually or at set intervals, management can measure improvements in responses over time.

Focus Groups

Focus groups are small, pre-selected groups of individuals who discuss specific topics in a relaxing environment. Focus groups are an excellent way to gauge employee opinions regarding the employment experience. Topics can include healthcare options, compensation, specific programs, work schedules, training, growth opportunities, supervisory relationships, promotion opportunities, or any other topic that an organization would like direct opinions on from the employees.

It is important to select participants from different departments, different positions, various tenures of service, and various age ranges to ensure diverse perspectives are offered during the focus groups. It may be necessary to have multiple focus groups discussing the same topics to gauge variances or similarities among the individuals in the groups and the groups themselves. When facilitating a focus group, it is vital to ensure that the participants know if the information will be confidential or available

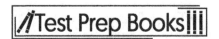

to decision makers. Some participants may not be as willing to share information for fear of retribution or retaliation if their comments and opinions are shared with others. If it is possible, removing names may be a best practice to implement to ensure open and honest dialog and feedback. Without this, a focus group may not yield the best information and ultimately not the best use of time or resources.

<u>Exit Interviews</u>

Individuals who are leaving a company are given an exit interview to uncover their reasons for parting ways with the organization. **Exit interviews** are typically conducted by a neutral party, such as an HR professional, rather than by the departing employee's direct supervisor. HR will typically summarize and analyze the data from exit interviews at regular intervals to share information with management regarding possible improvement opportunities.

Retention

After taking the necessary time to recruit the right employees, it is important for companies to work to retain them. Employee turnover has high costs associated with it—lost time and lost productivity. There are many ways that companies attempt to retain staff, and not one method works for all employees. For example, some employers feel that offering a competitive benefits package that includes healthcare, a retirement program, and life insurance is the best way to retain employees. However, sometimes low or no cost options that improve employees' work/life balance, such as flextime, telecommuting, and allowing employees to wear jeans to work every day (unless they are attending customer-facing meetings) are the best way to go. In addition, staff can be grateful for, and tend to stay longer at, workplaces that provide perks that are meaningful to them. Examples of these include on-site childcare, tuition reimbursement, dry cleaning pickup, and free doughnuts on Fridays.

Succession planning involves preparing current employees for future advancements or promotions by developing their knowledge, skills, and abilities. Ongoing training for any potential open position in the company ensures no loss of productivity or operational efficiency, should key employees leave.

Some common succession planning techniques employers use include special assignments, creating team leadership roles, and sending staff to internal and external training for their continued development. This can also be used as a retention tactic, as employees may recognize the benefit of staying with a company when they can see a clear path toward promotion.

Employers can stay in touch with how their employees are feeling about the work environment by conducting what is known as **stay interviews**. During these interviews, topics including why employees came to work for the employer, why the employees have stayed at the employer, what would make the employees consider leaving, and what the employees would want to see changed are discussed. This allows management to make necessary improvements before they find themselves conducting exit interviews.

Finally, in a workplace that is serious about retention, open communication between management and employees about the company's mission and future goals is key. It is also important for management to show concern for employees' continued development and to promote from within when possible.

Workplace Behavior Issues

Various issues can arise in a workplace that must be addressed by HR. It is extremely important to ensure that policies and procedures address as many of these issues as possible so that employees

understand expectations and appropriate behavior in the workplace. A common concern that many organizations deal with is absenteeism, the practice of not showing up for work or requesting time away from work, sometimes for dubious reasons. Organizations should have a detailed policy for employees to follow to request time away from work. Vacation leave, sick leave, bereavement, military leave, or other types of leave should be requested and approved by a supervisor before the leave is taken.

Although emergencies happen and an employee may not be able to submit a request for approval prior to taking leave, employees should know how to report these emergencies. This ensures that the organization can plan its workload while the employee is out. If an employee needs to be absent from work due to an illness, the organization should have policies and procedures in place for requesting this leave, especially if it is related to the Family Medical Leave Act or a state-specific illness leave. In some circumstances, employees may be abusing their leave and not following proper procedures to request time off. There may even be occasions where an employee uses certain types of leave fraudulently, such as taking sick leave but going to Disney World and posting pictures on social media. In the cases that an employer suspects an employee of fraudulent use of leave time, an investigation should be conducted and appropriate action taken. Counseling or progressive discipline may be warranted based on the circumstances and the findings of the investigation.

Aggressive behavior, employee conflict, and workplace harassment are all behavior issues that an organization may have to address and resolve appropriately. Regardless of the concern, the first step should be conducting a thorough investigation. The concern may be brought forward through a formal complaint process, or it could be discovered through other means such as having a conversation with an employee or through general knowledge of an incident.

The first step of the resulting investigation should be to interview the individuals involved, including witnesses and supervisors. The second step is to determine what occurred and whether the behavior violated company policy. If there was a violation, the appropriate steps should be taken to hold the individual accountable. Progressive discipline, counseling, training, or even termination may be warranted based on the circumstances of the incident and the egregiousness of the actions.

Afterward, it is important to communicate to the appropriate employees that the matter has been investigated, appropriate actions have been taken, and the matter is now resolved and closed. HR should also review the matter with a holistic lens to determine whether additional training is necessary to ensure that the behavior does not occur again the in the future. It may also be appropriate to communicate the policies, procedures, and expectations to all employees. By being as proactive as possible, employers can work to prevent future occurrences and ensure a safe and engaging workplace free from conflict, harassment, bullying, or other inappropriate behaviors.

Investigating Complaints or Grievances

Consulting Managers on How to Supervise and Handle Difficult Employees

Complaints or concerns should always be addressed in a fair and consistent manner regardless of the subject of the complaint. While specific complaints may require different processes due to complexity or legal issues, it is important to have standardized processes and practices. It is also important to understand when to inform leadership of issues and concerns. It may be appropriate to communicate a synopsis, including resolutions, at the end of a process for informational purposes only; however, based on the issue, severity, risks, and impacts, it may be necessary to communicate to leadership immediately after the complaint is received. Leadership may need to be involved in the investigation and process,

including the recommendations and action plan to resolve the concerns. It is important to understand the level of communication needed based on the issue.

Handling complaints, either informal or formal, should follow a structured process. Employees should have a full understanding of how and to whom a complaint can be submitted, how the process will unfold, and an estimate of the time needed to complete the process. Seeking to understand as much as possible about the issue should be at the core of the process. This is accomplished by investigating that involves asking questions, researching practices, analyzing data, and following up on additional pieces of information gained throughout the process. Being respectful, responsive, attentive, empathetic, and available will assist in ensuring an effective complaint handling process.

The goal of handling any complaint is to resolve the issue at the lowest level possible. To be successful, employees, especially supervisors, should be trained in conflict resolution methods. **Conflict resolution** involves the following:

- Identifying the problem that is causing the issue
- Identifying the feelings, perceptions, and opinions regarding the issue
- Identifying the potential impacts of the issue as well of any resolution implemented
- Identifying the recommendations and actions to implement to resolve the issue
- Working towards resolution of the issue
- Communicating the resolution with all parties as appropriate

If conflict resolution methods do not resolve the issue, then more formal approaches should be taken to escalate the issue. Ensuring that the issue is resolved in the most effective and efficient way possible is the goal of any process. Filing a grievance, submitting a formal complaint, or reaching out to other oversight organizations that investigate matters such as safety issues (Occupational Safety and Health Administration) or employment practices (Equal Employment Opportunity Commission) may be appropriate as a next step. However, it is important to note that depending on the issue, it may be appropriate to begin the complaint handling process at a more formal level. Examples of these issues would be sexual harassment, workplace violence, discriminatory practices regarding promotions, unsafe working conditions, or other concerns that deserve an escalated response. In each of these examples, leadership should be notified immediately to ensure that the issues are addressed promptly and appropriately. Once a case has been resolved, it may be appropriate to review applicable policies and procedures to ensure that necessary changes are made so that future incidents may be avoided.

Conducting Investigations into Employee Misconduct

Internal investigations are conducted when issues arise or complaints are submitted. Regardless of how an issue comes to the attention of Human Resources, an investigation should be conducted to ensure that any concerns or potential policy violations are corrected and that appropriate responses and actions are delivered. Employees should understand how to submit a complaint regardless of who it is against or what the subject matter. Internal investigations can be both informal and formal, but both should be conducted with good-faith efforts that result in a rational and supported conclusion. Informal investigations could turn into formal investigations to ensure that the issues are fully reviewed and understood. Additionally, a formal investigation could result in an external third-party investigation to ensure impartiality and a full vetting of the issues from an outside perspective. While it is a best practice to attempt to resolve issues and concerns at the lowest level possible, there will always be a need to investigate claims and concerns. Human Resources professionals should be properly and formally trained to investigate complaints.

Internal investigations should always include interviews with the employee making the complaint, the employee who the complaint is against (if any), all witnesses to the incident, and any other party that may have firsthand information and knowledge of the incident. While it is a good practice to have prepared questions for all interviews, it is also appropriate to ask additional questions if new information is presented during the interview to ensure that a full understanding of the incident is gathered. It may be necessary to schedule follow-up interviews based on the information that is gathered or new evidence that is gained. After gathering all of the information, interviewing all of the appropriate parties, and assessing the credibility of the investigation, Human Resources professionals should prepare a conclusion and recommendation to resolve the initial complaint.

Investigation conclusions should be rational, specific, and legally defensible based solely on the information gathered during the investigation. Resolution could be conflict resolution between two employees, changing policy or procedure to address a workplace issue, creating training programs for employees to work better together in a team dynamic, and/or discipline if appropriate. Multiple resolutions may be necessary to ensure that the issue is fully addressed and potential future occurrences are eliminated.

When conducting an internal investigation, there are various best practices to incorporate into the process to ensure a thorough and fair investigation. First, it is important to be proactive and not reactive. Investigators should take a proactive approach when gathering information from employees and researching data and details. Being proactive allows the organization to gather the most recent and current information available. Witnesses are more likely to remember details and specifics of an incident that is fresh and recent. It is harder to recount information regarding incidents that happened longer ago. Being proactive also includes being broad and open to identifying new resources that would have information pertinent to the case rather than relying on one individual's account of an incident. A common quote used to describe this is "follow the leads." If an investigator follows the leads and goes where the evidence leads, the investigation is more likely to yield an accurate assessment and conclusion of the incident.

Second, it is important to agree to the purpose and specific issue being investigated. When employees understand what the investigation is attempting to define or discover, they are more likely to be able to provide specifics about the incident. During the investigation, information may arise that is outside of the original scope, and it is important to ensure that either the initial investigation is expanded or a secondary investigation is conducted to review the new information.

Third, investigations should always be independent and impartial. Investigations should be conducted by individuals who can review the evidence and conduct interviews that are unbiased and open-minded. Depending on the professional relationship between the employee complaining and the Human Resources professional conducting the investigation, it may be appropriate to bring in an external investigator who can maintain impartiality. Not only does this allow for a fair and accurate investigation, conclusion, and proposed recommendation, but it also avoids allegations or the perception of conflicts of interest.

Fourth, completed investigations and recommendations should align with the organization's policies, procedures, and goals. If there is no alignment, based on the behavior of employees, the investigation may prompt a review and evaluation of the policies, procedures, and goals of the organization. Regularly reviewing these items against the behaviors of employees allows the organization to implement programs that can affect cultural change and promote appropriate and respectful behavior.

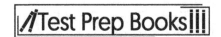

Finally, investigations should always consider the consequences and repercussions of the issues being brought forward and the effects of not handling and resolving the issues quickly and completely. Many states have laws that hold supervisors responsible for their behavior, as well as the organization, if appropriate actions are not taken to correct behavior or hold employees responsible. Modern society holds individuals to a higher standard regarding sexual harassment, and many federal statutes are being passed to ensure accountability, transparency, understanding, and consequences. In addition to this, many states are mandating frequent training and requirements regarding training for specific levels of employees. Supervisors may be required to frequently attend expanded training sessions to ensure a thorough knowledge and understanding of the responsibilities when supervising others. However, organizations are responsible for ensuring that training requirements are met and that actions are taken to address issues.By conducting fair, impartial, thorough, and proactive investigations, Human Resources professionals can protect employees and the organization.

Resolving Workplace Labor Disputes Internally

It should be the goal of HR professionals to resolve workplace disputes internally and at the lowest level possible. Sometimes, disputes between employees rise to a level that requires a third-party investigation; however, most matters can be resolved through a standard, internal conflict resolution process. As soon as HR is aware of an issue, it is important to act immediately and address the situation so that a resolution can be quickly and amicably achieved. Some issues may be resolved simply by having a conversation with involved individuals to correct any misunderstandings and move forward. Employees may just want to be heard and understood. No matter what approach was deemed appropriate, it is important to the process to ensure that all individuals could express their feelings, concerns, and ideas to resolve the issue and move forward. There may be occasions when issues are of a more serious nature and HR needs to launch a full investigation of the matter. However, when appropriate and necessary, HR should strive to implement conflict resolution techniques to resolve issues internally and at the lowest level possible.

Empowering Employees to Report Unethical Behavior

HR should ensure that all policies and procedures are available to employees from their first day on the job. Many organizations provide a hard copy of the employee handbook and require employees to read through it, ask questions, discuss the requirements, and sign an acknowledgement receipt. In this way, HR can be confident that employees are aware of the policies and expectations of the organization. One of the policies that should be fully communicated is how to report inappropriate behavior by another employee. This policy should include the process, privacy rights, and expectations of no retaliation for coming forward. Employees should be able to voice concerns without fear of retaliation, either by the organization or other employees. However, it is important to understand that if false complaints are submitted, the employee may be disciplined. Depending on the current culture in an organization, it may be important and necessary to create an anonymous reporting method or purchase a third-party service for reporting complaints.

Mitigating the Influence of Bias

An employee may come forward to complain about another employee, a supervisor, or a leader of the organization, and the HR professional may have a concern about their own bias in this situation. This could be for several reasons, such as the HR representative is friends with the employee, they have inside information or knowledge about the employee(s) or situation, the complaint is against their supervisor, or they simply do not know enough about the actual context of the situation. In these cases, it is best to be open and honest about the issue and potentially hire a third-party investigator to handle the complaint and formal investigation process. This will accomplish several things: 1) ensure a fair and

unbiased investigation; 2) provide an accurate representation of what is occurring; and 3) enhance credibility and trust in HR for acknowledging this potential bias and taking action to address it.

Grievance Procedures

A **grievance** is a complaint made by an employee that is formally stated in writing. A formal grievance procedure allows management to respond to employee dissatisfaction appropriately through formal communication. Additionally, if a unionized employee is being questioned by management in a situation where a disciplinary action may result, they have the right to union representation during that conversation, which is also known as Weingarten rights (after a famous court case). If that right is violated and the unionized employee is let go, they can be reinstated with back pay.

Every contract will lay out a slightly different process to address potential contract grievances. However, many will follow a similar pattern. The goal is always to remedy the situation before it escalates to the need for arbitration. Typically, employees first discuss the grievance with the union steward and the supervisor. Next, the union steward discusses the grievance with the supervisor's manager and/or the HR manager. The next step is for a committee of union officers to discuss the grievance with the appropriate managers in the company. Then, the national union representative discusses the grievance with designated company executives. If, after this process, the grievance is still not settled, it then goes to arbitration. Grievance arbitration is a process in which a third party is used to settle disputes that arise from conflicting interpretations of a labor contract. Decisions that are reached through this process are enforceable and cannot go to court to be changed.

Settling Discrimination Charges

Unfortunately, discrimination exists in some organizations, and sometimes official charges are brought forth. In these cases (and even in cases where the organization is confident that no wrongdoing has taken place), an organization has a decision to make. It can follow the process through the Equal Employment Opportunity Commission (EEOC) and be investigated by a Fair Employment Practices Agency (FEPA) at the local or state level. Or the organization may choose to settle the charges rather than face an investigation. Employee charges of discrimination must be filed with the EEOC within 180 days of the alleged incident.

If probable cause is found, then the EEOC will attempt conciliation, and the employer is required to settle. The complaint charge is either settled or the process may move to litigation with either the EEOC or a private court. If the EEOC is not able to determine probable cause, the employee can request a right-to-sue letter after the end of the 180-day period and must file suit in court within ninety days. Finally, if the EEOC does not find probable cause, the employer and employee are both notified. The employee can request a right-to-sue letter, and the EEOC's involvement with the case ends. The employee can then sue the employer in court.

There are several factors that can influence a company's decision to settle discrimination charges. One is the financial cost of an investigation. Lawyers and court fees can be a financial strain on a company's finances, not to mention additional obligations if the court rules against the company. There are also the challenges of the investigation itself to consider. If charges are brought to the EEOC or FEPA, a company may be required to devote considerable time and resources to cooperating with the investigation. Thus, an organization may decide that a one-time financial penalty is preferable to an extended period of disruption. A company must also weigh the risk of damage to its reputation when considering the best path of settlement.

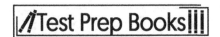

A long, drawn-out trial and investigation, potentially widely covered on social and traditional media, can do irreparable harm to the company's image. Even in cases where the company is found to be blame-free in the case, the general public may still associate the organization with the charges of discrimination. Therefore, a company may find it is better to accept the financial expense to avoid the potential long-term damage to its reputation. Finally, there are systemic problems to think about. If the company is aware of deeper issues of discrimination among its employees, it may choose to settle charges to avoid having the investigation uncover an ongoing pattern that may be hard to address.

Front Pay

If a company is found guilty of workplace discrimination, it is usually required to allow the individual in question to return to their position within the organization. However, in some instances, the court may rule that the company should require front pay. **Front pay** is money awarded to an individual in a workplace discrimination case and is generally equal to lost earnings. Front pay is usually required when the position is not available, the employer has not made any effort to address an ongoing issue of discrimination throughout the company, or the employee would be forced to endure a hostile work environment if they were to return to the original position.

Mediation Process

Mediation often serves as a precursor to the more official step of arbitration. In general terms, arbitration is sometimes thought of as a form of mediation, but legally there are important differences. Most notably, a mediator doesn't serve as a final "judge" of the dispute, but rather attempts to work with both parties to help them reach a resolution without having to take additional legal steps.

The mediation process usually begins with both parties agreeing to use a mutually acceptable mediator. The mediator sets the ground rules for the process and defines details such as what the dispute is about, who is involved, when and where the negotiations will take place, and the negotiation procedure. When the actual meeting takes place, the mediator reiterates the ground rules for the process. Both sides present their case and the mediator attempts to help both parties reach a compromise or find other solutions. If both sides agree to a compromise, a written document will be signed to ensure that both sides will follow through on the agreed-upon actions. If both sides do not agree, they may choose to pursue arbitration or litigation (court action).

Constructive Confrontation

Constructive confrontation is a type of mediation used in some extremely complicated or contentious disputes, particularly ones where neither party can agree to a compromise. Constructive confrontation can sometimes break these stalemates by temporarily skipping the main issue in dispute, and instead, focusing first on secondary issues. Sometimes, by first resolving these smaller details, a mediator can affect parties' willingness to compromise on bigger issues.

Arbitration

Arbitration is a way to settle disputes without taking the issue to court. In a general sense, arbitration is a form of mediation. However, arbitration typically refers to a more formal process that takes place after an initial mediation attempt has failed. In arbitration, a neutral third party (known as an arbitrator) decides based on the facts presented. There are different kinds of arbitration, decisions, and arbitrators.

In **compulsory arbitration**, the disputing parties are required by law to go through the arbitration process. This could be the result of a court order, but it could also arise from a contract that dictates that arbitration take place in certain situations.

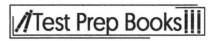

In **voluntary arbitration**, the disputing parties choose to undergo the arbitration process, usually because they cannot come to an agreement, but do not want to go through a potentially expensive and time-consuming lawsuit.

In a **binding decision**, the disputing parties are required by law to follow the decision reached as a result of the arbitration process. This means that the losing party must follow the actions laid out by the decision, such as payments or reinstatement to a disputed position. In addition, a binding decision marks the end of the legal process. Neither party may pursue further legal action after the decision has been reached.

As the name suggests, **non-binding decisions** do not carry legal weight. Either party may choose to follow or not follow the terms of the decision. In addition, a dissatisfied party may choose to pursue additional legal action after the decision of the arbiter is reached.

A **permanent arbitrator** is someone who routinely judges arbitration cases for a company or other organization. An arbitrator may be trained and certified by a professional organization or a mutually trusted individual to provide an unbiased opinion on the dispute.

An **ad-hoc arbitrator** may also be a certified professional or a mutually trusted third party. But unlike permanent arbitrators, ad-hoc arbitrators do not have a regular arbitration relationship with either party. Instead, they are chosen as a one-time solution to address only the unique dispute in question.

An **arbitrator panel** functions just like an ad-hoc arbitrator, but it is comprised of multiple arbitrators (usually three). They are sometimes called arbitral tribunals or tripartite arbitration panels.

Progressive Discipline

Warnings
Warnings are the first step in the progressive discipline process. Warnings can be both verbal and written; both are documented so that the discipline history is recorded. Verbal warnings can take the form of informal counseling or discussions to ensure that an employee understands the concern and knows the corrective action to take. At the conclusion of the verbal warning, it is important to ensure that the employee understands what will happen if the behavior is not addressed. Written warnings include official letters or memos documenting the behavior and concerns, with the necessary expectations outlined. Employees should have an opportunity to review the written warning, provide comments, and then sign and date to show a record of receiving the warning.

Written warnings should include the specific behavior that is being addressed with the details of the incident: date, time, witnesses, and concerns. Additionally, the policy that was violated should be specifically identified and communicated so that the employee understands why the warning is being issued. Like the verbal warning, written warnings should include the expectations of the employee and what will happen if the behavior is not addressed. Written warnings should indicate that progressive discipline, including and up to termination, will be administered if the employee's behavior does not change.

Escalating Corrective Actions
When verbal and written warnings do not address a behavior or performance concern, it may be necessary to escalate to more corrective actions. These actions can include suspensions, or time off without pay, mandatory training programs, demotions, and termination. Organizations are responsible

for ensuring their discipline policy outlines the various levels of corrective action. Many agencies have bargaining agreements with their represented employees that require multiple levels of suspension before progressing to termination. Below is another example of an extensive, multi-level escalating progressive discipline schedule:

- Verbal warning
- Written warning
- One-day suspension
- Three-day suspension
- One- week suspension
- Two-week suspension
- One-month suspension
- Termination

Regardless of the length of the schedule, each step should include a documented report indicating the inappropriate behavior or performance, expectations moving forward, the level of discipline being issued for the incident, and what will occur if the behavior does not change or if performance does not improve. It may be necessary to conduct a root cause analysis to determine whether additional insight is needed to provide a better course of action to get the employee on the right course. If the discipline is being issued due to poor performance, the primary issue may be training. The individual may be in the wrong position and steps may be necessary to transfer the employee to a more suitable position.

Termination

Termination is the final step in the progressive discipline process and when an employee is removed from their job. Terminations occur for behavioral issues, poor job performance, and policy violations. It is imperative that employees receive sufficient warning regarding the seriousness of their offenses prior to their termination.

Once the decision is made to end a staff member's employment, the actual termination takes place in a swift manner, typically during a face-to-face meeting. During the termination meeting, with the employee's manager and sometimes with a member of HR, the employee's building and systems access is deactivated, while the employee's co-workers are gathered in a conference room. This allows the terminated employee a few minutes of privacy to gather personal belongings under the supervision of building security, HR, or the employee's manager. Then the terminated employee is escorted out of the building.

In some situations, terminated employees are given formal contracts known as separation agreements. The agreements state that the terminated employees agree not to sue the employer in exchange for some previously agreed-upon severance pay and/or other conditions.

Off-Boarding or Termination Activities

When an employee exits an organization, it is important to have a clear set of steps and actions outlined to ensure that all areas are addressed. Off-boarding activities vary, depending on the type of termination. Employees who are voluntarily resigning or retiring have a different exit process from employees being terminated for inappropriate behavior or policy violations. In general, though, there are many similar pieces of information that should be conveyed to an individual leaving an organization. These items could include:

- Turning in security badges and keys
- Turning in all equipment such as computers, phones, or other items
- Turning in uniforms and other company issued items such as credit cards
- Disabling access to internet and email systems
- Enabling "out of office" messages for email and phone
- Reviewing benefits information such as when health coverage will end, COBRA terms and conditions, retirement options, vacation and other leave payouts, and other items of importance
- Discussing the final paycheck, what it will include, and when it will be issued
- Ensuring accurate contact information including mailing address, email address, and phone numbers

A common best practice for employees exiting an organization is conducting an exit interview. Usually, these are best conducted with an individual who is voluntarily departing the organization. An **exit interview** is a conversation with a departing employee, in which an HR professional asks questions related to work experience, salary and benefits, training, concerns, and other topics that the organization wants to learn more about improving for the future. This is an excellent opportunity for the organization to find out what could be done better and what may have changed the employee's mind to stay with the organization.

There are also several activities that should be conducted by internal departments to ensure that business can continue as usual. If the exiting employee is a supervisor and responsible for managing employees, it is important to ensure that there is continuity for these employees in having a supervisor. Items such as approving leave requests, scheduling overtime, submitting and authorizing timecards, and handing out paychecks are all vital to the business operations. Ensuring there is a plan for handling these responsibilities is important to the organization and to the individual employees.

Finally, HR should announce the departure of the employee and the plan that will be implemented moving forward, especially if the termination is unexpected. Plans for moving forward could include redistributing the workload to other employees, recruiting a new employee to backfill the opening, or appointing an employee to fill the vacancy while plans are finalized. Losing an employee for any reason can have a huge impact to operations and other employees. Taking steps to coordinate the exit in a smooth and transparent manner can help reduce the potential of problems.

Practice Questions

1. Which best describes corporate social responsibility?
   a. Corporate social responsibility is a policy mandated by the government to coerce corporations to improve their communities.
   b. Corporate social responsibility refers to the responsibility that corporations have toward shareholders.
   c. Corporate social responsibility is an issue of ethics, pursued by corporations that see the health of their business as contingent upon the health of their community.
   d. Corporate social responsibility refers to the social climate of the organization and the policies created to sustain the strength of that climate.

2. CSR can be evaluated on which three Ps of the "triple bottom line"?
   a. People, prizes, and proxy
   b. Planet, profit, and projects
   c. People, profit, and prizes
   d. People, planet, and profit

3. What is the purpose of a vision statement?
   a. A vision statement is a memo drafted by management that articulates that if company policy is breached, there will be severe consequences.
   b. A vision statement is a succinct explanation of how an organization plans to deliver quality products/services.
   c. A vision statement is a lengthy and detailed speech given by a CEO to shareholders and other investors.
   d. A vision statement is a short address that low-level employees give to management.

4. Regarding corporate social responsibility, the most common ways for a corporation to assimilate into a community includes all of the following EXCEPT?
   a. The most common way for a corporation to pursue social responsibility is to establish alliances with respected members of the community and outside organizations.
   b. The most common way for a corporation to pursue social responsibility is to deliver inexpensive goods and services for the community.
   c. The most common way for a corporation to pursue social responsibility is hiring as many locals as possible.
   d. The most common way for a corporation to pursue social responsibility is by maximizing their profits despite any consequences to the surrounding environment.

5. What is the primary purpose of organizational branding?

 I. The intent of organizational branding is letting customers know when they walk into a store.

 II. One purpose of organizational branding is to establish a distinctive image for consumers to automatically recognize.

 III. Organizational branding allows entities to create a perception of the values and ethics for which it stands.

 IV. Organizational branding focuses on promoting the benefits of the company in order to appeal to a target audience.

a. I, II, and IV only
b. I, III, and IV only
c. II and III only
d. I, II, and III only

Answer Explanations

1. C: Corporate social responsibility is an ethical standard pursued by corporations that see the health of their business as contingent upon the health of their community. This ethical issue emphasizes becoming a part of the community and its social fabric. Corporate social responsibility can engender controversy by suggesting that a business has an obligation greater than merely supplying goods and services at a low cost.

2. D: CSR can be evaluated by people, planet, and profit. *People* refers to the organization's treatment of their employees as well as members of the community. *Planet* refers to the impact the organization has on the environment. *Profit* refers to the organization's overall contribution to economic growth. Choices *A*, *B*, and *C* are all incorrect.

3. B: A vision statement is a concise statement that reflects organizational confidence and long-term aspirations about how the firm will achieve more than just economic success. Some questions that may be answered in a vision statement include: How does this firm fit into the marketplace? How would it positively change the world? Institutionally, how does the company plan to deliver their product or service cheaper and more efficiently than competitors? Ultimately, vision statements serve the purpose of boosting trust, confidence, and an image that the firm is engaging in a task larger than itself.

4. D: When practicing corporate social responsibility, there are several ways an organization can engage the community. First, a firm can establish alliances with influential members of the community or a respected local organization. Secondly, a firm can deliver on its promise of delivering low-cost goods and services to the community. Lastly, as one tenet of corporate responsibility is improving the quality of life in a community, it should hire as many locals as possible.

5. D: Organizational branding can serve multiple purposes. One is creating a distinctive logo that is easily identifiable to consumers. Furthermore, organizational branding represents an opportunity to establish a perception of values and ethics that consumers understand when they see the logo. The famous logo for the Michelin corporation is a jovial tire man, which articulates friendly service and exactly what the firm sells. Number IV is not part of branding, but more of a characteristic of marketing.

Compliance and Risk Management

Laws and Regulations Related to Recruitment and Selection

There are many federal laws to consider when planning for new hires. One is the Civil Rights Act of 1964—specifically, Title VII, which prohibits employers from discriminating against employees on the basis of sex, race, color, national origin, and religion. This act led to the creation of the Equal Employment Opportunity Commission (EEOC), which enforces and oversees laws against workplace discrimination. The definition of workplace discrimination has since been expanded to include protection from discrimination based on an employee's disability, children, sexual orientation, gender identity, genetic information, and reporting discriminatory practices. Title VII generally applies to employers with fifteen or more employees.

HR should keep EEOC rules in mind when crafting job descriptions and advertisements. For example, a job posting should not say that the company is only looking for workers in a specific age range (such as, "Only graduates from after 1999 should apply") or gender. These rules also need to be followed during all hiring procedures, including job interviews and background checks. Interviewers should not ask any questions related to the protected identities listed above. For example, questions like, "Do you have children?" or "Would you prioritize your children above your job duties?" are prohibited discriminatory questions.

The interviewer should consider what skills and capabilities are important, and rephrase the question accordingly—perhaps something like, "How do you prioritize competing obligations?" or "Are you able to work a flexible schedule?" This is also true when checking references and contacting past employers. For example, the interviewer would not be able to ask questions such as, "Can you describe the employee's medical history?" or "Did the employ take many sick days or have any health problems that made them unable to work?" because these questions would be discriminating based on disability. Better questions might be, "Did the employee have good attendance?" or "Did the employee complete all essential job tasks?"

In 1978, the EEOC along with the Department of Labor, Department of Justice, and U.S. Civil Service Commission adopted the Uniform Guidelines on Employee Selection Procedures (UGESP) to provide standards on what constitutes discriminatory hiring practices. UGESP established the four-fifths rule, which states that if the selection rate for any race, sex, or ethnic group is less than four-fifths of the selection rate for the group with the highest selection rate, the hiring practice is generally considered discriminatory. For example, from a pool of applicants, a company hires 8 percent of the men who applied, but only 2 percent of the women who applied. In this case, the selection rate for women is only 25 percent of the selection rate for men—less than four-fifths (or 80%). This would be deemed discriminatory hiring.

Another relevant law is the Fair Labor Standards Act of 1938 (FLSA), which establishes standards for a minimum wage, overtime pay, recordkeeping, and child labor standards. There are some exemptions to FLSA (for example, many tip-based professions such as food service), but it generally covers employers with at least $500,000 of business in a year. There are also other laws related to pay for specific professions. The Walsh-Healey Public Contracts Act of 1936 establishes labor rights for U.S. government contracts, and it applies to any contracts exceeding $15,000 for goods. Like the FLSA, it sets standards for overtime pay and child labor, prohibiting the employment of those under the age of 16. It sets a separate minimum wage using the prevailing wage, as determined by state departments of labor.

The prevailing wage is defined as the standard hourly wage, overtime, and benefits paid to most workers in a given area. Another contract act is the McNamara-O'Hara Service Contract Act of 1965 (SCA), which applies to contractors and subcontractors working on service contracts exceeding $2,500. Those contractors or subcontractors are also required to pay service employees no less than the prevailing wage. The Department of Labor oversees compliance with each of these laws.

The Rehabilitation Act was passed in 1973 to prohibit employment discrimination based on physical or mental disabilities. This legislation charges employers with taking affirmative action to hire qualified disabled persons. The act further requires that reasonable accommodation(s) be made for the disabled unless the employer can show an undue hardship based on business necessity or financial cost (spending in excess of $1,000 per employee). The Civil Service Commission, Department of Labor, Department of Veterans Affairs, and the Department of Health and Human Services administer this law, which applies to the federal government, federal contractors with contracts over $10,000, and companies who are in receipt of funds in excess of $10,000 by a company that receives federal monies.

Under this law, disability is defined as a physical or mental impairment that substantially limits one or more major life activities. Examples of reasonable accommodations that can be made under the Rehabilitation Act consist of the following:

- A change in job design: eliminating tasks that are not necessary to perform the job

- Qualifications: getting rid of unnecessary job specs for everyone, such as requiring a medical exam prior to employment (which will allow the disabled to be hired)

- Job accessibility: adding wheelchair ramps, brail in elevators, etc.

- Nondiscriminatory treatment: eliminating hiring decisions based on people's fear of, or uneasiness with, disabilities

Adverse Impact

There are two types of discrimination: disparate treatment and disparate or adverse impact. Disparate treatment occurs when an employer treats protected classes differently than other employees. Examples of disparate treatment include holding genders to different standards, sexual harassment, and blatantly rejecting a member of a protected class due to stereotypes.

A famous disparate treatment case was McDonnell Douglas Corporation vs. Green. Green was a black employee who was laid off during a regular reduction in force. He protested at the company (as part of a group), chained and locked company doors, and blocked an entrance to company property. His activities did not please the company. When the company began hiring again, they advertised, and Green reapplied. He was denied, and the company continued looking for candidates. Green claimed the rejection was due to his race and his involvement in civil rights activities.

This was a precedent-setting EEO case that established criteria for disparate treatment and ruled that a *prima facie* (at first glance) case can be shown if an employee:

- Belongs to a protected class
- Applied for a job when the employer sought applicants
- Was qualified and yet rejected
- Was rejected but the employer kept looking

In disparate treatment cases, an individual must prove:

- They are a member of a protected class
- They applied for a job for which they were qualified and for which the employer was seeking applicants
- They were not hired even though they were qualified
- After they did not get the job, the position remained open, and the employer continued to receive applications

Disparate or **adverse impact** refers to a form of discrimination where an employer's policy seems neutral but in fact has an adverse impact on a certain group or a certain characteristic such as race, sex, or disability. This was identified by the Supreme Court in 1971 in the case of Griggs v. Duke Power Co., where it was proven that the requirement of a high school diploma for higher-paid positions was unfairly affecting African American employees in lower-paid labor positions who had a history of receiving inferior education.

As another example, if an employer requires a potential employee for a position to be at least 5'10'', it may exclude an entire group, such as women. Because statistically men are taller, this requirement is based solely on biological reasons rather than if the candidate can adequately perform the required role.

An employer discriminating based on certain physical elements, however, can be justified if it is in correlation with job requirements. For example, it is necessary for a fire department to discriminate based on height, facial hair, or grooming to ensure the safety of its employees.

Employee and Employer Rights and Responsibilities

Employment-At-Will

Employment-at-will refers to the employment of employees who do not have a contract indicating the terms of employment and who can be discharged by an employer at any time for any reason. While there are some legal protections for employees who have filed complaints regarding harassment, discrimination, retaliation, or whistleblowing, in general an at-will employee can be terminated from employment without notice and without cause. The term "cause" in this context refers to actions that are considered violations of policy which could include inappropriate behavior, fraud, misappropriation of funds, untruthfulness, or other actions that would warrant termination. Depending on the organization and its agreements and policies, some employees may be at-will employees and others may have protections established through union representation or other contractual terms.

It is important to remember that employment-at-will does not allow an employer to fire someone at will. Employees still have rights and protections afforded to them under federal and state legislation.

Employers must understand how an employment-at-will situation aligns with these protections when considering terminating an employee who has at-will employment status.

Defamation

Defamation refers to intentionally injuring another individual's name or reputation by spreading lies or untruths through slander and/or libel. **Slander** specifically refers to a verbal statement or gesture that defames an individual, and **libel** specifically refers to a written or recorded statement that defames an individual. Regardless of the intention behind defamation, individuals and organizations can be held accountable for their actions when they cause injury to another's reputation. Slander and libel are not protected under the First Amendment, or freedom of speech, and those guilty of defamation are held accountable for their actions. Organizations often deal with defamation in various ways and levels of severity. Rumor mills and gossip chains, regardless of the intention, are common, everyday forms of defamation that can cause stress, poor working relationships, and negative work environments. Many organizations have begun to implement policies that combat gossip to ensure that employees are working in a safe and healthy environment, free from defamation in any form.

Employer/Employee Rights Related to Substance Abuse

Substance use is a dependence on an addictive substance such as illegal drugs. This dependency not only impacts the individual but also may affect families and communities. Programs specifically designed to combat substance use can be extraordinarily beneficial. Because substance use is not limited to adults, programs may be introduced that focus on children and adolescents as well. In addition to the physical dangers of substance use, subsequent behavioral patterns compound issues. If treatment is not sought, the likelihood of a life of crime and poverty greatly increases.

Effective substance use policies protect both employers and employees in the workplace. Privacy policies generally authorize employers to conduct random drug tests if the employee has given prior consent. The employee should be clearly notified when hired that these tests may be administered by the employer. Employee substance abuse is damaging to the workplace and often results in inappropriate conduct with co-workers, insubordination, and fatal injuries due to improper use of machinery.

Through the Americans with Disabilities Act, federal guidelines exist to protect both employers and employees in regard to substance abuse. Employers do have the right to ensure a drug-free workplace by prohibiting the use of illegal drugs and alcohol. Employers may test for illegal drug use but must meet state requirements to do so. If an employee tests positive for current drug use through proper testing procedures, employers have the right to terminate that employee.

The ADA gives protection to employees who have successfully rehabilitated from past drug use but are no longer engaged in the illegal use of drugs. Employers cannot discriminate against any employee who has either completed a rehabilitation program or is undergoing rehabilitation. Reasonable accommodation efforts should be extended to those individuals who are rehabilitated or are undergoing current treatment.

Ergonomics refers to the ability of a person to fully utilize a product while maintaining maximum safety, efficiency, and comfort. Ergonomic risk factors in the workplace can lead to musculoskeletal disorders such as carpal tunnel, rotator cuff injuries, muscle strains, and lower back injuries. In order to reduce these risks, employers should evaluate workplace ergonomics and educate employees about potential issues. An ergonomic evaluation tests a product to determine its ease of use and potential safety risks.

When employers identify and address ergonomic concerns in the workplace, they protect their workers and likely prevent serious injuries.

Laws and Regulations Related to Training and Development Activities

Copyright Act of 1976

The **Copyright Act of 1976** is the foundational law in the United States regarding property ownership of film, radio, musical and dramatic works, literary and pictorial works, and architectural structures. Superseding local and state copyright laws, the statute establishes a standardized and universally applied measure to the country's major social and technological transformations in media. Hitherto the act, there were deficient authorship protections that had the capacity to safeguard creative works and lawfully secure remunerative rewards. Written with a broad intent, the landmark legislation is applicable to "original works of authorship fixed in any tangible medium of expression."

In order to lawfully reproduce, disseminate, modify, publicly display, or perform copyrighted material, one must hold a copyright over such material, published or unpublished. Stipulated by the Copyright Act of 1976, a copyright lasts for the duration of the author's life, plus an additional seventy years after their death. However, the law incorporates a policy of "fair use." Fair use enumerates some instances in which a person may use copyrighted material.

Fair Use

The Copyright Act of 1976 specifies instances in which protected material can be used without threat of infringement. These selective requirements fall into the jurisdiction of "fair use." The first qualification is the intended purpose of the work. Is it intended for commercial gain or for non-profit education? Secondly, fair use is determined by the nature or type of work in question. Thirdly, the amount or proportion of the copyrighted work is evaluated. Lastly, the potential variation in market value of copyrighted material is determined. Educational purposes, research, criticism, scholarship, comment, teaching, or news reporting are the categories specifically noted that would determine the applicability of fair use.

Public Domain

When any of the works delineated have no copyright, they enter the public domain. In the public domain, any person can use these works freely. For a work to not be protected by federal copyright law, it needs to meet one of two conditions. If the federal government publishes the work, it is regarded as public, and therefore is exempt from copyright infringement. Expiration is the only other way an article would lose copyright protection. Works created on or after January 1, 1978, are protected for the life of the author and seventy years after their death; anonymous works, works-made-for-hire, and articles are protected for 95 years from the date of creation or 120 years after being published. Works-made-for-hire includes works made by employees or works that are specially ordered or commissioned.

Title 17

Title 17 is a United States copyright law enacted in 1947. It applies to authorship of any tangible medium of expression. Specific works that fall under Title 17 are literary works, architectural works, musical recordings, pictures and graphics, choreographic works, musical works, motion pictures, and audio works.

U.S. Patent Act

The **U.S. Patent Act** expressly prohibits the unauthorized use, sale, reproduction, or distribution of the product without the consent of the patent holder. The legislation's broad composition is designed to preserve and protect the property of inventors. Furthermore, one of two conditions must be met for protections to be granted by the act to apply: the invention in question must be created in the United States or the invention must be imported into the country. Although the law explains several prohibitions regarding the unsanctioned use, sale, reproduction, or distribution of an invention, it does not specify any legal recourse in the event of infringement of a particular patent.

Patent Types

There are three types of patents in the United States: utility, design, and plant. The most common type of patent is a utility patent. A **utility patent** involves anything technological, mechanical, chemical, pharmaceutical, or software-related. Utility patents are valid for twenty years after the date the patent is filed. In order to obtain a utility patent, one must provide a written and meticulously detailed description of the product. The second type of patent is a **design patent**. These patents are valid for fourteen years after the date they are filed. Unique to the United States, this patent comprises ornamental design –specifically, the way a product looks (aesthetics) and how it works. For instance, when applying for a design patent for a bookcase, the inventor must exhibit how it is assembled, how much weight it can withstand, and the size screws that must be used to give it requisite support. A **plant patent** can be filed for an asexually reproducible plant discovered in a cultivated area. These patents last for twenty years after the date they are filed. Plant patents are the least common type of patent.

Trademark Act

The **Trademark Act** was created to provide for the protection and registration of trademarks and service marks.

Title VII

Title VII is a federal law within the Civil Rights Act of 1964. It stipulates that no person shall be discriminated against on the basis of sex, race, color, national origin, and religion. Although Title VII is a federal law, it applies to state and local governments as well. Moreover, the law applies to private and public colleges and universities, private sector employment, and labor unions. Under this law, all employees are guaranteed equal access to career development and training.

The Collective Bargaining Process

Collective bargaining is the act of negotiation between an employer and its employees, where a union represents the employees' interests. The NLRA addresses the collective bargaining process and lays out legal definitions for negotiating in good faith, both on the part of the employer and the union. Some examples of negotiating in bad faith include employers making contract proposals directly to employees without working through the union that represents them, employers urging employees to engage in activities that would weaken the union's negotiating power (for example, encouraging employees to decertify the union), and employers making unfavorable changes to workplace terms and conditions (such as pay, hours, and special pay) during the process of collective bargaining. Additional examples of negotiating in bad faith include unions refusing to disclose critical information during the collective bargaining process, unions refusing to reasonably cooperate in the logistics of the negotiation process (for example, time and location), and unions engaging in an unfair labor practice, as defined by the Labor Management Relations Act.

The NLRB helps define and limit the subjects that can be discussed during a collective bargaining negotiation. Illegal subjects cannot be discussed during negotiations and generally involve actions that fall outside the realm of contract negotiations. Examples include hot cargo agreements, security clauses, or any illegal activity on the part of the employer or union. Mandatory subjects must be discussed during negotiations. Mandatory subjects typically involve the basics of employees' working conditions and terms, covering areas such as hours, benefits, pay, and worker safety concerns. Voluntary subjects are topics that parties are permitted to discuss but may choose not to. Voluntary subjects include all issues not covered under the categories of illegal or mandatory subjects.

The goal of collective bargaining is to develop a mutually agreed-upon collective bargaining agreement (CBA). The CBA should address basic terms and conditions including the following:

- Hours, benefits, pay, and workplace safety

- The contract grievance process, which is a clear statement of the procedures to be followed in case of a dispute as well as the actions the organization can take if employees do not follow the terms of the contract

- A zipper clause stating that the CBA has been agreed to and is final. The zipper clause also dictates that any issues not covered in the current contract cannot be discussed until it expires.

There are several strategies that are commonly employed by unions during a collective bargaining negotiation. **Single-unit bargaining** occurs when union representatives meet with one employer at a time and don't attempt to use the process as a springboard in separate negotiations. **Coordinated bargaining** takes place when unions within an organization meet with the employer to negotiate beneficial results for the groups they represent (also called multi-unit bargaining). **Multi-employer bargaining** occurs when a union with employees in multiple companies meets with all of those companies as a single negotiation. Finally, **parallel bargaining** occurs when a union successfully negotiates an agreement with a company, then uses the result of that negotiation as another example while dealing with a different company (also called leapfrogging or whipsawing).

Organization or union representatives typically use one of two approaches when engaging in a collective bargaining process. **Distributive bargaining** takes place when a group negotiates with the goal of achieving specific objectives (also called positional bargaining). **Principled bargaining** occurs when a group negotiates while remaining mindful of the key issues to each side of the process. The negotiation then becomes a process of searching for solutions from both sides in hopes that an agreement can be reached.

The Collective Bargaining Process

While collective bargaining is required by law for both parties to negotiate in good faith, success is only achieved when both parties are willing to listen, understand, and compromise. **Good faith bargaining** refers to the duty of both parties to demonstrate a sincere and honest intent to reach agreement, be reasonable, communicate honestly, and negotiate in the best interest of the employees. It is important to note that collective bargaining is a group action that many refer to as an art form. Collective bargaining should not be a competitive process, but rather a continuous and logical process that involves strategy and understanding.

There are various objectives that collective bargaining seeks to achieve:

- Settle disputes or conflicts regarding wages, benefits, working conditions, or safety concerns

- Protect employees' interests

- Resolve differences over difficult and stressful issues

- Negotiate voluntarily and as needed, without the influence or interference of an outside third party who is not as familiar with the organization and employees

- Agree to amicable terms and conditions through a give-and-take strategy

- Co-exist and work together peacefully for the mutual benefit and morale of all employees

- Maintain employee and employer relationships

A best practice that many negotiators utilize at the bargaining table is to establish ground rules at the beginning of the process. **Ground rules** refers to a set of items agreed upon by both parties to assist the negotiations process. Ground rules establish respect for both parties, the time and efforts each puts forth, and other specific areas that may arise during negotiations. Ground rules should establish the following:

- Who speaks for the parties and the individuals representing each party

- When subject matter experts will be called in and the specific purpose

- Where, when, and how long the parties will meet

- A cut-off date for submitting new proposals

- How formal proposals and responses will be made

- Communications plans regarding media or external communications

- What form of agreement will be acceptable: full and complete document or an itemized list of agreed upon changes

- Any other specific details pertinent to the negotiations

There are five basic steps to the collective bargaining process: prepare, discuss, propose, bargain, and settlement. While this process is conceptualized as a linear process, there can be multiple twists and turns when bargaining in real life. Negotiators should be prepared for surprises and unexpected events that could derail negotiations.

Prior to beginning the negotiation process, it is vital for both sides to prepare and determine what needs to be changed, added, updated, deleted, or remain status quo. Each side should come to the negotiation table well prepared and ready to begin discussions. During discussions, new ideas may be presented from the opposing side that require additional preparation before they can be conducted. These should be discussed, and a plan to engage in further discussions should be agreed upon.

Proposals should be given that are thoughtful and based on the needs of the party. They should be clear, concise, and fully communicate the intent of the suggestion as well as provide an understanding of the effects of the change. The employer usually bears the responsibility of costing out a contract and determining the expenses related to new proposals. As each new proposal is discussed, the open dialogue should include transparency regarding the costs associated with each. If an organization only has authorization to spend a certain amount of money to settle a contract, negotiations will need to be conducted about how to spend that money. If every proposal comes with a cost, the sides may have to agree to the proposals that will meet the cost allocation provided and have the most positive impact on the organization and employees.

Another example of this is proposing a five percent increase in wages and additional time off that would equate to an additional two percent increase in cost. If the organization is only approved to negotiate an increase of four percent, the parties may want to negotiate a smaller increase to both wages and time off so that both areas are receiving an increase while the overall cost is within the approved cost threshold. When situations like this arise, a vital piece of information is understanding the needs and wants of the employees so that the best decision can be made. When all of the proposals have been discussed and bargaining has occurred for each, the parties can agree to the terms and conditions through a formal settlement.

Each side should have the opportunity to review the final documents before signing. Once the official settlement has occurred, the union representatives must then begin the education and communication process with the membership for ratification of the proposal. **Ratification** is the process in which represented employees vote to approve or deny the proposed settlement. If the settlement is ratified, then the organization will move forward to receiving final approval through a board or executive authority and then finally implementing the terms of the settlement.

Once a final settlement is achieved and ready for implementation, it is important to roll out a communication plan so that employees will understand what will happen and when. Employees should clearly understand what changed, what stayed the same, and, if appropriate, why.

ADR Processes

Alternative dispute resolution (ADR) refers to many different processes and techniques that assist two parties in resolving their issues without filing a lawsuit or going to court. ADR processes include informal and voluntary processes such as negotiation and mediation as well as formal and mandatory processes such as conciliation and arbitration. The more informal the process, the more control each party has regarding recommendations to the resolution. The two parties are generally negotiating between themselves without intervention. As the process becomes more formal, there is less control by either party as an arbitrator, judge, or jury determines the resolution. The goals of ADR are to expedite the exchange of information and decision-making, while lowering costs and achieving resolution quickly and confidentially. The techniques used in ADR are flexible and can be customized to the parties involved and the specific issue that requires resolution. **Negotiation** is a voluntary agreement that works out a solution directly between the two parties involved. **Mediation** is a facilitated negotiation that works out a solution between the two parties through a neutral third party or mediator.

Conciliation is a non-binding formal process in which a conciliator explains the law and provides the parties with non-binding recommendations to resolve the issue. **Arbitration** is a formal process in which an arbitrator considers evidence presented by each party and determines a solution that is binding and final. It is a common practice to work through the four ADR processes respectively, as described above. Progressing through the four ADR processes above prior to filing a lawsuit or claim is an appropriate

path to follow if the matter cannot be resolved. Human Resources is an important resource for each of these steps as HR professionals can provide insights and information that can assist with negotiating an agreement at any of these levels.

Making Recommendations for Addressing Employee Representation

The first major labor statute passed in the United States was the **Norris-LaGuardia Act** of 1932. The Norris-LaGuardia Act endorsed collective bargaining as public policy and established government recognition that the job to a worker is more important than a worker to a corporation. Establishing this relationship was vital in showing that the only real power an employee has is in impacting employers through concerted activity. While this act did not create new rights, it curbed the power of courts to intervene in labor disputes and declared that unions could operate free from corporate control and interference.

The **National Labor Relations Act (NLRA)** is the basic law governing relations between labor unions and employees, giving employees the right to organize and bargain collectively. The NLRA is also known as the **Wagner Act** and was passed in 1935. The NLRA prohibits both employers and unions from violating the basic rights of employees, which include the following:

- The right to self-organize a union to negotiate with the employer
- The right to form, join, or assist labor organizations
- The right to bargain collectively about wages, working conditions, and other subjects
- The right to discuss employment terms and conditions of employment
- The right to choose representatives to bargain
- The right to take action to improve working conditions by raising work-related complaints
- The right to strike and picket, as appropriate
- The right to engage in protected activities
- The right to refrain from any of the above

Additionally, the NLRA stipulates that employers cannot prohibit employees from soliciting for a union during nonwork time or from distributing union literature or communications during nonwork time. The NLRA also prohibits the union from threatening employees with termination or other unjust actions unless union support is given. Finally, the NLRA established the **National Labor Relations Board (NLRB).** The NLRB certifies organized labor unions, supervises elections, and has the power to act against unfair business practices.

The NLRA establishes that both parties must negotiate and bargain in "good faith." **Good faith bargaining** refers to the honest attempt made by both the employer and union to reach an agreement. Good faith bargaining does not obligate either the employer or union to specific concessions or proposals. The basic requirements for bargaining in good faith include approaching negotiations with sincere resolve to reach an agreement, meeting regularly and at reasonable times, putting agreements in writing if requested, and having authorized representatives available and present at the scheduled times. The NLRA also establishes that mandatory subjects of bargaining must be negotiated between labor and management. **Mandatory subjects of bargaining** include wages, benefits, time off, hours, seniority, safety conditions, working conditions, employee testing protocols, disciplinary procedures, and recruitment issues such as promotion and demotion.

In 1947, the **Taft-Hartley Act**, or the **Labor-Management Relations Act,** was passed to amend the NLRA and limit employee labor rights. The Taft-Hartley Act provided protections for employers and stated that

they too have the right to go to the NLRB. This act prohibited unions from engaging in the following behavior:

- Forcing employees to support and join the union
- Refusing to bargain in good faith with employers
- Carrying out certain kinds of strikes
- Charging excessive union fees
- Going on strike during certain periods of time

It also provides for a cooling-off period in negotiation. Additionally, this act allowed states to pass "right-to-work laws," banned union contributions to political campaigns, required that union leaders swear they were not communists, and allowed for government intervention in certain circumstances. Finally, the Taft-Hartley Act established the **Federal Mediation and Conciliation Service (FMCS)** to help resolve negotiating disputes.

In 1959, the Landrum-Griffin Act, or the Labor-Management Reporting and Disclosure Act, was passed to amend the NLRA again. The Landrum-Griffin Act increased reporting requirements, regulated union affairs, and protected union members from improper union leadership to safeguard union member rights and prevent inappropriate practices by employers and union officers. This act is a bill of rights for union members, and it provides election procedures, accounting practices, and leadership oversight. This act was intended to protect the interests of the individual union members. This act provides union members the right to:

- Identify and propose candidates for office
- Vote in elections to select a board of representatives
- Attend and participate in union meetings
- Vote on union business
- Review and audit union accounts and records for transparency and accountability
- File grievances against union officers as appropriate to protect the integrity of the union

The history of unions in the United States goes back to ensuring that employers provide a safe workplace and a fair wage for a day's work. Employees should leave work in the same physical condition that were in when they arrived. While there are various federal laws enacted to protect worker's rights as discussed above, as well as laws that protect wages, working conditions, safety and wellness, and other areas of concern, some individuals still want unions to represent their interest with employers.

While there are many misperceptions about why employees might consider and want a union, the following are the most common reasons for unionizing a workforce:

- Poor communications
- Poor leadership and management
- Supervisors and employee treatment
- Stagnant wages and benefits
- Healthcare and retirement plans
- Safety and working conditions
- Workload and stress
- Job security
- Employee morale
- Lack of employee recognition and appreciation

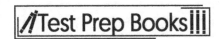

There is usually not one specific reason that a group of employees may look to unionize, but rather a culmination of multiple factors that lead to a disengaged, unmotivated, and dissatisfied group of employees.

Collective Bargaining Activities

Unions

In its broadest sense, a **union** (also known as a labor union) is simply a formally organized group of employees who work together to accomplish goals. These goals usually involve working conditions, pay, and other aspects of a common trade, but can vary widely depending on the union and the particular situation.

Types

A **local union** refers to either a union for a small organization or a union for a smaller geographic area. In many cases, the local union serves as a branch of the larger national union for a particular trade. A **national union** is often comprised of smaller, local unions. These groups represent a wide geographic area. A national union could represent employees of a single organization or employees of multiple organizations that happen to be working in the same trade. A **federation** is made up of different national unions representing different industries that nevertheless share some commonalities and have common goals. Finally, an international union represents workers in multiple countries.

Organizing Process

Unions must go through a specific process to be officially organized and recognized as a legitimate representative for a group of workers. Employees must demonstrate an interest in participating in the union and must sign authorization cards indicating their interest in the union. At least 30 percent of eligible employees are required to sign authorization cards by the NLRB before they can order an election. The union must inform the employer of the employees' desire to unionize. If at this point the employer refuses, the union may take action through the NLRB. The NLRB then holds an election where employees vote on whether to be represented by the union. Employees are eligible to vote in the election if they were on the company's payroll during the pay period directly prior to the calling of the election and during the pay period immediately preceding the election date. Any employees who were striking and then were permanently replaced are allowed to vote in an election that is conducted within twelve months following the end of the strike.

Picketing

Picketing is an act of protest where a group of people (picketers) gather in front of a business to raise awareness of an issue or to discourage people from entering a building to work or do business. The NLRB outlines what kinds of picketing activities unions may legally participate in. Employees may engage in **informational picketing**, where they picket to announce to the public that they are not represented by any one authority and thus plan to organize. Employees may also engage in **organizational picketing**, where they picket to convince employees to join or support their union. Finally, employees may engage in **recognitional picketing**, where they picket to encourage the employer to recognize their union as the employees' representative.

While in disputes with an employer, unions may engage in **common situs picketing**. This is where employees picket at a location used by the targeted employer as well as other organizations. This is legal as long as the picketers make clear which employer is being protested, so that other organizations are not adversely affected by the picketing. Unions may also use **consumer picketing**, where employees picket to discourage the public from doing business with the employer in question. Finally, unions can

take advantage of **double breasting picketing**, where employees picket at a location where the employer's workers are not unionized. This is only legal in certain situations.

Decertification

If a company's employees feel that their union is not doing a good enough job to represent them, they can go through the process of **decertification**, which strips the union of its official status as the employees' representatives. To decertify the union, 30 percent of employees must first sign a petition. Then, the employees can file the petition with the NLRB. The petition cannot be filed less than twelve months after the union was officially certified. If the NLRB approves the petition, then it holds a decertification election among the company employees. The union is decertified if a majority of the voting employees vote in favor of the decertification (a tie vote also means the union is decertified).

Deauthorization

Deauthorization is a process of removing a union's security clause and its authority to negotiate. A security clause is basically a condition in a contract that requires employees to join a union. The deauthorization process is identical to that of decertification. First, 30 percent of employees must sign a petition in favor of deauthorization. Then, the employees file the petition with the NLRB. If the NLRB approves the petition, then it holds a decertification election among the company employees. Deauthorization is approved if a majority of the employees who are eligible to vote vote in favor of deauthorization. In this instance, a situation where employees who are eligible and do not exercise their right to vote equates to a vote against deauthorization.

Laws Affecting Employment in Union and Nonunion Environments

Labor Management Relations Act (Taft-Hartley Act)

Passed in 1947, the **Labor Management Relations Act** (LMRA) focuses on union activities that qualify as unfair labor practices. For example, unions cannot force employees to join. Employees also have the right to choose their union representative. Unions must bargain with the employer or its representative. Unions also cannot interfere with the negotiation and enforcement of an employer's contract. Unions cannot discriminate against non-union participants, or those who publicly oppose the union. Unions cannot encourage a secondary boycott (an attempt to encourage non-union members to cease business with an organization) or a hot cargo agreement (an attempt to force an employer to stop doing business with another company or individual). Unions also cannot charge unreasonable membership fees.

The LMRA also established the **Federal Mediation and Conciliation Service**. This piece of legislation granted power to the United States president to obtain an injunction ending a strike or lockout for an eighty-day "cooling off" period if the continuation of the strike could "imperil the health or safety of the nation."

Labor Management Reporting and Disclosure Act (Landrum-Griffin Act)

Passed in 1959, the goal of the **Labor Management Reporting and Disclosure Act (LMRDA)** was to protect employees from corrupt unions. This piece of legislation allowed for a closed shop exception for construction trades. The LMRDA also provided for a Bill of Rights for union members, which gave members the right to secret ballot elections for union offices, protection from excessive dues, freedom of speech in union matters, and the right to sue the union.

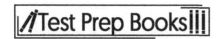

WARN Act

The **Worker Adjustment and Retraining Notification (WARN)** Act of 1988 requires that a minimum of 60 days' notice be given in advance of plant closings and mass layoffs. The notice must be given to local government, state dislocated worker units, and workers or their representatives. This piece of legislation applies to employers with one hundred or more full-time employees, or employers who have a total of full-time and part-time employees working 4,000 hours per week (not counting overtime) at all their employment sites combined.

A plant closing is the temporary or permanent shutdown of an entire site or one or more facilities or operating units within a single site that results in an employment loss during any thirty-day period of 50 or more full-time employees. A mass layoff is a reduction in force (not a plant closing) during any thirty-day period that results in an employment loss at a single site for either 50 or more full-time employees, if they make up at least 33 percent of the workforce at the employment site, or 500 or more full-time employees. Employment loss is the involuntary termination of employment (other than for cause), layoff for more than six months, or at least a 50 percent reduction in hours for each month of a six-month period.

The WARN Act provides for three situations in which the sixty-day notice is not required, but the burden is on the employer to show that the reasons are legitimate and not an attempt to thwart the intent of the act. First, the "faltering company" exception applies only to plant closures in situations where the company is actively seeking additional funding and has a reasonable expectation that it will be forthcoming in an amount sufficient to preclude the layoff or closure, and that giving the notice would negatively impact the ability of the company to obtain the funding. The "unforeseeable business circumstance" exception applies to plant closings and mass layoffs and occurs when circumstances take a sudden and unexpected negative change that could not have reasonably been predicted. Finally, the "natural disaster" exception applies to both plant closings and mass layoffs occurring as the result of a natural disaster such as a tornado, earthquake, or hurricane.

Glass Ceiling Act

The **Civil Rights Act of 1991** was enacted to address workplace discrimination, specifically, the practice of preventing employees from reaching higher-level positions of management based solely on race, color, religion, sex, or national origin. The **Glass Ceiling Act** is part of Title II of this Act and established a commission to study how businesses filled management positions, and whether there were significant barriers to protected groups (such as women and minorities) that were preventing them from reaching those positions.

The commission did indeed find significant barriers in a number of organizations and divided the barriers into three categories. Governmental barriers occur when companies do not enforce existing equal opportunity regulations, thus preventing protected individuals from advancing to management positions. Internal structure barriers occur when company cultures (through official policies or unofficial but normal practices) prevent protected individuals from advancing to management positions. Societal barriers occur when protected individuals cannot receive the necessary education for management positions, or when pre-existing prejudice toward the protected group prevents expected advancements. (Note: societal barriers can refer to the larger society beyond that of the company in question).

Norris-LaGuardia Act

The **Norris-LaGuardia Act** (1932) is designed to protect workers' rights to form and join a union, as well as their right to strike. The act also protects all non-violent union activities from court injunctions. Lastly,

the act protects employees from having to sign what are known as "yellow-dog" contracts, which are contracts that prevent employees from joining unions.

National Labor Relations Act (Wagner Act)

Passed in 1935, the **National Labor Relations Act (NLRA)** grants specific rights to workers who already belong to, or wish to join, a union. In addition to reinforcing the rights covered by the Norris-LaGuardia Act, this piece of legislation also grants employees the right to participate in collective bargaining activities, even if they are not a member of the union in question. There are some restrictions, however, such as the NLRA does not affect the special restrictions of the Railway Labor Act. In addition, the NLRA does not affect certain individuals who may make decisions on behalf of an employer, such as managers, supervisors, independent contractors, and immediate family.

The NLRA also defines what constitutes a legal and an illegal strike. A strike is considered legal when employees are seeking a better work environment, benefits, or compensation, or when an employer is using an unfair labor practice. A strike is considered illegal when employees have signed a contract with a no-strike clause, employees are striking to defend a union's unfair labor practice, or there is a significant concern that the striking employees are expected to cause property damage or bodily harm.

The NLRA also dictates what can be considered unfair labor practices, such as an employer doing one or more of the following: stopping workers from joining or participating in a union, taking control of a union or showing favoritism to any particular union, discriminating against union participants, discriminating against a worker who has filed charges with the National Labor Relations Board (NLRB), and refusing to bargain with the union representing its employees.

In addition, the NLRA created the National Labor Relations Board (NLRB) to encourage union growth. This board is primarily responsible for investigating potential unfair labor practices. The NLRB focuses on protecting employees from unfair treatment by employers or unions. The NLRB has the authority to take various actions to combat unfair labor practices, including the following: forcing employers to rehire employees, forcing employers to negotiate with a union, disbanding employer-controlled unions, forcing unions to refund excessive membership fees, forcing unions to negotiate with an employer, and forcing unions to reinstate members.

Rules and Regulations Related to Compensation and Benefits

Payroll Vendors

Some of the reasons that companies may elect to outsource their payroll function include the following:

- Freeing up staff time to allow resources to be more strategic in nature
- To reduce costs
- To improve compliance
- Possibly to avoid fines associated with incorrect/late payments or IRS filings
- To have the ability to offer direct deposit of payroll checks to employees

An employer can choose to outsource its entire payroll function or only one or more areas of its payroll function, such as W-2 form printing services. When outsourcing payroll, an employer should select a vendor with an excellent reputation for paying employees on time and providing a high level of customer service.

In an effort not to create additional work, it is important to determine if the vendor's systems are able to effectively integrate with the employer's systems—e.g., time tracking and self-service technologies used to update employees' personal data and payroll-related information. An employer should ensure that the vendor chosen will be able to provide the level of service that the company requires at an affordable cost.

COBRA Administration

When administering COBRA, the length of time that an employee is eligible for coverage is determined by the type of qualifying event. For example, eighteen months is the period of eligibility for an employee's reduction in hours or an employee's termination. If you or one of your qualified beneficiaries has a disability, they may be able to get an 11-month extension, for a maximum period of 29 months. If you have a second qualifying event, such as a divorce/legal separation or death of an employed spouse during your 18-month period of coverage, you may be granted a maximum 18-month extension (36-month maximum total). Employees and their family members have sixty days to elect COBRA coverage from the time that a qualifying event has taken place.

Covered employers are required to provide an initial COBRA notice within ninety days of the date an employee/spouse is covered under the plan. Employers are also required to provide a notice of unavailability of continuation of coverage within fourteen days of the date of the qualifying event if the employee/spouse is not covered. Employees must be notified of their coverage ending before the maximum continuous period allowed.

Employee Recognition Vendors

Due to a lack of staff resources, time, or in-house expertise, companies may choose to outsource their employee rewards program to a trusted recognition vendor. Since a vendor can, ultimately, determine the success or failure of a company's rewards program, there are a number of items that an employer should evaluate when entering this type of relationship.

An exceptional recognition vendor will take the time to learn about a company's culture, business goals, employee rewards needs, and program budget. The recognition vendor should have an offering of high-quality awards and be able to accommodate rush orders and unique awards, if needed.

Additionally, world-class customer service is the key to employees receiving timely reward fulfillment and recognition for their efforts and achievements. An employer should be assured that the company will receive correct invoices and accurate reporting from the vendor. The ultimate goal for both the employer and the recognition vendor is to ensure that employees feel valued and remain loyal.

Non-Cash Rewards

Managers are frequently being asked to do more with less, including stretching their compensation budgets. This is where non-cash rewards can be factored in with cash compensation to motivate the workforce effectively. Non-cash rewards include such items as personalized thank-you notes for a job well done, company merchandise, and gift cards. Some organizations have factored non-cash rewards into their formal recognition programs, making them more meaningful.

For example, there are peer-to-peer recognition programs in place, where one employee can send a personalized thank-you eCard to another employee for a job well done. In that same system, managers can acknowledge an employee for their extra effort on a project by assigning recognition points, along with sending an eCard. Once an employee accumulates a bank of recognition points, they can cash in the points to receive either a gift card or an item from the company store.

Confidentiality and Privacy Rules

Secure data storage is a difficult but necessary policy to prevent corruption from malware and hackers. Data corruption is a widespread concern for firms of all sizes and locations. Organizations with sensitive and confidential data, such as government agencies, continue to take steps to strengthen their data security. Data backup requires copying and archiving current information to separate drives to restore information in the event of data corruption. Data storage and backup are essential to protect organizational plans, policies, and secrets in the event of a data breach.

Legal and Regulatory Environment

HR professionals need to be familiar with relevant employment laws and regulations. Applicable laws may vary based on organization type, size, and other factors, but there are many regulations that apply to most organizations. Several important regulations are administered by the Equal Employment Opportunity Commission, or EEOC. One of these is Title VII of the Civil Rights Act of 1964, which applies to employers with fifteen or more employees and prohibits discrimination based on race, color, religion, sex, or national origin. EEOC also oversees the Age Discrimination in Employment Act of 1967 (ADEA), which prohibits discrimination against anyone forty years old or older in terms of hiring, promotion, wages, termination, and denial of benefits. The ADEA also prohibits mandatory retirement in many sectors. The Equal Pay Act (EPA) prohibits wage discrimination based on sex for people in the same organization performing the same or similar jobs (in terms of skills and responsibilities) under the same or similar conditions. In addition, the EEOC administers ADA, discussed earlier in this study guide.

Domestic and Global Employment Laws

Other important regulations include the Fair Labor Standards Act (FLSA) which establishes rules such as minimum wage and overtime pay, standards for child labor, and definitions for exempt and non-exempt employees. The Family and Medical Leave Act (FMLA) outlines standards for when employees are permitted to take unpaid, job-protected family and medical leave. The Occupational Safety and Health Act of 1970 created the Occupational Safety and Health Administration (OSHA), which ensures that employers provide a safe and healthy workplace. Examples of OSHA regulations include things like eliminating or reducing hazards when possible, providing free safety equipment, informing employees about chemical hazards, providing comprehensive and comprehensible safety training, keeping records of work-related injuries and illnesses, and displaying the official OSHA poster describing employees' rights and employers' responsibilities.

Alignment of HR Programs, Practices, and Policies

HR programs, practices, and policies must align and comply with these laws and regulations and others. This means staying current on local, state, and federal regulations, as well as any international laws that may be applicable. It also means being proactive and circumspect about where laws need to be applied. This ensures that the organization is providing a safe and fair workplace for employees, while also ensuring that the organization avoids any fees, fines, lawsuits, or other liabilities that may arise from not following the law. For example, when posting a job advertisement, HR must ensure that there are no references to restricting hiring based on things like age, race, or sex. The same applies to the interviewing and hiring stages, even until terminating employees.

Illegal and Noncompliant HR-Related Behaviors

Because these decisions and practices can extend beyond HR, HR professionals are also responsible for coaching employees at all levels about how to avoid illegal and noncompliant behaviors. One way to

keep employees informed is by displaying posters related to applicable laws and regulations; as previously mentioned, employers are required to display certain information (related to things like OSHA and FLSA), depending on such factors as the size, location, and type of organization. The U.S. Department of Labor (DOL) offers resources to help organizations determine what information they are legally obligated to display for employees.

HR can also coach employees who are responsible for things like hiring and terminating decisions in order to avoid illegal terminations, for example, or illegal questions during job interviews. Interviewers should be sure to ask only questions that are job-related and determine qualifications that are justified by a business purpose (also known as bona fide occupational qualification, or BFOQ). If interviewers and hiring managers are screening employees based on factors that are not covered by BFOQ, it can present grounds for complaints of discrimination (for example, when an employer requires a higher level of education than is necessary for a position, and then uses this requirement as a basis to screen applicants of certain racial or socioeconomic backgrounds).

Interpretation of Employment Laws
HR professionals can also consult legal experts as needed when it comes to the interpretation and application of employment laws. Whether those legal services are internal or external may depend on the nature of the organization. Smaller organizations may be more likely to consult with outside services, while large organizations are more like to have in-house legal services. However, particularly when an organization begins operation in a new area (for example, in a new state or country), it would be a prudent move to consult with experts who have experience in local laws.

HR Policies and Procedures

Americans with Disabilities Act
The Americans with Disabilities Act (ADA) is a federal law that outlaws discrimination based on disability. The ADA precludes discrimination based on race, sex, national origin, and religion. Moreover, the law requires that employers provide reasonable accommodations to employees who have a disability. For instance, this could require employers to build a wheelchair accessible ramp for disabled employers to enter and leave the building. Also, the ADA stipulates that public spaces be accessible for disabled persons. Under this law, all employees are guaranteed equal access to career development and training.

Additionally, all employees are also guaranteed equal access to career development and training under the Age Discrimination in Employment Act (ADEA) and the Uniformed Services Employment and Reemployment Rights Act (USERRA).

Pregnancy Discrimination Act
The **Pregnancy Discrimination Act**, passed in 1978, was an amendment to Title VII of 1964. The act applies to all employers with fifteen or more employees and states that while pregnant women are working, they are to be treated in the same way as other employees who are performing their jobs. Therefore, pregnancy must be treated in the same manner as any other type of temporary disability.

Under this legislation, an employer:

- Cannot refuse to hire a pregnant woman
- Cannot force a woman to take leave or terminate her employment because she is pregnant

- Must give a woman a comparable position to the one that she held prior to her maternity leave (if the company already does so with employees taking short-term disability) upon her return to work
- Must provide a pregnant woman with reasonable accommodation(s) if she is unable to do her job and approaches her manager to that effect
- Cannot discriminate against a woman who has undergone an abortion

When a pregnant woman is interviewing for a job position, she is not required by law to disclose the fact that she is pregnant. If it is obvious that a female interview candidate is pregnant, a prospective employer can only state the job requirements for the position (ignoring the pregnancy) and ask the candidate when she is available to start work.

Uniform Guidelines on Employee Selection Procedures

The **Uniform Guidelines on Employee Selection Procedures**, passed in 1978, were designed to prohibit selection procedures that have an adverse impact on protected groups. Adverse impact occurs when the rate for a protected group is less than 80% of the rate for the group with the highest selection rate. This is also known as the 80% rule, or the four-fifths rule. Below are two examples:

Example 1
Four hundred white candidates applied and two hundred were hired – 50 percent
One hundred Hispanic candidates applied and forty-five were hired – 45 percent
80% of 50 = 40
There is no adverse impact here. If the number was lower than forty, there would be.

Example 2
Sixty male candidates interviewed and thirty were hired – 50 percent
Forty female candidates applied and ten were hired – 25 percent
80% of 50 = 40
Yes, there is adverse impact here, since there were only 25 percent females hired. Females must be hired at a selection rate of 40 percent.

Under these guidelines, procedures that have an adverse impact on women and minorities must be proven to be valid in predicting and/or measuring performance, so as not to be viewed as discriminatory. The **"bottom line" concept** was an outcome of these guidelines, meaning that an employer is not required to evaluate each component of the selection process individually if the end result is shown to be predictive of future job performance.

If adverse impact is found (which is not always intentional), the employer has alternatives:

- Abandon the procedure
- Modify the procedure to eliminate adverse impact
- Demonstrate job relatedness
- Conduct validation studies
- Keep detailed records
- Investigate alternatives with less adverse impact
- Show the business necessity associated with the need to keep the procedure (which is difficult to do)

Immigration Reform and Control Act (IRCA)

The **Immigration Reform and Control Act (IRCA)** was passed in 1986 and amended in 1990. This act was created to prevent discrimination against individuals based on national origin or citizenship on elements such as employment, pay, or benefits, so long as they are legally able to work in the United States. Employers are also required to verify new employees by having them complete an employment eligibility verification form (I-9) and receiving proof of lawful status within their first three working days. The back of the I-9 form lists each of the documents that can be used to show legality to work in the United States, verifying an individual's right to work and identity. Employers must retain I-9 forms for three years, or for one year after an employee's termination, whichever comes later. In addition, this act established civil and criminal penalties for hiring illegal immigrants.

Furthermore, the IRCA instituted categories for visas, such as immigrant visas or green cards. While permanent or indefinite visas and are obtained through family relationships or employment, nonimmigrant visas are temporary. Another example is the H1-B visa, for which there is a yearly cap. This type of visa is set aside for certain kinds of working professionals who travel to the United States for a specified period of time.

Sexual Harassment in the Workplace

There are two types of sexual harassment that occur in the workplace: quid pro quo and hostile work environment. The translation of quid pro quo is "this for that." **Quid pro quo sexual harassment** takes place when a superior conditions employment (e.g., promotional opportunity, raise, etc.) on sexual favors.

The type of sexual harassment known as **hostile work environment** takes place when sexual or discriminatory conduct creates a work environment that a "reasonable person" would find threatening or abusive (e.g., unwelcome advances, offensive gender-related language, and sexual innuendos). It is important to remember that male employees can also be victims of sexual harassment.

There are four well-known court cases that stemmed from sexual harassment in the workplace:

- **Meritor Savings Bank vs. Vinson**: The court held that sexual harassment violates Title VII. This case dealt with an employee who was plagued with unwanted sexual innuendos. The court said that the plaintiff did not need to prove concrete psychological harm, just an abusive or intimidating environment.

- **Harris vs. Forklift Systems, Inc.**: This case established the "reasonable person" standard for hostile environment sexual harassment.

- **Oncale vs. Sundowner Offshore Service, Inc.**: The court ruled that same-gender sexual harassment is actionable. This case dealt with all male gender working on an offshore oilrig, where a heterosexual male was threatened with rape.

- **Faragher vs. City of Boca Raton**: The court stated that employers can be held liable for supervisory harassment that results in an adverse employment action. This case dealt with female lifeguards who were sexually harassed. The city was held liable because the lifeguards' supervisors were not informed of the policy (it was not communicated effectively).

The following items are key elements to put in place in order to prevent sexual harassment from occurring in the workplace:

- Provide staff with a written, zero tolerance policy on sexual harassment that contains clear definitions and examples
- Provide a complaint procedure for staff to utilize
- Hold training sessions for employees and document attendees
- Investigate all sexual harassment complaints
- Follow through with corrective action (up through and including termination), if necessary
- Communicate the policy on sexual harassment to everyone in the company using multiple methods

Equal Opportunity Employment (EEO) Reporting

Annual workforce data reporting is required by the Equal Employment Opportunity Commission (EEOC) for all employers with one hundred or more employees and federal contractors with at least fifty employees and government contracts of at least $50,000. The EEOC sets the due date for reporting each year, with the 2023 report being due by June 4, 2024. In addition, these employers must place EEO posters and notices in prominent locations within their workplaces. EEO reporting aids employers in determining their workforce composition, to ensure they are not discriminating against protected classes.

The various EEO reports collect data by some type of job grouping about race/ethnicity and gender. There are nine EEO job reporting categories:

- Officials and managers
- Professionals
- Technicians
- Sales
- Office and clerical
- Craft workers (skilled)
- Operatives (semiskilled)
- Laborers (unskilled)
- Service workers

As another example, the EEO-1 Report, which is also known as the Employer Information Report, categorizes data by race/ethnicity, gender, and job category. This report applies to employers who are required to file an annual report of employee sex and race/ethnic categories under Title VII of the 1964 Civil Rights Act. Government guidelines for the reporting of race are detailed in the EEO1 report form, which is jointly produced by the EEOC and the Office of Federal Contract Compliance.

Progressive Discipline

Progressive discipline is a system that, rather than defining a single "one size fits all" response to an employee infraction, attempts to address each incident as a unique situation, and then develops consequences accordingly. Typically, factors like severity and frequency (in other words, "how bad" and "how often") are key in determining the appropriate response. Many organizations make use of a five-stage process. Coaching is the first stage, where the manager discusses the behavior problem with the employee. This stage is typically used for small or first-time infractions. Then the employee receives a first warning. This is also called the counseling stage and usually involves the employee receiving a

verbal warning. Then the second warning follows, which is also called the formal warning stage. This stage progresses to the employee receiving a written warning. A disciplinary action follows. At this stage, the employee is suspended for their behavior. Finally, if the chain of progressive discipline has not corrected the behavior, the final step in the progressive discipline process is to terminate the individual's employment.

Job Classifications

Employee Classification

The FLSA requires employers to classify all employee positions into two categories, exempt and non-exempt, depending on the type of work the employees do, the amount of money the employees are paid, and how the employees are paid.

- **Non-exempt** positions fall directly under the FLSA regulations. These employees earn a salary of less than $35,568 per year or $684 per week. Non-exempt positions do not involve the supervision of others or the use of independent judgment; they also do not require specialized education.

- **Exempt** positions do not fall under the FLSA regulations. These employees are paid on a salary basis and spend more than 50 percent of their work time performing exempt duties. Exempt level duties fall into three main categories: executive, professional, and administrative.

  - **Executive employees** are responsible for directing the work of two or more full-time employees. Management is a key focus of their role, and they have direct input into the job status of other employees, such as hiring and firing.

  - **Professional employees** can fall into the category of learned professionals, meaning their positions require knowledge in a specific field of science or learning, such as doctors, lawyers, engineers, and accountants. Professional employees can also fall into the category of creative professionals, meaning their positions involve the invention, imagination, originality, or talent in a recognized field of artistic or creative endeavor—e.g., writing, acting, and graphic arts.

  - **Administrative employees** are responsible for exercising discretion and judgment with respect to matters of significance, which can be directly related to management of the general business or in dealings with the customers of the business.

Employees and Independent Contractors

It is important for employers to be able to discern between employees and independent contractors who are performing work for them for the purpose of withholding taxes, paying overtime and on-call pay with regard to the Fair Labor Standards Act (FLSA), providing benefits, and granting legal protection to the appropriate individuals, all of which apply only to employees.

Employers can use independent contractors to grow and reduce their workforce as needed while reducing their legal liability. There can also be a significant cost savings associated with having independent contractors complete work as they can typically be paid less than regular, full-time staff, and they do not receive healthcare benefits.

The Internal Revenue Service has developed a list of twenty factors that fall under three categories for employers to use to determine if an individual working for them is an employee or an independent contractor:

IRS 20-Factor Test
Behavioral Control
1. Instruction: A company-employee relationship could exist if the company dictates where, when, and how the employee works.
2. Training: A training relationship indicates the company has control over the type of work done by the employee.
3. Business Integration: Workers are likely to be considered employees if the success of the business depends on the work they do.
4. Personal Services: Independent contractors are free to assign work to anyone. Likewise, a company-employee relationship may dictate a particular person to carry out a specific task.
5. Assistants: An independent contractor may hire, supervise, and pay their own assistants, while a company-employee relationship may indicate that the company has control over the hiring, supervising, and paying of the worker's assistants.
Financial Control
6. Payment Method: Usually, hourly, weekly, or monthly payments indicate a company-employee relationship. Independent contractors are usually paid by commission or upon project completion.
7. Business or Travel Expenses: Employers who pay business or travel expenses for their employees are usually part of a company-employee relationship.
8. Tools and Materials: A company-employee relationship usually exists if the company provides the worker with tools and materials.
9. Investment in Facilities: Independent contractors usually invest in their own facilities, while employees for companies are usually provided facilities.
10. Profit or Loss: Workers who realize profits or losses are usually independent contractors.
Type of Relationship
11. Continuing of Relationships: An ongoing relationship between a company and a worker could indicate an employment relationship.
12. Set Hours: The implementation of a set schedule indicates that a company-employee relationship exists.
13. Full-Time: While independent contractors choose to work when and for whom they choose, employees sometimes must devote their schedules to full-time work for employees.
14. On-Site Services: If the work must be done on company property, a company-employee relationship probably exists.
15. Sequence of Work: A company-employee relationship is indicated if the worker must perform work in order of company preference and is not able to choose the sequence themselves.
16. Reports: If a worker is required to give oral or written reports to a company, this may indicate a level of control the company has over an employee.
17. Multiple Companies: Workers who provide services for multiple companies at one time are usually considered independent contractors.
18. Availability to Public: Workers who make their work available to the general public are often considered to be independent contractors.

| 19. Right to Discharge: Employers who have the right to discharge employees indicate a company-employee relationship. |
| 20. Right to Terminate: Independent contractors are usually under contract to work, so they cannot terminate their employment as easily as employees. |

Workforce Reduction and Restructuring Terminology

Workforce Reduction (Downsizing)

Workforce reductions are the planned elimination of some personnel in order to make an organization more competitive.

Once a company realizes it has a talent surplus, Human Resources can take the following steps to implement a workforce reduction:

- Reduce employees' hours
- Implement a hiring freeze
- Institute a voluntary separation program, also known as an early retirement buyout program

Although workforce reductions help companies cut costs in the short term, they often hurt productivity. For an organization to successfully implement a workforce reduction, it should communicate with employees throughout the entire process, and provide downsized employees with outplacement services to assist with resume writing, career counseling, and interview preparation. It can also provide referral assistance to exiting employees. Companies should strive to build the trust and commitment of the remaining employees to boost employee morale, especially during a downsizing situation.

Employees who are laid off are typically asked to sign a document known as a **separation agreement and general release**. This document, when signed, is a legally binding agreement that states the employee cannot sue or make any claims against the company in exchange for agreed upon severance benefits. Severance pay is not required by law, but most companies will pay employees who are laid off a set number of weeks of salary continuation, based upon their years of service (typically one or two weeks' pay per year of service), to ease their financial burden and to preserve the organization's image. Some companies also include a continuation of healthcare benefits for a set period.

An employee is given the agreement during their exit meeting and is allowed to take it home and review it with a lawyer. They have twenty-one days to sign and return the agreement for an individual separation and forty-five days to sign and return the agreement in cases of a group reduction in force. Once the agreement is signed, an employee still has seven days to revoke their signature.

Mergers and Acquisitions (M&A)

Corporate restructuring that involves mergers and acquisitions require complying with certain laws and regulations and performing due diligence to evaluate a business contract before making any big decisions. Due diligence is typically performed when a company is buying another company (acquisition) and helps to uncover any potential liabilities or evaluate business and financial risk.

The due diligence process may involve spending time at the business location, reviewing sales numbers, learning about future plans for expansion, and carefully studying documents with vendors such as purchase order and sales agreements. An attorney may be hired to assist with the due diligence process to check for any discrepancies and verify the validity of certain documents and contracts.

In order to cut costs, reduce inefficiencies, or recover financially from a recent downturn, a company may decide to dispose of some or all its business units by selling the company to another company, closing permanently, declaring bankruptcy, or relocating overseas (offshoring). This is known as divesting a business. **Divestitures** can help a company better manage its portfolio of assets by closing some units to focus on others, or by selling off one or more business units to recover from a loss.

Outplacement Practices

Outplacement practices are a best practice for dealing with outsourcing or reductions in force. Although severance packages are excellent tools that can include extensions of salary and benefits to assist with a transition out of an organization, it is also important to look at other options that can help employees with this difficult phase. Specialized services can include job search services with career counselors, resume writing workshops, training programs to develop new and in-demand skills, or even financial planning to deal with the loss of an income.

Although it is never possible to meet every need of every employee, organizations who try to provide additional support and resources during transition periods will see easier transitions. These smooth transitions can result in less disruption to services and to the remaining employees. It is also important to address the needs of the remaining employees; they are facing a difficult transition as well. Their work may be changing, their former colleagues are no longer in the workplace, and the work environment in general changes. It is important to be cognizant of these issues and provide support as needed to those remaining with the organization.

Employee Records Management

Companies should maintain maximum security while possessing the personal information of customers and employees. Each organization should utilize an apparatus that monitors and reports security breaches, notifying employees, customers, and various authorities. In addition, internal privacy policies must comply with current laws and regulations. These laws are intended to deter security breaches.

A company's internal privacy policy should address sensitive information such as addresses, telephone numbers, credit reports, medical reports, employee records, company technology, and data systems that collect personal information. An effective privacy policy explains the purposes of investigations and monitors the conduct of employees. Episodic privacy tests can be useful, particularly if management has reason to believe that employee misconduct has occurred. A company should communicate regularly with its employees about security issues and technology. Additionally, written policies must exist to protect employers from employee claims of privacy invasion. Employees should be notified of these policies and agree to all conditions. An effective privacy policy will identify and monitor employees suspected of violating protocol and procure the necessary information to review the employee's practices.

Identity theft occurs when a person wrongfully obtains and uses another individual's personal information, typically for financial gain. This form of fraud can be very damaging and is difficult to prevent. In order to commit identity theft, a perpetrator does not need a person's fingerprint. The criminal simply needs a Social Security number, credit card number, bank statements, or any piece of information that will allow access to personal documents. The expense of identity theft to the victim can be shocking, and in some cases may be in excess of $100,000. Identity theft primarily occurs in public places through methods such as "shoulder surfing." This technique involves watching over somebody's shoulder when they are using an ATM machine or rummaging through someone's garbage in search of confidential material that was not disposed of properly.

Data protection is the process of securing personal information from identity theft or other corruptive activities. Data protection involves storing important materials and can be done through a variety of means, such as file locking, disk mirroring, and database shadowing. The principal purpose of data protection is to maintain the integrity and proper storage of information. Two effective means of achieving maximum data protection while ensuring availability is to pursue data lifecycle management (DLM) and information lifecycle management (ILM), which may provide better data protection in the event of a virus or hack. A feasible data protection plan is also applicable to disaster recovery and business continuity.

Workplace monitoring is a policy that employers use in order to monitor a suspicious person and gather information. Employers may use a workplace monitoring program to discover activities that threaten the integrity and interests of the firm. Monitoring techniques involve wiretapping, reviewing Internet content usage, GPS tracking, checking employees' social media accounts, and interviewing other employees about suspicious activity. Management surveillance programs are easier to execute if employees are required to use company phones and computers. However, before such actions are taken by an employer, all employees should be given ample documentation of rules and regulations. This will ensure that any breach of protocol is intentional and deliberate on the part of the employee.

Recordkeeping

Implementing a Record Retention Process
Internet Applicants
The **Office of Federal Contract Compliance Programs (OFCCP)** created a recordkeeping rule, known as the **Internet Applicant Rule**, to determine what records need to be kept by federal contractors who have Internet applicants applying for their open positions. Under this rule, a job seeker is classified as an Internet applicant by a contractor if they meet four criteria:

- They have expressed an interest in employment over the Internet or through another related electronic data technology

- The employer considers the individual for employment in a particular position

- The individual's expression of interest indicates that they possess the basic qualifications for the open position

- The individual does not remove themselves from consideration at any point during the contractor's selection process

The following record retention requirements are based on federal guidelines. However, individual states may also have record retention requirements that need to be followed.

Pre-Employment Files
Selection, hiring, and employment records are to be kept for either one year after their creation or following the hire/no hire decision (whichever date is later). Federal contractors must keep these same types of records for three years. The following items are examples of what are included in these types of records:

- Employment applications
- Resumes

- Interview notes
- Records related to promotions, transfers, and terminations
- Requests for reasonable accommodations
- AAP records related to hiring benchmarks

I-9 forms are to be kept for three years after the date of hire or one year after the date of termination (whichever date is later).

Credit reports have no record retention requirement. However, the law requires an employer to shred all documents containing information from such a report.

Drug test records are to be kept for one year from the date the test was administered, or up to five years for any job positions related to the Department of Transportation.

Medical Files

Records associated with family medical leave (for a company with fifty or more employees) are to be kept for three years. The following items are examples of what is included in these types of records:

- Basic employee data
- Dates of leave taken
- Hours of leave taken for intermittent Family and Medical Leave Act of 1993 (FMLA) leave
- Copies of employee notices
- Records of premium payments of employee benefits
- Records of any disputes regarding designation of leave

Benefits Files

Records associated with employment benefits are to be kept for six years. The following items are examples of what are included in these types of records:

- Summary plan descriptions
- Annual reports
- Plan amendments
- Plan terminations

There are no record retention requirements for documentation associated with employees and their dependents who wish to continue group healthcare coverage under the Consolidated Omnibus Budget Reconciliation Act (COBRA) after a qualifying event. However, it is recommended that companies maintain these records for six years to be consistent with the requirements of the Employment Retirement Income Security Act (ERISA).

Statutory Reporting Requirements

The Occupational Safety and Health Act, passed in 1970, established the Occupational Safety and Health Administration (OSHA) of the federal government in 1971. This agency creates and enforces workplace safety standards. Employers who are engaged in commerce and have one or more employees must observe the regulations established by OSHA. However, partial exemptions are allowed to employers with fewer than 10 employees. These employers do not need to keep OSHA injury and illness records unless requested, however, work-related fatalities, hospitalizations, and amputations must still be reported. Not only does OSHA set minimum standards, but the agency also ensures job training for

workers in a language they can understand. Additionally, OSHA protects employees who work in substandard conditions and informs them of their rights. A critical provision of OSHA is the protection of employees who reach out to OSHA to open an investigation of their working conditions. These employees are protected by OSHA from employer retaliation. OSHA regulations empower employees to help accomplish safety and security.

Employee Retirement Income Security Act (1974)

The Employment Retirement Income Security Act (ERISA) establishes the minimum standards for benefit plans of private, for-profit employers. It states that in order to receive tax advantages, these plans must conform to the Internal Revenue Code's requirements.

This law also established the federal agency known as the Pension Benefit Guaranty Corporation (PBGC). In return for the plans or their sponsors paying premiums to the PBGC, it guarantees payment of vested benefits up to a maximum limit to employees covered by pension plans.

Vested benefits are simply benefits from a retirement account or from a pension plan belonging to an employee that they get to keep regardless of whether they remain employed at the company. Companies have different rules regarding the number of years at which benefits vest; many are five years. Therefore, if an employee resigns after the vesting period of five years, then they can retain the benefits.

Minimum eligibility requirements were also established by ERISA. In order to participate in a plan, an employee must be at least twenty-one years of age and have completed one year of service with the company. However, company plans may be more generous concerning these minimum eligibility requirements.

ERISA established minimum vesting schedules for graded and cliff vesting. **Graded vesting** is a set schedule where employees are vested at a percentage amount less than 100 percent each year, until they accrue enough years of service to be considered 100 percent vested. **Cliff vesting** refers to employees becoming 100 percent vested after a specific number of years of service. ERISA established that employees are always 100 percent vested in their own contributions towards their retirement plans. The vesting schedules differ based on the type of retirement plan an employer is offering.

Minimum reporting standards for benefit plans were set up by ERISA. The act requires benefit plan sponsors to prepare and distribute summary plan descriptions (SPDs) to participants at least once every five years. Participants must also receive a summary annual report (SAR) that contains financial information about the plan.

Employers who fail to comply with this act may face both civil and criminal penalties. Some criminal penalties can cost companies as much as $710,310 and up to ten years in prison.

Laws and Regulations Related to Workplace Health, Safety, Security, and Privacy

Workplace policies should strictly follow federal laws in order to legally secure a workplace that satisfies minimum health, safety, security, and privacy standards. Failure to meet federal standards can result in fines or the loss of a license. Federal laws and regulations function as minimum standards that all workplace policies must meet. Employers are allowed to pursue policies that go beyond what is legally required if they believe such policies will benefit the organization. Many employers strive to understand the delicate balance between meeting federal guidelines and maintaining high profit margins.

Therefore, organizations often find innovative ways to meet federal standards while using efficient business strategies.

Five federal agencies and laws regarding workplace issues are the Occupational Safety and Health Administration (OSHA), the Drug-Free Workplace Act, the Americans with Disabilities Act, the Health Insurance Portability and Accountability Act, and the Sarbanes-Oxley Act.

The **Occupational Safety and Health Act (OSHA)** regulations focus on employer and employee rights and responsibilities. Employers are required to meet all OSHA safety standards, attempt to reduce hazards to workers, and supply free protective equipment to workers. Additionally, they must provide safety training and prominently display OSHA posters that detail employee rights. Employers must keep accurate records of any injuries or illnesses that occur in the workplace and notify OSHA promptly of any injuries. Furthermore, employers may not retaliate if an employee uses their right to report an OSHA violation.

OSHA regulations provide specific rights to employees. Examples of these include the right to obtain information concerning work hazards, request a workplace inspection without fear of employer retaliation, and meet privately with a licensed OSHA inspector. Additionally, OSHA regulations allow employees to refuse work that may be abnormally dangerous or life-threatening.

The **Drug-Free Workplace Act of 1988** requires organizations to establish a drug-free workplace, provide a copy of this policy to their employees, and institute a drug awareness program. This law applies to federal contractors with contracts of $100,000 or more and all organizations that are federal grantees. Different penalties exist for employers who do not comply with the act, including contract suspension or contract termination. Although an employer may discuss alcohol and tobacco use in its policies, the Drug-Free Workplace Act does not address the use of these substances.

The **Americans with Disabilities Act (ADA)** is a federal law that prevents discrimination based on disability. This law requires employers to provide reasonable accommodations to employees with a disability. For example, an employer may accommodate a disabled employee by building a wheelchair accessible ramp to enter and exit the building. Additionally, the ADA stipulates that public entities be accessible for disabled persons. The ADA does include both mental and physical medical conditions, and temporary conditions may qualify as a disability. ADA protections apply to every aspect of job application procedures, employment, and promotions.

The **Health Insurance Portability and Accountability Act of 1996 (HIPAA)** addresses issues of healthcare access and portability as well as aspects of healthcare administration. HIPAA provisions allow workers that change jobs or become unemployed to transfer and continue their healthcare coverage. Additionally, HIPAA regulations establish standards for healthcare administration in order to reduce waste, fraud, and abuse. HIPAA laws strengthen privacy standards and provide benchmarks for medical records in areas such as electronic billing.

HIPAA is applicable to health insurance plans issued by companies, HMOs, Medicare, and Medicaid. Moreover, these regulations apply to healthcare providers who conduct transactions electronically and healthcare clearinghouses that process certain information. HIPAA's Privacy Rule gives rights to the insured regarding the disclosure of medical information, such as the ability to view health records and request an edit of inaccurate information. Additionally, individuals may file a complaint if rights are denied or health information is not protected. Patient information with heightened protection is placed in the insurer's database and may include conversations about patients between medical professionals

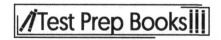

and billing information. Lastly, HIPAA creates strict rules regarding how healthcare information is disseminated and specifies who is given access.

The **Sarbanes-Oxley Act of 2002**, or **SOX**, is federal legislation that is designed to establish higher levels of accountability and standards for U.S. public institution boards and senior management. The act was passed in reaction to major global corporate and accounting scandals such as WorldCom and Enron, companies that were caught engaging in dubious financial practices. Sarbanes-Oxley specifically targets senior executives responsible for accounting misconduct and record manipulation. The law protects shareholders from any activity that conceals or misleads investors about the firm's finances. The firm has a mandate to report financial information transparently and accurately either to shareholders or the Securities and Exchange Commission (SEC). Moreover, SOX imposes more stringent penalties for white-collar crime and requires detailed reporting to the SEC if a company's finances significantly alter.

Claims Processing Requirements

Organizations should ensure that the process for filing a claim is clear, concise, and fully understood by all employees. Employees should know what they need to do and when. Supervisors should also know what they need to do and when in the case that one of their employees is injured. Most claims processes require the following steps:

- 1. Employee immediately reports the injury to employer.

- 2. Employee is seen by a doctor immediately, either a physician as identified by the employer, the employee's primary care physician, or an urgent care facility.

- 3. Claim forms are completed by the employee, including the following information:

    o Date and time of injury

    o Witnesses, if any

    o Specific details of the injury including body part(s) and damage

    o Specific details of how the injury occurred

- 4. Claim forms are reviewed by the supervisor, with the supervisor adding additional information if necessary.

- 5. Claim forms and medical reports are returned to the administrator of the program.

- 6. The administrator reviews the claim and reports and file with the insurance adjustor.

- 7. If the employee is to be off work to recover, HR communicates with supervisor about the timeframe for time off.

- 8. If the employee is to return to work with restrictions, HR communicates the restrictions to the supervisor and determines if the organization can accommodate the employee.

- 9. If accommodations cannot be made to return the employee to work, the employee is placed on leave pending new restrictions or a return to work.

- 10. Prior to returning to full duty, employees have a follow-up review with the physician who will determine when the return to full duty can occur.

While the above is a sample process, it is vital to ensure that your organization's procedures, forms, and requirements are frequently communicated to employees. Employees should understand their responsibilities in reporting injuries and which actions need to occur and when. Employees should know where to locate the forms and who the main administrator of the program is. They should also be aware of their rights and of the available resources. If a claim has been rejected, employees should understand their appeal rights and how to request a review of the rejected claim.

After a worker's compensation claim has been initiated, it is vital that an organization review the incident and what occurred. After this review has been completed, the organization should act, if appropriate, to ensure that the injury does not occur again in the future. This could include additional training, new safety equipment, or a change in a process. Organizations that are proactive in safety measures are less likely to have injuries and workers compensation claims.

Risk Mitigation in the Workplace

Protecting employees, minimizing loss, and developing effective safety procedures are central goals for a successful organization. In order to meet these goals, firms must establish robust and creative policies, procedures, and standards.

Corporate Governance Procedures and Compliance

In business, **governance** refers to how senior executives direct and control an organization. Particularly in large organizations where executives cannot be directly involved in every detail of every department,

it's important to have a clear process for communicating the most crucial management information to executives so they can continue to make informed decisions. Governance also includes the processes by which executive decisions are communicated to and implemented throughout all levels of the organization.

Compliance refers to following requirements while carrying out business activities. These requirements could be from industry regulations, corporate policies, contract agreements, or local or federal laws. In order to avoid potential legal problems or fines, organizations should be up-to-date on all relevant laws and regulations and ensure that all departments comply. The Sarbanes-Oxley Act of 2002 (also known as Sarbox or SOX) established new regulations for corporate accounting and created the **Public Company Accounting Oversight Board (PCAOB)**. Some of its other major elements include auditor independence (to prevent conflict of interest) and executive responsibility for corporate financial reports (to increase overall corporate responsibility for accurate accounting). Whenever a new law like SOX is created, the organization's policies must be reviewed and, if necessary, revised to ensure compliance.

Governance and compliance are often grouped together with risk management under the term **GRM** (governance, risk management, compliance). By grouping GRM together, an organization can avoid redundancies in procedures and increase the effectiveness of communication between each area.

Lawsuits

Employers should protect themselves from the risk of lawsuits by complying with all applicable state, federal, and local labor laws. Knowledge of labor laws is not specifically the purview of Human Resources (HR), either; HR leaders should ensure that leaders throughout the organization are familiar with key regulations. This can be achieved through communication initiatives such as training sessions or posting notices about labor regulations as required by law. There are many laws protecting workers' rights. The Occupational Safety and Health Administration (OSHA) oversees and enforces workplace safety regulations. One such regulation is the Hazard Communication Standard, which includes standards for safety measures such as the labeling of workplace hazards. Title VIII of the Sarbanes-Oxley Act of 2002 (also known as Sarbox or SOX) provides protections for corporate whistleblowers and describes the penalties for interfering with fraud investigations. Title I of the Americans with Disabilities Act (ADA) applies to employers with fifteen or more employees and outlines legal protections for qualified employees with disabilities, including their legal right to reasonable accommodation in the workplace if it does not place an undue hardship on the employer.

Emergency Response, Business Continuity, and Disaster Recovery Process

Emergency Response

All organizations must have procedures that secure an orderly response in the event of an emergency. **Emergency response plans** incorporate several elements of maintaining safety and order. These elements may include practiced evacuations, reserved resources to preserve organizational function, and a plan that seeks to minimize property damage. An organization with no emergency response plan is vulnerable to instability, disorder, and distrust. An effective emergency response plan not only protects lives and property but provides security that management has control over the situation. This knowledge provides an element of calm in an otherwise stressful emergency situation, which can be as important as the response protocol.

An emergency response is planned and practiced protocol used during an emergency. These strategies should be planned rationally and practiced frequently in order to mitigate the impact of a disaster. Workplace emergency responses should plan for a wide range of scenarios, such as machinery

malfunctions or workplace violence. Once created, emergency response plans should be communicated to all staff, frequently tested by the organization, and kept up to date.

An **evacuation** is a coordinated and planned exit from a place that is considered to be dangerous. It is a principal component of general health and safety policies. Conditions that may prompt evacuation are fire, flood, or violence. The most effective way to orchestrate an orderly and calm evacuation is through practice of an evacuation plan. This routine practice familiarizes staff with expedient exit routes and ensures that exits remain visible and unobstructed.

Hazard communication is the notification of employees concerning the noxious health effects and physical dangers of hazardous chemicals in the workplace. Workers should be clearly notified of any physical hazards (corrosion or flammability) or health hazards (skin irritation and carcinogenicity) that they will come into contact with in the workplace. OSHA created the Hazard Communication Standard (HCS) to ensure that chemical information is accessible to all individuals who may interact with the substance. In addition to the HCS, all employers are required to implement a hazard communication program that encompasses training, access to material safety data sheets (MSDS), and labeling of hazardous chemical containers.

Developing Business Continuity and Disaster Recovery Plans

In the event of a crisis, an organization may face multiple challenges such as mitigating casualties, protecting property, and testing disciplinary protocol. Aside from protecting human life, the most challenging priority during a crisis is maintaining business continuity. Business continuity maintains productivity during and after a potential disruption.

Business continuity plans identify potential threats and their associated impacts in order to maintain organizational productivity during an operational interruption. These plans establish procedures to handle disruptions and/or loss of business functions. There are four components to a business continuity plan: business impact analysis, recovery strategies, plan development, and testing and exercises. A business impact analysis (BIA) assesses the potential consequences of a disruption and collects information to develop recovery strategies. A BIA is a risk assessment tool, and information can be gathered by means of a questionnaire. The second step is to identify, document, and implement the most comprehensive of the proposed strategies. Recovery strategies frequently identify gaps in necessary resources. The third step, plan development, builds a business continuity team and crafts the business continuity plan. Finally, extensive training and testing are conducted to test strategies, personnel, and the business continuity plan.

Business continuity plans respond to a variety of crisis scenarios, such as a loss of administrative capacities, a hack into the operating system, and threat of workplace violence. These plans must be observed by all staff to ensure the plan's effectiveness. If an employee does not comply, disciplinary measures should be enforced by the organization.

A **disaster recovery plan (DRP)** is a set of procedures that prepares for a disaster so that destructive effects are reduced, and essential data can be recovered. A DRP increases a firm's ability to recover from an unexpected, devastating incident. A DRP assists the organization in resuming normal business functions as quickly as possible. As information technology systems become more sophisticated and complex, solving critical organizational technology questions becomes more difficult. The ability of hackers and viruses to infiltrate these systems makes an effective organizational DRP more important than ever.

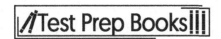

Technological increases have created viable scenarios for employers to offer alternative work locations. If a corporation offers alternative work locations, these employees are allowed to work from home or another off-site location rather than a traditional office space. Communication between organizations and its remote employees generally takes place through the Internet and phone calls. Alternative work locations can be helpful in disaster recovery because organizational data is decentralized and more difficult to corrupt entirely.

A procedure is a recognized and established way of accomplishing a desired goal. Procedures provide a plan of action for organizations in a time of vulnerability or crisis. The business continuity plan, disaster recovery plan, and any additional organizational policies should be studied and practiced frequently by employees.

Business Continuity and Disaster Recovery Plan Training

A business continuity plan or disaster recovery plan is only as good as the organization's ability to implement the plan. If all levels of employees and management are not familiar with the plan, they will not be able to execute it when the need arises. Employees and management must possess unwavering familiarity with the DRP. The best defense against disruption is training that allows the workforce to react according to the DRP, maximizing the allocation of resources and reducing panic.

The organization should devote sufficient time and resources to ensure proper training for its employees. This training should begin with an awareness of the plan and its components. Employees should understand the plan's framework and their role in the plan. If a staff member has a specific role in the plan, this staff member may require additional time and training.

Scenario training is the next essential step in ensuring a successful business continuity and/or disaster recovery plan. Employees and management respond to mock scenarios that provide them opportunities to utilize their training. These scenarios may also be used as an opportunity to test critical backup systems, applications, and facilities. During scenario training, all areas of response should be documented for further evaluation and review.

After scenario training is complete, the organization can review what aspects of the plan were successful and unsuccessful. This evaluation assists in determining potential changes to the plan and updating the plan as necessary. All areas of management should review the scenario training to determine the best possible course of action.

Risk Management

An organization engages in risk management when it identifies, targets, and strives to minimize unacceptable risks. While a variety of different risks may arise, an organization's principal risks are generally workplace health, safety, security, and privacy. Failure to protect from these risks can result in serious consequences and may lead to negative company publicity, low employee morale, and burdensome expenses. Organizations must prioritize risk management and comply with federal laws and regulations. By doing so, employers will increase productivity and build sustainable relationships between employees and management.

Cost-Benefit Analysis (CBA)

A **cost-benefit analysis** (**CBA**) is an important factor in many business decisions. A CBA compares the cost of a particular option with the benefits it will bring to the organization. A CBA has two main uses. First, it helps to determine whether a particular option is worthwhile (Do the benefits sufficiently offset the costs?). Secondly, it's a method of comparison when making a decision that has several options.

Of course, any cost-benefit analysis involves a certain level of uncertainty because it's predicting future values under future conditions. For example, a change in the cost of a certain resource or the exchange rate of foreign currency could impact the results of a CBA. For this reason, a CBA usually includes a sensitivity analysis, which determines how much a change in uncertain variables will affect the CBA. This sensitivity analysis takes into account the expected conditions (what will happen if everything proceeds according to the status quo?) as well as worst-case conditions (what will happen if all possible problems arise in this situation?). In this way, a CBA can also reveal the level of risk involved in a decision. An option that appears attractive at first may seem less certain after a sensitivity analysis.

A cost-benefit analysis can also be approached differently based on the view of the analysis—short-, mid-, or long-term. For many business decisions, the costs are upfront while the benefits may appear immediately or after a longer period. For this reason, a short-term and long-term CBA could yield very different results. If an organization needs a quick return on benefits, it might place more emphasis on a short-term CBA. However, if it's willing to wait longer to reap the benefits of a decision, it might compare its options based on long-term CBAs.

Enterprise Risk Management (ERM)

No matter how carefully an organization conducts research, carries out analyses, and develops strategic plans, the organization will always face unknowns. There are risks that activities will fail, outside obstacles will appear, or new threats will emerge. **Enterprise risk management** (ERM) is a method of managing unknowable risks by anticipating potential risks, focusing on those with the greatest likelihood or potential impact, and planning a response strategy for when risks become realities.

An organization could choose four different responses to a particular risk: reduce the effects of the risk, share it, avoid it, or accept it. In order to reduce the effects of the risk, the organization finds ways to decrease its likelihood or to soften its potential harmful impact. If the organization wants to avoid the risk altogether, it will simply cease all activity associated with that risk. Finally, an organization might decide to go ahead and accept a risk; this might happen when cost-benefit analysis has determined that the benefits greatly outweigh all potential risk to the organization.

Risk management is especially important in human resources, which can account for a significant portion of an organization's financial risk, especially in terms of liability and legal concerns. For example, the organization can be held liable for compliance (or non-compliance) with labor laws, proper management of employee information, and legal concerns of employees like workplace safety and sexual harassment. HR can identify which risks are the most pressing for their organization and plan accordingly, perhaps through an HR audit. Like any audit, an HR audit is an inspection—in this case, of an organization's HR policies and practices. The purpose of an HR audit is to check that policies are in line with all applicable laws and regulations and are properly followed by all employees.

Workplace Violence Conditions

Workplace violence is any act of physical violence, intimidation, threat, or verbal abuse that occurs in the workplace. This behavior is disruptive both physically and psychologically. Employees may demonstrate violent behavior as a result of a history of violence, a troubled upbringing, issues of substance use, and psychological illness. These conditions may foster violent behavior from an employee but do not make violent behavior inevitable. Workplace violence not only interrupts immediate employees, but can cause an organization to lose clients, suppliers, and advertisers. Furthermore, a firm can suffer devastating economic consequences as a result of negative publicity from incidents of workplace violence. Workplace violence attacks the foundation of trust and safety that all workplaces need to operate successfully.

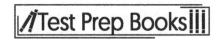
Although an employer cannot eliminate the possibility of workplace violence, several steps can be taken to avoid these incidents. One example is a mental health program, such as an Employee Assistance Program (EAP), which provides employees the option to improve their psychological wellbeing. Additionally, offering company parties and functions in alcohol-free locations may reduce the likeliness of workplace violence. Violence may also be introduced in the workplace from the public. In areas with high crime rates, statistics show a higher probability of violence for employers who operate at night. Finally, organizations should establish and enforce a zero-tolerance policy for on-site weapons and acts of violence.

Workplace Safety Risks

Minimizing injuries in the workplace is a primary concern for employers. Accidents and injuries triggered by safety risks diminish productivity and reduce savings because of costly workers' compensation payments. Furthermore, failure to adequately protect workers can result in employer penalties and fines. Two common workplace safety risks are tripping hazards and blood-borne pathogens.

Trip hazards cause a person's foot to hit an object that does not budge, plunging the person forward involuntarily. Tripping can occur in the workplace for many reasons such as obstructed views, poor lighting, excessive clutter, uneven walking surfaces, wrinkled carpeting, or unsecure wires. Tripping may result in injuries such as sprains, broken bones, or torn ligaments. Employers should maintain an orderly workplace and arrange for bright lighting to reduce the likelihood of tripping. Accordingly, employees should pay attention when walking, make wide turns when walking, and walk with feet pointed outward.

Bloodborne pathogens are infectious microorganisms in human blood that can cause disease in humans. Specifically, some of these pathogens are hepatitis B virus (HBV), hepatitis C virus (HCV), and human immunodeficiency virus (HIV). One potential cause of spreading bloodborne pathogens is through improper usage and/or disposal of needles. Occupations such as nursing, healthcare professionals, medical first responders, and housekeepers who work in medical environments are the most likely to encounter a needle with bloodborne pathogens. Due to growing concerns within the medical field, The Needlestick Safety and Prevention Act of 2000 revised OSHA's Bloodborne Pathogens Standard. This law provides requirements in selecting medical devices and establishes oversight through a sharps' injury log, which details all sharps-related workplace injuries.

Additional workplace safety risks with OSHA regulations are occupational noise exposure, emergency exit procedures, control of hazardous materials, lockout/tagout procedures, machine guarding, and confined space environments.

Workers' compensation laws are designed to protect employees who are injured in the workplace. The primary purpose of workers' compensation is to provide injured employees with fixed monetary sums. Workers' compensation benefits cover medical expenses due to workplace injuries. Furthermore, workers' compensation benefits are extended to dependents of employees killed by an injury or illness that occurs in the workplace. In addition to employee protection, some workers' compensation laws protect employers by limiting the amount of money that can be distributed to employees. The program also has provisions that restrict co-worker liability in most workplace accidents. Most workers' compensation programs are structured at the state level by legislative bodies and agencies. However, worker's compensation exists at the federal level, where it is limited to federal employment and industries that considerably affect interstate commerce.

Security Risks in the Workplace

Security Plans

Obtaining a safe and secure working environment is not accomplished by simply strategizing. The staff of an organization must have adequate training to appropriately respond to diverse situations. Workplace security plans and policies address a variety of issues from a sudden crisis to an act of intentional harm. A clear understanding of security plans and policies can minimize unpredictability and panic and teach employees how to respond to a crisis.

Employees should understand security plans and how they address the physical security needs of the work environment. Workplace security plans and policies may include security measures such as control badges, keycard access systems, backup communication systems, locks on various rooms and closets, and concealed alarms. When developing workplace security plans, a team approach is vital to ensuring its success. Representatives are needed from human resources, legal counsel, security, and facilities to provide a comprehensive perspective of security needs. Once the security plans and policies are established, employees should be trained annually to review the plans and their importance.

Theft

Theft is the act of taking property without the consent of the owner. Theft can occur by deception or force, with or without the knowledge of the owner. Theft can be very costly to an organization, and management should take steps to prevent any opportunity for theft. Such measures may include hidden video cameras, a private security force, and incentives for employees who disrupt incidents of theft. Theft can be accomplished by employees, management, and customers. Therefore, prevention policies should apply to all levels of the organization.

Corporate Espionage

Corporate espionage is a form of spying that occurs between competitive companies. The principal purpose of corporate espionage is to obtain industrial secrets and learn about a competitor's plans, future products, business strategies, or total profits. Knowing these secrets can give a competitor an unfair advantage when trying to increase market share. A company must hire trustworthy employees, particularly employees privy to classified information. A firm should employ strategies to test employee loyalty and offer incentives that encourage employees to report suspicious activity.

Sabotage

Sabotage is the act of purposely weakening or corrupting a country or a company. In the workplace, sabotage is the intentional thwarting of successful planning models to create dysfunctional conditions at odds with the organization's best interests. Those who commit sabotage are known as saboteurs, and they generally conceal their identity and intentions. Sabotage is debilitating to a company and can cultivate an environment of distrust and hostility. Therefore, management must conduct frequent tests to ensure that all members and employees act in good faith.

Practice Questions

1. What is the main purpose of a cost-benefit analysis?
    a. When evaluating a policy or program, a cost-benefit analysis empirically tests its efficacy to ensure that resources aren't squandered.
    b. Cost-benefit analyses are rarely conducted because they are expensive and unreliable.
    c. When evaluating a policy or program, a cost-benefit analysis is conducted that rationally tests its efficacy to ensure that resources aren't squandered. However, because cost-benefit analyses are antiquated, management typically decides on the policy or program based on its organizational popularity.
    d. A cost-benefit analysis is the empirical testing of a policy or program. However, management is typically disdainful of them because of a belief that the testers are inherently biased.

2. Which of the following best describes enterprise risk management (ERM)?
    a. Enterprise risk management is when each department crafts its own policies and procedures for handling issues of risk and loss.
    b. Enterprise risk management policies are crafted only by senior executives and then handed down to all departments to follow.
    c. Enterprise risk management is the process of establishing a broad but comprehensive protocol for handling issues of risk and loss.
    d. Enterprise risk management is when a company participates in a high-risk situation in order to maximize profits for the good of the company.

3. All of the following are necessary for an organization to pay attention to the legislative and regulatory environment EXCEPT?
    a. To anticipate changes and craft corporate governance policies that address new regulations and legislation
    b. To engage in lobbying efforts in order to fight proposed changes that could be damaging to the corporation
    c. To modify new legislative and regulatory changes and make them more palatable
    d. To examine competitors and match their own legislation to that of other corporations

4. Which definition most accurately explains a whistle-blower?
    a. A whistle-blower is a person who reports any unethical information about an organization.
    b. A whistle-blower is a person hired by an organization to cover up illicit or unethical activity.
    c. A whistle-blower is a person who reports or publicizes any illegal or unethical information about the institution. Whistle-blower status is only granted when the organization is private.
    d. A whistle-blower reports or publicizes any illegal or unethical information about the institution. Whistle-blower status is only granted when the organization is public.

5. Which of the following best describes mergers and acquisitions (M&A)?
   a. Mergers occur temporarily in order to consolidate resources and beat out a competitor; acquisitions occur permanently.
   b. Mergers occur when one company purchases another without a new company being formed. Acquisitions occur when two companies combine to form a new one.
   c. Mergers occur when two companies combine to form a new one. Acquisitions occur when one company purchases another without a new company being formed.
   d. Mergers and acquisitions often occur temporarily in order to consolidate resources and beat out a competitor; then the actions are rescinded, and the entities disband.

Answer Explanations

1. A: A cost-benefit analysis is an objective empirical study of the precise effects of a specific policy or plan. Cost-benefit analyses are critically important because they indicate if a policy or plan will save resources or squander them. If the costs outweigh the benefits, then an action isn't financially sensible. But if the analysis indicates that benefits will outweigh costs, then the policy can be pursued with confidence.

2. C: Enterprise risk management (ERM) are comprehensive policies and procedures that dictate how an organization handles risk and loss. The purpose of ERM is to coordinate and create a harmony of responses to problems facing an organization. ERMs lead to greater levels of stability and structure.

3. D: Choice *D* mentions legislation, but does not fit the question otherwise. It's imperative that firms anticipate potential changes in public policy because they must adjust. The success of this adjustment will depend upon institutional preparedness. Furthermore, if anticipated changes are expected to be damaging, a firm will want to engage in lobbying efforts to modify and amend the policies.

4. A: A whistle-blower reports or publicizes any illegal or unethical information about an organization or industry. Another example of a whistle-blower is former tobacco industry official Jeffrey Wigand, who confessed in a televised interview that the tobacco industry was intentionally packing cigarettes with addictive levels of nicotine. Whistle-blowers are generally perceived as villains by institutions, while others believe they risk their livelihood for a just cause. Whistle-blowers can operate in public or private institutions.

5. C: One notable merger occurred in 1999, when Exxon and Mobil merged to form ExxonMobil. It can be helpful to think of mergers as consolidations.

Practice Test #1

1. All of the following are part of the core meaning of competitive advantage EXCEPT:
   a. Competitive advantage is the practice of constantly attempting to increase market share by exploiting advantages.
   b. By constantly developing a labor force and technology, competitive advantage is pursued by all corporations in order to edge out competitors in the market.
   c. It's mandatory that organizations pursue policies of competitive advantage because they all want to maximize output and increase market share.
   d. Competitive advantage is a type of benefit that customers believe they could not get anywhere else.

2. Josiah is processing the final exit paperwork for an employee who is retiring. Which two of the following documents must he include in the termination paperwork?
   a. Employment contract
   b. Leave balance payouts
   c. Benefits eligibility and leave accruals
   d. COBRA information

3. Which of the following is a quantitative method of job evaluation?
   a. Job ranking
   b. Paired comparison
   c. Factor comparison
   d. Job classification

4. The employee value proposition (EVP) reflects employees' perceived valuing of the tangible and intangible rewards and benefits of working for an organization. What is an example of an intangible benefit?
   a. Holiday bonus
   b. Annual paid company retreat
   c. Flexible schedule options
   d. Retirement savings plan

5. The vice president of an organization has noticed that a particular employee, Ben, has been working extremely hard and has made a positive impression on a large majority of the organization's leadership. The vice president meets with Ben and asks him about his work. Ben shares all of the accomplishments that his team has achieved in the last quarter. What is Ben displaying during this meeting?
   a. Ego
   b. Individualistic behavior
   c. Team-oriented culture
   d. Humility

6. Which of the following is an exception to the concept of employment-at-will?
   a. An employee who decides to willingly sever the employment relationship
   b. An employee who is terminated for whistle-blowing or for reporting unlawful conduct by the employer
   c. An employer who lets an employee go who does not have an employment contract
   d. An employee who is fired for willful misconduct

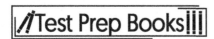

Practice Test #1 | Error! No text of specified style in document.

7. Under federal guidelines, for what length of time is an employer required to keep employment applications and resumes?
   a. Three years
   b. One year
   c. Three years after creation or following the hire/no hire decision (whichever date is later)
   d. One year after creation or following the hire/no hire decision (whichever date is later)

8. During a project meeting, Mary creates a table that includes a detailed description of every task needed for the project, a deliverable date for each task, and the owner of each task. Each member can access and update the table with status updates. What is Mary doing?
   a. Helping each member feel accountable
   b. Micromanaging
   c. Modeling ethical behavior
   d. Collecting data

9. A company must set a placement goal when which of the following situations occurs?
   a. Minorities and women are assigned to jobs that are not challenging at the company.
   b. The company experiences adverse impacts in its hiring practices.
   c. The company is unable to determine its applicants' ethnicities.
   d. The company is found to employ a smaller number of minorities and women than is indicated by their availability.

10. What are business metrics?
   a. Business metrics are quantifiable measures that describe the productive capacity of a policy, program, or product.
   b. Business metrics are informal activities that management occasionally conducts in order to discover the feasibility of a policy, program, or product.
   c. Business metrics are typically utilized to weed out underperforming employees.
   d. Business metrics are meetings with representatives from each department to voice concerns and establish harmonious, firm-wide standards and practices.

11. All of the following is true about offshoring EXCEPT:
   a. Offshoring is typically done to reduce the costs of business.
   b. Offshoring involves shifting business operations to a country where business can be conducted at lower costs.
   c. The only beneficiary of offshoring is the company itself.
   d. Offshoring is one aspect of corporate restructuring that permits a company to remain competitive.

12. Which of the following are part of the seven C's of effective communication? Select all that apply.
   a. Courteous
   b. Concise
   c. Consistent
   d. Correct

13. Which of the following is NOT a key component of a business plan?
    a. Annual goals
    b. Projected growth targets
    c. Net income expectations
    d. Bonuses for executives

14. Public domain is a copyright provision that posits which of the following?
    a. Under no circumstances can a previously copyrighted work be used without authorization.
    b. Any work published by the federal government can be used freely without authorization.
    c. Items that are works-made-for-hire never fall into the public domain.
    d. Works protected by a copyright can be used without consent if they are used for a public purpose.

15. Before extending a contingent offer of employment, an employer should obtain which of the following?
    a. Medical records and completion of a physical examination
    b. Signed consent from the candidate to check work references
    c. Verbal consent from the candidate to check work references
    d. Polygraph test

16. Which two of the following choices constitute the first step of the talent acquisition process?
    a. Evaluate the needs of the department.
    b. Source and review candidates.
    c. Conduct assessments and interviews.
    d. Create a job posting.

17. Where should an employee first encounter an organization's ethical standards and policies?
    a. During on-the-job training
    b. During the first interview
    c. In the job posting for their role
    d. By reading a company press release

18. Which of the following pieces of legislation established a commission to study how women and minorities face significant barriers and are prevented from reaching management positions?
    a. Title II
    b. The Civil Rights Act of 1991
    c. Equal Pay Act
    d. The Glass Ceiling Act

19. Which of the following best represents 360-degree feedback?
    a. A method by which employees receive anonymous feedback from their managers, peers, direct reports, and customers
    b. A method by which employees perform a self-appraisal regarding their own performance at several different points over the course of a year
    c. 360-degree feedback features reviews only by fellow employees. This is most effective because learning how employees interact with each other is indicative of their attitudes and efforts.
    d. 360-degree feedback uses reviews only by management. Only management can assess an employee's suitability in an organization by evaluating productivity levels.

Test Prep Books!!!

Practice Test #1 | Error! No text of specified style in document.

20. Which of the following situations would likely warrant a written employment contract?
    a. An employee who is a salesperson
    b. A full-time telecommuting employee
    c. An employee who is a department manager
    d. An employee who is a graphic artist

21. Which of the following pieces of legislation guarantees that all employees have equal access to career development and training?
    a. Title VII of the Civil Rights Act of 1964
    b. Fair Labor Standards Act (FLSA)
    c. Older Workers Benefit Protection Act (OWBPA)
    d. Davis Beacon Act

22. What is the best way for HR leaders to communicate acceptable and ethical behaviors in the workplace?
    a. Provide written protocols about what constitutes ethical and unethical behavior.
    b. Relay that employees are continuously monitored with in-house cameras, so they should be especially mindful of their work behavior.
    c. Model acceptable and ethical behavior themselves, as much as possible.
    d. Tell employees at their new-hire orientation.

23. Which of the following court cases dealt with sexual harassment in the workplace? Select all that apply.
    a. Faragher v. City of Boca Raton
    b. Harris v. Forklift Systems, Inc.
    c. Oncale v. Sundowner Offshore Service, Inc.
    d. McDonnell Douglas Corporation v. Green

24. To reduce operating costs, a company has decided to maintain its domestic headquarters and open an overseas manufacturing plant. What is the best word to describe this move?
    a. Outsourcing
    b. Downsizing
    c. Offshoring
    d. Globalizing

25. What is a true statement about alternative work locations?
    a. No companies have experimented with alternative work locations, so their benefits cannot yet be evaluated.
    b. Alternative work locations are generally discouraged since it is difficult to trust employees to work outside of the office.
    c. Alternative work locations have been proven to reduce employee productivity.
    d. Because alternative work locations help decentralize operations, the organization is better protected from the destructive efforts of a single person.

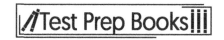
26. Which of the following employees could qualify to be exempt under the Fair Labor Standards Act (FLSA)?
   a. The employee earns over $80,000 a year but makes routine decisions.
   b. The employee earns less than $23,000 a year but makes non-routine decisions.
   c. The employee is regularly supervising two or more employees and has management as their main job duty.
   d. The FLSA lets employers decide who is and isn't exempt.

27. Which of the following pre-employment activities can assist companies with protecting themselves from lawsuits or damage to their reputation?
   a. Interviewing
   b. Selection tests
   c. Reference and background checks
   d. Employment agreements

28. Which of the following tools would NOT be used to determine why goals were not achieved or why there was a discrepancy between expected outcomes and actual outcomes?
   a. Six Sigma
   b. Gap analysis
   c. Root cause analysis
   d. Cause-and-effect diagram

29. A pension plan that meets the minimum standards set by the Employee Retirement Income Security Act (ERISA) must do which one of the following?
   a. Allow new hires to participate beginning in their first month of employment.
   b. Provide plan participants with a copy of the summary plan description once every 10 years.
   c. Include schedules for graded and cliff vesting.
   d. Allow the employer to keep pension plan assets together with other company assets.

30. What is the compa-ratio for a salary range of $10–$22 and an entry-level employee salary of $12.50?
   a. The compa-ratio is 70%.
   b. The compa-ratio is 78%.
   c. The compa-ratio is 1.04%.
   d. The compa-ratio is .96%.

31. Based on the compa-ratio determined by the previous question, which of the following can be deduced about the employee and/or the company's pay strategy?
   a. The employee is new to the job and/or the organization, is a low performer, or is working for a company that has adopted a lag-behind-the-market pay strategy.
   b. The employee is new to the job and/or the organization, is a high performer, or is working for a company that has adopted a lag-behind-the-market pay strategy.
   c. The employee is long-tenured, a high performer, or is working for a company that has adopted a lead-ahead-of-the-market pay strategy.
   d. The employee is long-tenured, a low performer, or is working for a company that has adopted a lead-ahead-of-the-market pay strategy.

Practice Test #1 | Error! No text of specified style in document.

32. Which of the following is used to describe the knowledge, skills, abilities, education, and experience that are essential to performing a specific job?
    a. Job analysis
    b. Job description
    c. Job specification
    d. Job evaluation

33. Under the WARN Act, in which of the following situations is the employer required to provide a minimum of 60 days' notice to their employees in advance of a plant closing or mass layoff?
    a. An employer shuts down a plant facility that employs 50 total employees, 25 of which are working part-time. The company employs over 100 full-time employees.
    b. 30 full-time employees are laid off by a company at a single site that employs 120 full-time individuals for a three-month period.
    c. A company lays off (for more than a six-month period) 250 full-time employees at a single site that employs 650 full-time individuals.
    d. An employer shuts down a plant facility that has already been partially idled for quite some time. Only 40 employees remain working at the site. The company employs over 100 full-time employees.

34. What is the most crucial aspect of successfully implementing organizational change?
    a. Work ethic
    b. Leadership buy-in
    c. Highly compensated employees
    d. Terminating employees who do not agree

35. Which of the following is a crucial factor in the new generation of employees selecting their job field?
    a. Compensation and benefits
    b. Retirement programs
    c. Flexible staffing schedules
    d. Social impact and engagement

36. After conducting an engagement survey, you review the data and find that your marketing department is disengaged compared to the rest of the company. The information is not precise enough to see why. What would you recommend as a next step?
    a. Wait until a few employees resign and conduct exit interviews.
    b. Make the first Tuesday of every month Marketing Appreciation Day.
    c. Increase the pay for the marketing staff.
    d. Conduct stay interviews with your current staff to find out more information.

37. _____ is the complete strategic process that forecasts an organization's current and future employment needs.

38. Under the Taft-Hartley Act, which of the following is illegal?
    a. Creating a company-sponsored labor union
    b. An employee deciding to contribute to a charity instead of paying union dues, due to their religious objection
    c. An employer filing an unfair labor practice charge against a union
    d. A union representing nonunion employees in the bargaining unit

39. The details of the behaviors that are expected of employees and the behaviors that are prohibited are called a _____.

40. Put the following ways to handle conflict resolution in order from best to worst:
    a. Identifying the potential impacts of the issue and any resolution
    b. Identifying the recommendations and actions to resolve the issue
    c. Identifying the feelings, perceptions, and opinions regarding the issue
    d. Working toward resolution of the issue

41. Once a salary survey is completed, what is the term used for weighting the data for jobs included on the survey that are similar, but not identical, to positions with the organization? This process is done to create a more accurate match.
    a. Aging
    b. Benchmarking
    c. Leveling
    d. Wage compression

42. Which of the following are part of a company's strategic planning process with regard to HR? Select all that apply.
    a. Development
    b. Evaluation
    c. Formulation
    d. Implementation

43. Considering they have met all the necessary requirements, which of the following individuals is eligible to take unpaid, protected leave from work under the Family and Medical Leave Act (FMLA)?
    a. An employee who is non-weight bearing, recovering from ankle surgery, and will have multiple follow-up appointments with his surgeon and numerous physical therapy visits to attend
    b. An employee who is out of the office for three days sick with the flu
    c. An employee who wants to take care of her aunt who is suffering from end-stage lung cancer
    d. An employee who wishes to travel to China to support her sister who is in the process of adopting a child in that country

Test Prep Books

Practice Test #1|Error! No text of specified style in document.

44. In performance management, what is a principal function of rating?
    a. Rating allows management to identify their most productive workers and provide them with incentives to stay at the company.
    b. Because of its narrow statistical application, rating is generally an infrequent practice by management.
    c. Rating provides a way for management to designate their most favored employees.
    d. By having employees rate management, they can more accurately decide for whom and under which conditions they wish to work.

45. Which of the following statements is true regarding Title VII of the Civil Rights Act of 1964?
    a. Equal working conditions must be provided for all employees.
    b. Discrimination against sex and race is prohibited.
    c. All employees must be provided with an equal opportunity to participate in training.
    d. Sexual harassment training must be provided to all employees.

46. LaShonda is exploring noncash compensation that can be added to the compensation package for a new position at her company. Which two of the following would be considered noncash compensation?
    a. Bonus programs
    b. Cafeteria-style healthcare plans
    c. Flextime scheduling
    d. Monthly and annual employee award programs

47. Which of the following is NOT a federally protected class of the Equal Employment Opportunity Commission (EEOC)?
    a. Pregnancy status
    b. Genetic information
    c. Disability
    d. Being between 18 and 26 years old

48. Which of the following is an exception to Title VII of the Civil Rights Act of 1964?
    a. An employer with only 20 employees
    b. A new seniority system that is being implemented at a workplace
    c. A bona fide occupational qualification
    d. A work-related requirement that is not truly legitimate

49. The CEO of a company holds biweekly meetings with his entire organization to relay new information about company performance, trends, and personal opinions relating to the industry. What is this an example of?
    a. Transparency
    b. Overshare
    c. Validation
    d. Process control

50. Under federal guidelines, for what length of time is an employer required to keep employee records associated with employment benefits?
    a. Six years
    b. Three years
    c. Five years
    d. One year

51. The statement "We value lightheartedness" is an example of a:
    a. Mission statement
    b. Value statement
    c. Vision statement
    d. Slogan

52. What is an example of a factor that influences workforce supply?
    a. Worker attrition
    b. Number of customers
    c. Seasonal workload
    d. Economic downturn

53. Which of the following is an example of a short-term strategy to develop workforce competencies?
    a. Increase the academic and professional qualifications in job postings.
    b. Enroll targeted employees in a high-potential development program.
    c. Reassign underperforming employees to positions that better fit their skills.
    d. Organize a week-long training class focused on the desired skill development.

54. Which of the following results in a violation of the Uniform Guidelines on Employee Selection Procedures? Select all that apply.
    a. 200 white candidates applied, and 80 were hired; 100 Hispanic candidates applied, and 40 were hired.
    b. 50 female candidates applied, and 15 were hired; 60 male candidates applied, and 15 were hired.
    c. 150 Latino candidates applied, and 30 were hired; 100 white candidates applied, and 50 were hired.
    d. 200 male candidates applied, and 120 were hired; 250 female candidates applied, and 50 were hired.

55. Which of the following are considered alternative dispute resolutions? Select all that apply.
    a. Negotiation
    b. Mediation
    c. Conciliation
    d. Arbitration

56. What are the three types of organization development interventions?
    a. Human process intervention, sociotechnical intervention, techno-structural intervention
    b. Human process intervention, employer intervention, techno-structural intervention
    c. Managerial intervention, human process intervention, techno-structural intervention
    d. Employer intervention, sociotechnical intervention, techno-structural intervention

57. Which of the following items is inferred from an employer's actions or conduct?
    a. Express contract
    b. Employment-at-will
    c. Golden parachute clause
    d. Implied contract

Practice Test #1 | Error! No text of specified style in
document.

58. Michael leads an HR department at a federal agency. He is in the planning stage for the new fiscal year and is thrilled that he has created initiatives that are highly detailed and comprehensive and use the resources of contracts his agency currently has in place. He is very attached to the outcomes of these initiatives. However, a presidential election is taking place in one month that will likely affect the contracts that are awarded to his agency. What can Michael do to protect his new fiscal year plans?
   a. Ensure there is leftover money from the previous fiscal year to serve as a cushion should he not receive expected contracts.
   b. Create backup plans for all the contracts that may be affected, while calmly accepting that some changes may be unanticipated and out of his control.
   c. Nothing, he has already distributed them to employees and archived them on the organization's servers.
   d. Find a new job.

59. An organization is trying to improve its parental leave policy. Who in the organization could be considered key stakeholders for this initiative?
   a. Pregnant female employees
   b. Male employees
   c. Managers of both sexes
   d. All of the above

60. What term is defined as a qualification that is determined to be justified by a business purpose?
   a. Bona fide occupational qualification
   b. Minimum required qualification
   c. Preferred qualification
   d. Essential job function

61. Which of the following statements is true about the Landrum-Griffin Act?
   a. This act outlawed yellow-dog contracts.
   b. This act established the Federal Mediation and Conciliation Service.
   c. This act created the NLRB to encourage union growth.
   d. This act created a Bill of Rights for union members.

Read the following scenario and answer questions 62–65.

In order to free up more time for assisting with strategic objectives, the HR department of a large communications company has decided to implement new automation processes. They are currently evaluating specific functions for automating. One function under consideration is performance evaluations. Currently, the company conducts traditional annual performance reviews in which department leaders and other supervisors give feedback to subordinates. However, HR is considering adopting an employee engagement app that allows real-time, anonymous feedback between employees at all levels.

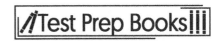

62. From an employee engagement standpoint, what would be the most important advantage of adopting the new app?
    a. It lends a game-like appeal to evaluations by allowing employees to use smartphones during work.
    b. It gives more timely and dynamic feedback to employees and helps solve performance problems as soon as they arise.
    c. It increases the appeal of working for the company by advancing its brand as a leader in modern business technology.
    d. It allows supervisors to put less effort into managing subordinates by creating a self-managed feedback system.

63. Which of the following is LEAST likely to be a drawback of using this new technology?
    a. It could create a channel for bullying and harassment.
    b. Some employees might feel overwhelmed by constant feedback.
    c. Some employees might have difficulty learning how to use the system.
    d. The app will prove to be expensive and cost prohibitive compared to traditional performance evaluations.

64. Alyssa has decided to use the ADDIE model to design a new employee training program. Put the following steps in the order that she should follow:
    a. Design the structure of the program.
    b. Develop the training materials.
    c. Complete a determination of needs.
    d. Assess the effectiveness of the program in meeting the company's needs.

65. How can HR encourage employee buy-in of the new performance management method?
    a. Hold a demonstration of how the technology works in different situations, including information about user resources.
    b. Require supervisors to phase out all traditional performance evaluation activities within the next six months.
    c. Buy new smartphones for employees whose devices are not up to date enough to run the new app.
    d. Post user testimonial videos on the company intranet.

66. Soliciting feedback from stakeholders is an important part of which of the following process stages?
    a. Evaluation
    b. Control
    c. Testing
    d. Documentation

67. Which of the following is a direct result of broadbanding?
    a. Green-circle rates
    b. Taller organizational structures
    c. Red-circle rates
    d. Flatter organizational structures

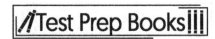

68. Which type of interview occurs when an interviewer has guided conversations with applicants that involve broad questions and new questions that come about from the discussions that take place?
    a. Semi-structured
    b. Structured
    c. Non-directive
    d. Unstructured

69. The _____ methodology requires that all plan objectives be specific, measurable, achievable, realistic, and time-targeted.

70. Which of the following employees would NOT be eligible to vote in an upcoming union election?
    a. An employee who is temporarily laid off
    b. An employee who is out sick with the flu
    c. An employee who is out on military leave right before the election
    d. A staff member who is out of the office on a medical leave of absence and who will not be returning to work

71. Each fiscal quarter within a fiscal year is an example of which of the following?
    a. Benchmarking
    b. Milestone
    c. Calendar divide
    d. Bonus assessment period

72. What is one of the primary benefits of an individual development plan (IDP)?
    a. It gives all the development responsibility to employees, freeing up HR professionals for other strategic work.
    b. It closely evaluates employees and documents mistakes to avoid wrongful termination complaints when employees are fired.
    c. It provides managers with greater control over workers' daily tasks.
    d. It helps workers become more invested in their professional development.

73. _____ refers to employees who do not have an employment contract indicating the terms of employment and who can be terminated by an employer for any reason.

74. Which of the following types of compensation is given to employees when they work during holidays or vacation days?
    a. Reporting pay
    b. Shift pay
    c. Premium pay
    d. Emergency shift pay

75. New employees must take in a great deal of information during the onboarding and orientation process. Which two of the following are part of the four areas of orientation?
    a. Compensation and benefits
    b. Tools, equipment, and software
    c. Assigning mentors
    d. New employee training

76. Which of the following pieces of legislation dictates what are known as unfair labor practices?
    a. The Wagner Act
    b. The Norris-LaGuardia Act
    c. The Taft-Hartley Act
    d. The Railway Labor Act

77. Which of the following is indirect compensation?
    a. Bonus
    b. Incentive pay
    c. Pension plan
    d. Hourly wage

78. Which of the following statements LEAST describes corporate governance?
    a. Corporate governance is the established policies, rules, and standards that an organization follows in order to fulfill its vision and goal as a for-profit entity and a stakeholder in the broader community.
    b. Public policy influences corporate governance (e.g., the Sarbanes-Oxley Act).
    c. Corporate governance addresses rules, practices, and institutions that protect and manage ecosystems in relation to the environment.
    d. Corporate governance is necessary to establish an organization's self-image and can be used as an instrument to restore institutional trust.

79. Which of the following is an example of a defined benefit plan?
    a. Cash balance plan
    b. 401(k) plan
    c. 403(b) plan
    d. Section 125 plan

80. Arrange the following items into the appropriate order in the talent acquisition process:
    a. Conduct employee onboarding and orientation.
    b. Give assessment tests and conduct interviews.
    c. Perform a screening review of the candidate pool.
    d. Sort candidates into groups based on qualifications.

Read the scenario and *answer questions 81–82.*

> After several high-profile cases of other large companies dealing with issues of harassment and misconduct, HR professionals at one company have decided to prioritize training to address these issues with their organization's employees.

//Test Prep Books|||

Practice Test #1 | Error! No text of specified style in document.

81. Which of the following would be the most effective way to present information about workplace misconduct to employees?
    a. Give employees a checklist of workplace DON'Ts based on EEOC guidance.
    b. Show news stories of the recent high-profile cases, along with commentary from legal experts about corporate liability and other worst-case scenarios concerning violations of workplace conduct policies.
    c. Set up a self-paced, remote training session to allow for greater flexibility, so the information can reach as many employees as possible.
    d. Schedule mandatory in-person training with employee involvement, such as skits, role plays, and mock juries, to encourage engagement and focus on real-world implications.

82. Who would be the best featured speaker(s) for this training?
    a. A panel of employees who have made workplace misconduct complaints in the past
    b. Someone from the C-suite (e.g., CEO, CFO, or COO)
    c. A Department of Justice representative
    d. The HR professionals who organized the training

83. Which type of interview utilizes questions that are developed from an applicant's answers to previous questions?
    a. Unstructured
    b. Non-directive
    c. Semi-structured
    d. Structured

84. In a cost-benefit analysis of a proposed project, a project worker's salary is an example of what?
    a. A stakeholder
    b. A cost
    c. A benefit
    d. A dependent variable

85. How can HR determine ROI on a total rewards package design?
    a. Consult market data on total rewards best practices.
    b. Analyze relevant performance metrics (such as sales per quarter).
    c. Conduct a total remuneration survey.
    d. Defer to business executives in determining employee value to the organization.

86. How long does an employer need to retain an I-9?
    a. Three years after hire date
    b. One year after the employee terminates
    c. Three years after hire date or one year after the employee terminates, whichever is later
    d. Seven years after hire date or one year after the employee terminates, whichever is sooner

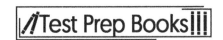

87. What is a hazard communication program, and is it legally binding?
    a. A hazard communication program is a guideline that gives employers the option to inform employees when they are working with hazardous materials. It is not legally binding.
    b. A hazard communication program is a mandate from OSHA that requires employers to inform employees when they are working with hazardous materials, as well as the nature of each material. It is legally binding.
    c. A hazard communication program is an evacuation procedure that is intended for emergencies. It is legally binding.
    d. A hazard communication program is an educational training program that OSHA offers to employers regarding dangerous chemicals. It is not legally binding.

88. Layla is responsible for increasing her company's diversity among all positions and within all departments of the organization. This objective aligns with the organization's corporate social responsibility plan to reflect the social demographics of the metropolitan area. She has been diligently working toward this goal with every recruitment, and the HR director has requested a report to determine the status of this initiative. Which of the following should Layla focus her attention on in this report?
    a. Key performance indicators for all HR metrics
    b. Employee demographics compared to other organizations in the area
    c. Recruitment concerns from the previous five recruitments
    d. Campus recruitment initiative program status

89. Why should a company create a mission statement and a vision statement?
    a. To establish an intentional culture across a large company and many employees and to help influence all actions employees and leaders in the company take
    b. To generate external support for the company by creating goodwill from customers
    c. They are required when you register a business.
    d. Both A and B

90. What is the main difference between downsizing and furloughs?
    a. Downsizing refers to a considerable reduction in the workforce; furloughs are a smaller volume.
    b. Downsizing is only used for reducing costs; furloughs are for restructuring.
    c. Employers are only required to provide notice when downsizing, not during furloughs.
    d. Downsizing is a permanent reduction in staff; furloughs are temporary.

Answer Explanations #1

1. D: A type of benefit that customers believe they could not obtain anywhere else is differential advantage, not competitive advantage. Competitive advantage is the strategy of maintaining maximum competitiveness by pursuing policies and programs that increase one's advantage. Examples of competitive advantage include implementing new technology, offshoring to lower business costs, and shedding underperforming or unnecessary laborers.

2. B, D: Exit paperwork, regardless of the reason for employment termination, should include the employee's final paycheck details, payouts for any leave balances, unemployment information, and insurance information, including COBRA. Choices *A* and *C* are information that should be included with an employment package when a new employee is hired.

3. C: Quantitative job evaluation methods use a scaling system and provide a score that indicates how valuable one job is when compared to another job. Job ranking, Choice *A*, is when an organization defines the value of a specific job relative to other jobs in the organization. Paired comparison, Choice *B*, is when an individual and their position are compared to another individual and their position. Job classification, Choice *D*, is a system designed to evaluate the duties and authority levels of a job.

4. C: Tangible benefits and rewards include things with monetary value like salaries and bonuses. Intangible benefits, by contrast, may not have a quantitative value, but are still important to employees. These include things like flexible schedules, telework options, and a sense of contributing to meaningful work.

5. C: Rather than speaking about all his hard work and contributions, Ben chose to share his team's accomplishments without singling anyone out. This is a display of a strong team-oriented culture in the workplace.

6. B: An employee who is terminated for whistle-blowing or for reporting unlawful conduct by the employer is an exception to the concept of employment-at-will, since these activities are protected under the law.

7. D: Under federal guidelines, an employer is required to keep employment applications and resumes for one year after creation or following the hire/no hire decision (whichever date is later).

8. A: Mary is providing clear, visible expectations of project tasks and completion dates. By sharing who is assigned to each task, it provides a sense of transparency and ownership. Together, these help individual members feel accountable for the role they play on the project.

9. D: A company must set a placement goal when it is found to employ fewer minorities and women than is indicated by their availability. This is known as underutilization.

10. A: Business metrics are quantifiable ways to assess and measure the efficacy of specific policies, programs or products. Like cost-benefit analysis, these metrics are objective and inform the firm whether an action should proceed. Metrics should be used when speaking to consumers and investors in order to establish trust and confidence.

11. C: Offshoring can have many positive effects that transcend the corporation. Offshoring reduces the costs of business, which leads to lower prices for consumers. Lowering business costs doesn't just lead to lower prices—it also frees up revenue to participate in philanthropic activity.

12. A, B, D: To be effective, communications should be clear, concise, correct, complete, considerate, concrete, and courteous. Choice *C* is not considered one of the seven C's.

13. D: A business plan has a variety of different projections. Some of these projections are annual goals, projected growth targets, and net income expectations. However, bonuses for executives aren't calculated in a business plan, which is intended to increase the firm's profitability and productivity.

14. B: Public domain is a provision in federal copyright law stating that work that meets designated criteria can be used without authorization. There are two possibilities where one can use material without obtaining consent. First, if the federal government publishes a work, then it is public, thus falling into the public domain. Second, copyrights can expire. Material that is created on or after January 1, 1978, is protected for the remainder of the author's life plus 70 years after death. Anonymous material, works made for hire, and articles are protected for 95 years from the date of creation or 120 years after being published.

15. B: An employer should obtain signed consent from the candidate to check work references before extending a contingent offer of employment. This is because many companies have been sued by job applicants who have discovered that they have been given poor references. Physical examinations cannot be required by an employer until after a job offer has been made. Finally, polygraph tests cannot be required by most employers.

16. A, D: When filling a vacancy, HR must evaluate the needs of the department and create an appropriate job posting for the position that needs to be filled. Choices *B* and *C* are the second and fourth steps in the recruitment process, respectively.

17. C: The job posting is the first place to share the company's mission, vision, and ethical standards. This attracts candidates with similar values to apply. Ethical standards should be reviewed again during the interview process and new-hire orientation to ensure good fit and promote the values.

18. D: The Glass Ceiling Act established a commission to study how women and minorities face significant barriers and are prevented from reaching management positions. This act was part of Title II of the Civil Rights Act of 1991, Choices *A* and *B*. Choice *C*, Equal Pay Act, is a law that seeks to abolish the wage disparity based on sex.

19. A: 360-degree feedback is a method by which employees receive anonymous feedback from their managers, peers, direct reports, and customers. Choice *B* is incorrect since 360-degree feedback involves much more than employee self-appraisals. Choices *C* and *D* are incorrect since 360-degree feedback is not reviews by only fellow employees or by only management.

20. A: An employee who is a salesperson would likely warrant a written employment contract to outline information such as salary (including guaranteed or discretionary bonuses), commission structure and payment processes, and clauses referencing noncompete agreements.

21. A: Title VII of the Civil Rights Act of 1964 guarantees that all employees have equal access to career development and training. The Fair Labor Standards Act (FLSA) was put into effect to establish employee classification (exempt/non-exempt) and regulate minimum wage, overtime pay, on-call pay, associated recordkeeping, and child labor. Under the Older Workers Benefit Protection Act (OWBPA), it is illegal for

employers to discriminate based on an employee's age in the provision of benefits, such as pension programs, retirement plans, life insurance, etc. Finally, the Davis Beacon Act requires contractors and subcontractors working on federally funded contracts in excess of $2,000 to pay all laborers at construction sites associated with such contracts at least the prevailing wage and fringe benefits that individuals working in similar projects in the area are receiving.

22. C: Modeling ethical behavior is the most effective way to show employees what is acceptable in the workplace. The other methods listed can help, but they may not be very effective on their own.

23. A, B, C: The Faragher case, Choice *A*, held that employers could be held liable for supervisory harassment. The Harris v. Forklift Systems, Inc. case, Choice *B*, established the standard for a "reasonable person," while the Oncale case, Choice *C*, ruled on same-gender sexual harassment. The case of McDonnell Douglas Corporation v. Green, Choice *D*, was a disparate treatment case.

24. C: Offshoring refers to the relocation of some or all of an organization's processes to an international location, either internally or through third-party vendors. Choice *A* is not correct because outsourcing refers to moving an organization's processes outside the company by contracting third-party vendors. Outsourcing can take place either domestically or internationally. Outsourcing and offshoring may often coincide, but they are not necessarily the same thing. Choice *B* is also incorrect; an organization downsizes when it reduces its operations and eliminates previously staffed positions. Finally, Choice *D* is incorrect because globalizing is a very broad term for engaging in operations on an international scale; it is not the best term to describe this specific situation.

25. D: Alternative work locations permit organizations to decentralize operations, thus minimizing the possibility for a person to cause significant destruction.

26. C: Employees that supervise other employees and have management as a significant part of their job are considered exempt. To classify as exempt, employees need to make over $23,600 per year and pass the duties test. The duties test needs to include either executive job duties, professional job duties, or exempt administrative job duties. These two requirements eliminate Choices *A* and *B*, as Choice *A* does not meet the duties test and Choice *B* does not meet the salary level test. Choice *D* is incorrect, as an employer must justify why an employee is exempt.

27. C: Reference and background checks are pre-employment activities that can assist companies with protecting themselves from lawsuits or damage to their reputation (for example, in the event of negligent hiring claims). Interviewing candidates, Choice *A*, may not reveal all pertinent information. Choices *B* and *D*, selection tests and employment agreements, do not provide information that would protect the company's interests.

28. A: Six Sigma is a specific technique that works to improve business processes by implementing various tools and concepts to reduce errors and eliminate waste. Gap analysis, root cause analysis, and cause-and-effect diagrams, Choices *B*, *C*, and *D*, are incorrect because they are all tools that would be used to determine why goals were not achieved or if there was a discrepancy between the expected results and actual results.

29. C: The plan must include minimum vesting schedules for graded and cliff vesting. For a pension plan to meet the minimum standards set by ERISA, employees must be at least 21 years of age and have completed one year of service with the company in order to participate in the plan. Plan participants

must be provided with a copy of the summary plan description at least once every five years. Additionally, the pension plan assets must be kept separate from other company assets.

30. B: The compa-ratio is computed by finding the mid-point of the salary range, which is $16 in this example. Then, the pay level of the employee ($12.50) is divided by the midpoint of the salary range ($16) to receive a compa-ratio of .78 or 78%.

31. A: Since the compa-ratio in the previous question is 78 percent and, thus, below 100 percent, the employee is paid less than the midpoint of the salary range. This can be attributed to the fact that the employee is new to the job and/or the organization, is a low performer, or is working for a company that has adopted a lag-behind-the-market pay strategy.

32. C: Choice *C*, job specification, is used to describe the knowledge, skills, abilities, education, and experience that are essential to performing a specific job. Choice *A*, job analysis, is the process used to identify the job requirements and duties and their relative importance. Choice *B*, job description, is a general written statement for a specific position based on a job analysis. Choice *D*, job evaluation, determines the relative worth of each job position by creating a hierarchy.

33. C: In Choice *C*, the employer has 100 or more full-time employees. The mass layoff is expected to last for at least six months, and at least 33 percent of the workforce at the employment site is being laid off.

Under the WARN Act, an employer is required to provide a minimum of 60 days' notice to their employees in advance of a mass layoff if the following criteria are met:

- The employer has 100 or more full-time employees (or a total of full-time and part-time employees working 4,000 hours per week, not counting overtime, at all of their employment sites combined).
- The layoff will result in an employment loss at a single site for either 50 or more full-time employees, if they make up at least 33 percent of the workforce at the employment site, or 500 or more full-time employees, and the layoff is for more than six months.

The WARN act also requires that an employer provide a minimum of 60 days' notice to their employees in advance of a plant closing if the following criteria are met:

- The employer has 100 or more full-time employees (or a total of full-time and part-time employees working 4,000 hours per week, not counting overtime, at all of their employment sites combined).
- The plant closing will result in the temporary or permanent shutdown of an entire site, or one or more facilities or operating units within a single site, that results in an employment loss (during any 30-day period) of 50 or more full-time employees.

34. B: Leadership buy-in promotes top-down change; without leaders in the company supporting new initiatives, it is highly unlikely that subordinate employees will embrace change. They are more likely to resist if they feel those in leadership positions do not find the change valuable.

35. D: A crucial factor for the future generation of new employees in determining their job field is the social impact and engagement of the work they will do and the organization that will employ them. Although compensation and benefits, Choice *A*, retirement programs, Choice *B*, and flexible work options, Choice *C*, are important when joining an organization and picking a career, they are not the primary focus of the next generation coming into the workforce.

36. D: Conducting stay interviews is a great way to get engagement information from your current staff in a targeted way. If you are unable to find the cause for the disengagement, it is crucial that you gather more information before trying to make a change. Without input from the department, you could lose great employees or not address the problem. Choices *B* and *C* try to recommend a solution without knowing the problem. Choice *A* could have you lose valuable staff before solving the problem.

37. Workforce planning: This is the process that forecasts an organization's employment needs, both current and future, including determining a plan to fill these needs and implementing the hiring plan. It consists of forecasting, conducting a critical skills gap analysis, recruitment and onboarding of new employees, and succession planning.

38. A: Under the Taft-Hartley Act, creating a company-sponsored labor union is illegal, making Choice *A* correct. The actions listed in Choices *B*, *C*, and *D* are not addressed by the Taft-Hartley Act.

39. Code of conduct or code of ethics: Companies develop a code of acceptable behavior that also includes prohibited behaviors or actions and the consequences of violating these rules. It often addresses things like conflicts of interest, confidentiality, privacy, and personal use of company property. Violations of the code are also explained and can include disciplinary action up to and including termination of employment. This set of guidelines and expectations is referred to as the code of conduct or the code of ethics.

40. C, A, B, D: When working through conflict resolution, first, the problem that is causing the issue should be identified. Then, the feelings, perceptions, and opinions of those involved should be identified. The potential impact of the issue and any resolutions should be considered, followed by identifying recommendations and actions to resolve the issue. Work toward that resolution, and finally, communicate the resolution with all involved parties as appropriate.

41. C: Leveling can be used if a job included on a salary survey is similar, but not identical, to a position within the organization. The data for that job can be weighted or leveled to create a better match. Choice *B*, benchmarking, is used to evaluate something by using a comparison. Choice *D*, wage compression, is when a new employee is paid at a higher wage than an individual who is currently employed in a similar position and with similar skills.

42. A, B, C, D: All four of these are part of a company's strategic plan. In order, they are strategy formulation, strategy development, strategy implementation, and strategy evaluation. Formulation involves determining the company's vision and mission statement as well as its values and future goals. Development involves collecting information and developing and defining plans for the company's long-range goals. Implementation involves creating short-range plans for the coming year and allocating necessary resources. Evaluation involves reviewing the implementation process, noting changes, and taking any necessary corrective action.

43. A: FMLA only covers unpaid, protected leave for the following reasons:

- The birth of a child, adoption or foster-care placement

- The serious health condition of a spouse, child, or parent

- The serious health condition of the employee

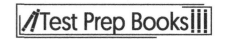

- Military caregiver leave, or leave to care for a covered service member with a serious injury or illness

Employees are to be granted up to 26 weeks of job-protected, unpaid leave during a 12-month period to care for a covered service member.

44. A: There are multiple functions of rating in performance management. The first purpose of rating is to give management the opportunity to identify the best performing employees. Once this is done, these employees can be rewarded in various ways, making Choice *A* correct. Conversely, rating is a technique used by management to distinguish poorly performing employees. Underperforming employees can be dealt with in many ways: they can receive a decrease in pay, be forced to attend additional training programs, or ultimately have their employment terminated.

45. B: Title VII of the Civil Rights Act of 1964 prohibits discrimination against sex and race.

46. C, D: Flextime scheduling and noncash employee award programs are ways employers can attract and keep valued employees when the company's maximum financial compensation has been reached. Choices *A* and *B* are both types of monetary compensation.

47. D: While you should not discriminate for any reason, the EEOC guideline on ageism protects those aged 40 and over.

48. C: A bona fide occupational qualification is an exception to Title VII of the Civil Rights Act of 1964. This act applies to most employers with 15 or more employees. A new seniority system implemented in the workplace and work-related requirements that are not truly legitimate are not exceptions to Title VII of the Civil Rights Act of 1964.

49. A: Transparency allows employees to know what is going on in most, if not all, aspects of the organization as it relates to their job. High transparency is associated with employees who feel valued and validated and report high morale.

50. A: Under federal guidelines, an employer is required to keep records associated with employment benefits for a period of six years.

51. B: This would be an example of a value statement. Value statements are a list of statements that the company holds itself to and creates policies around. Choice *A*, mission statement, is what the company does, while Choice *C*, vision statement, is what the company sees itself doing in the future. Choice *D*, slogan, would be used in a commercial for a company or used internally to build an employment culture.

52. A: Workforce supply may refer to the number of workers available for a specific position or for the industry. Worker attrition, or the number of workers who leave due to things like retirement or resignation, affects the workforce supply. The other choices all refer to factors that influence workforce demand, or the number of workers needed by an organization at a given time.

53. D: Although building the skills, knowledge, and competencies of the workforce is an ongoing responsibility of the HR department, sometimes there are short-term skills gaps that need to be closed. In this case, organizing a class or workshop to directly target the missing skill is a practical and effective approach. For example, if many employees are struggling with adopting new workplace software, a few training courses can help them get up to speed. Choice *A* is not the best choice because interviewing and onboarding new employees is very time-consuming and not the best short-term strategy. Choice *B*

is also not the best choice because a high-potential development program should carry employees throughout the time at an organization until they are positioned to become leaders; again, this is a long-term rather than short-term development strategy. Finally, Choice *C* is not the best choice because, while internal reassignment can help employees to find positions that best fit their competencies, this choice does not solve the problem because it removes underperforming employees without replacing them or building the skills of remaining workers.

54. C, D: The 80% rule dictates that the hiring rate for a protected group must be at least 80% of the rate for the highest selection group. In Choice *C*, the rate of hire for Latinos is 20 percent, while the rate of hire for whites is 50 percent, resulting in a hiring ratio of just 40 percent, which is a violation. In Choice *D*, 60 percent of the male applicants were hired. Following the 80% rule, at least 48 percent of the female applicants should have been hired. However, in this example, just 20 percent of the female applicants were hired, which is a violation. In Choice *A*, 80 of 200 candidates is a 40 percent hire rate for the white candidates. The hire rate for the Hispanic candidates is also 40 percent, which is an equal hiring rate for both groups, resulting in no violation. In Choice *B*, 30 percent of the female applicants were hired, and 25 percent of the male applicants were hired. The rate of hire for the lower selection group is still at least 80% that of the higher selection group, so there is no violation.

55. A, B, C, D: All of the choices are examples of alternative dispute resolution options. Negotiation, Choice *A*, is a voluntary agreement between the involved parties. Mediation, Choice *B*, is a negotiation facilitated by a neutral third party. Choice *C*, conciliation, is a formal settlement based on the law and nonbinding recommendations provided by a conciliator. Arbitration, Choice *D*, is a formal process conducted by an arbitrator who determines the final, binding solution to the dispute.

56. A: The three types of organization development interventions are human process interventions, sociotechnical interventions, and techno-structural interventions. Human process interventions are coordinated efforts to correct inefficiencies through human contact. Specific types of human process interventions include coaching, mentoring, training, and using a third party to mediate disputes. Sociotechnical interventions attempt to integrate new machinery and technology into pre-existing organizational models. Lastly, the goal of techno-structural interventions is to use technology to its most productive capacities.

57. D: An implied contract is inferred from an employer's actions or conduct. An express contract, Choice *A*, is based on an employer's written or oral words. Employment-at-will, Choice *B*, is a common-law doctrine that states employers have the right to hire, promote, demote, or fire whomever they choose, provided there is not a law or contract in place to the contrary. Under this doctrine, employees are also free to leave an employer whenever they choose to seek other employment. Finally, a golden parachute clause, Choice *C*, is an agreement between an employer and an executive that guarantees the executive the right to certain benefits if their employment is terminated.

58. B: Even with the most diligent planning, HR leaders should expect the unexpected and never be too emotionally attached to outcomes. Michael should realize that all baseline plans are fluid and manage his expectations accordingly, while also preparing contingency plans for his operations. Most federal funds cannot roll over from fiscal years, and simply communicating information about plans does not set them in stone.

59. D: Pregnant mothers, male employees who have, are expecting, or want children, and managers who must manage operations with decreased staff are all affected by decisions made to parental leave policies.

60. A: A bona fide occupational qualification, or BFOQ, is a qualification that has been determined to be justified by a business purpose. Minimum qualifications should be related to the job and established to reflect what experience would be needed in order to do the job being recruited for.

61. D: The Landrum-Griffin Act created a Bill of Rights for union members. The Norris-LaGuardia Act outlawed yellow-dog contracts, Choice *A*. The Taft-Hartley Act established the Federal Mediation and Conciliation Service, Choice *B*. Finally, the Wagner Act created the NLRB to encourage union growth, Choice *C*.

62. B: One of the drawbacks of conducting annual performance evaluations is that they may take too long to address critical issues with performance; in other words, the damage has already been done or inefficient work practices have already been established. This app provides more opportunities for feedback from more perspectives. Choice *A* is not the best choice because encouraging phone use at work does not really contribute to productivity or engagement. Choice *C* could be a potential advantage to this new program, but technology for technology's sake is not the primary objective of any new processes in the workplace. Choice *D* is not the best choice either because the program should encourage better engagement, not allow supervisors to disengage from the workers they manage. In other words, it presents an opportunity for a different type of feedback rather than removing supervisors from the feedback process altogether.

63. D: Generally, most moves toward automation present opportunities to cut costs and operate more efficiently by removing hours of manual labor and paperwork, so this is least likely to be a major drawback of adopting an automated system. Choice *A* represents a major potential problem that HR should work to address: How can they prevent constant feedback from turning into an opportunity to bully or overly criticize some employees based on personal feelings? The same applies to Choice *B*. Choice *C* is also a potential hurdle HR should overcome because any new technology requires some time for users to learn how to operate and optimize the system's functionality.

64. C, A, B, D: An analysis of the needs of the organization, and thus the goals of the training, should be completed first in the ADDIE model. The two Ds in the ADDIE model are design and development. Designing the program involves determining what information must be included, who will be undergoing the training, and how the training program might be implemented. Developing the program means creating the content and materials that will be used to convey the information. Evaluation or assessment is the final step of the model. It involves evaluating the effectiveness of the training and validating its future use. Evaluations are often done in the form of participant surveys and feedback.

65. A: With any new workplace technology, employees need to fully understand how to use the new system before they can engage with it. Holding a demonstration that addresses different scenarios can give employees ideas of how to integrate it into their work; offering user resources gives employees a way to find answers and solutions afterward. Choice *B* is not the best choice because it doesn't consider the needs of all stakeholders; for example, some supervisors may prefer to use both performance evaluation methods, or some employees may need longer than six months to adjust to a different management style. Choice *C* is also not the best choice because it isn't very practical and doesn't address engagement for employees who already have phones. Choice *D* is not a good choice because the videos are not likely to reach all employees who are using the app.

66. A: Feedback is an important part of the evaluation stage, which examines if processes were implemented smoothly and effectively and provided value.

67. D: Broadbanding occurs when employers decide to combine multiple pay levels into one, which results in only a handful of salary grades with much wider ranges. This type of pay structure is easier to administer and eliminates green- and red-circle rates. Broadbanding also leads to a flatter organizational structure, which encourages employees' horizontal movement through skill acquisition versus the traditional vertical movement through promotions to new pay grades.

68. A: A semi-structured interview occurs when an interviewer has guided conversations with applicants that involve broad questions and new questions that come about from the discussions that take place. A structured interview, Choice *B*, is controlled by the interviewer, who has a list of specific, job-related questions prepared prior to the start of the interview. The same questions are asked of all applicants. A non-directive interview, Choice *C*, utilizes questions that are developed from an applicant's answers to previous questions. Finally, Choice *D*, an unstructured interview, takes place when an interviewer improvises and asks applicants questions that were not prepared prior to the start of the interview.

69. SMART: The SMART methodology is used to ensure that goal achievement can be accurately defined and described. Thus, goals must be Specific, Measurable, Achievable, Realistic, and Time-targeted. Using this method, goals are clearly defined with the appropriate means of determining completion and measuring success.

70. D: An employee who is temporarily laid off, an employee who is out sick with the flu, and an employee who is out on military leave right before the election would all be eligible to vote in an upcoming union election.

71. B: Milestones are progressive periods by which certain business activities are expected to be completed.

72. D: IDPs help workers become more invested in their professional development. Although many development programs may be extended throughout an organization or limited to specific business areas and departments, an IDP is tailored to an employee's specific needs and created with their input and objectives in mind. This makes workers more invested and involved in their own future success. Choice *A* is not correct because HR should still be involved with helping employees create and manage their IDPs. Choices *B* and *C* are not correct because the purpose of an IDP is to give employees a roadmap for their own development, not to create opportunities for punitive measures or micromanagement.

73. Employment at will: Employees who do not have a contract with their employer and who can be discharged by the employer at any time and for any reason are said to be employment-at-will employees.

74. C: Premium pay can be given to compensate employees as a higher rate of overtime pay for working on holidays or vacation days. Some employees receive shift pay, Choice *B*, for working second or third shifts or for being called into work during an emergency, also known as emergency shift pay, Choice *D*. Reporting pay, Choice *A*, can be paid to employees who arrive at their place of employment and find that there is no available work for them to perform.

75. A, B: The four areas of new employee orientation (NEO) are compensation and benefits; onboarding, which includes receiving the tools, equipment, software, and resources necessary for the job; health and safety information; and policies and procedures. While assigning mentors and training, Choices *C* and *D*, may be an additional part of the company culture when bringing on a new employee, they are not among the four primary areas of NEO.

76. A: v The Taft-Hartley Act, Choice *C*, established the Federal Mediation and Conciliation Service. The Railway Labor Act, Choice *D*, resolves labor disputes by substituting bargaining, arbitration, and mediation for strikes.

77. C: Indirect compensation, most commonly referred to as employee benefits, includes such elements as healthcare coverage, retirement/pension plans, paid time off from work, and short-term and long-term disability.

78. C: Rules, practices, and institutions that address ecosystems in relation to the environment are known as environmental governance. Corporate governance refers to the policies and institutional code that a firm establishes in order to fulfill its role as a for-profit entity and an integral stakeholder in the community. Of course, firms are not the only actors that shape its governance laws—public policy has a salient role. The Sarbanes-Oxley Act mandated a new protocol that senior executives must follow in order to increase transparency and accountability. Moreover, corporate governance can serve as a valuable tool for cultivating a firm's self-image.

79. A: In defined benefit plans, employers agree to provide employees with a retirement benefit amount based on a formula. Cash balance plans are a specific type of defined benefit plan. Advantages of defined benefit plans are that the benefit is known to the employee, and the employer bears the burden of the financial risk. However, the cost is unknown. These plans tend to create higher rewards for longer tenured employees.

80. C, D, B, A: After the need to fill a vacancy has been determined, a job posting created, and candidates sourced, the candidates should first be evaluated through an initial screening to see which ones meet the job requirements. Next, those candidates should be further screened and grouped based on their qualifications, such as from most to least qualified. The most qualified candidates should then be assessed with tests and interviews, and when a final candidate is chosen, HR should complete the onboarding and orientation process.

81. D: Workplace conduct is a topic that HR should emphasize for all employees with a high level of engagement. HR has made the right first step in deciding to proactively address workplace harassment and misconduct; however, establishing clear guidance and creating a culture of civility comes from true engagement with employees. For this reason, Choice *C* is not the best choice, because employees will be passive learners. Also, while Choice *A* might be a good supplementary resource, employees also need positive modeling and information about how they should behave in the workplace, rather than just negative information about how they should not behave. Finally, Choice *B* is not the best choice because abstract legal implications may not have a strong connection to employees. Instead, Choice *D* gives employees a chance to explore situations that affect their everyday workplace interactions.

82. B: An organization's culture of civility must be rooted in its leadership. If employees sense that rules about workplace conduct do not apply to an organization's executives or are applied inconsistently, standards of civil behavior are less likely to take hold throughout the organization. It is important to engage leaders from the C-suite to lead by example. Choice *A* is not the best choice because some

employees may prefer to keep their complaints confidential; experience with harassment may be personal and hurtful to share with a large audience. Choice C is not the best choice because, while guidance from the Department of Justice could be helpful, it is better to begin with leadership from inside the organization. Finally, while HR should be involved with all levels of this training, it is important to reach outside HR to leaders in other areas of the organization.

83. B: A non-directive interview utilizes questions that are developed from an applicant's answers to previous questions. An unstructured interview, Choice A, takes place when an interviewer improvises and asks applicants questions that were not prepared prior to the start of the interview. A semi-structured interview, Choice C, occurs when an interviewer has guided conversations with applicants that involve broad questions and new questions that come about from the discussions that take place. Finally, a structured interview, Choice D, is controlled by the interviewer, who has a list of specific, job-related questions prepared prior to the start of the interview. The same questions are asked of all applicants.

84. B: The worker's compensation is calculated as one of the costs needed to get the project done. If the worker is not paid, he or she cannot be used as a resource on the project. The worker is not necessarily a stakeholder. The worker's salary is a benefit to the worker directly in return for their work, but it is not considered a benefit for the purpose of a cost-benefit analysis. The worker's pay is also fixed as a salary and is not considered a dependent variable for the purpose of the analysis.

85. B: When it comes to total rewards design, ROI is determined by taking the value an employee adds to the organization and comparing it to the amount that is spent to retain that employee. In this case, metrics that can demonstrate this added value (such as number of sales, completed projects, new clients, etc., depending on the type of work) help HR and other stakeholders to develop a rewards package that fairly compensates employees. Choices A and C can both be eliminated because best practices and total remuneration surveys both consider standards for compensation throughout the industry, but they do not reflect rewards relative to the value that employees add to the company. Choice D is also not the best choice because HR should take the lead in determining and communicating employee value.

86. C: When it comes to document retention, the answer is always whichever rule has the longest retention policy. Choices A and B are partially correct, but you must follow both rules and use the one that retains the document the longest to avoid a violation. Choice D is incorrect, as I-9 retention lasts three years after the start date.

87. B: A hazard communication program stipulates that dangerous health effects and noxious physical effects must be communicated to employees before they begin a specific job. The provision of OSHA that deals with hazard communication is the Hazard Communication Standard (HCS). In addition to the HCS, all organizations containing hazardous chemicals must provide hazardous material training to employees, access to material safety data sheets (MSDSs), and proper labeling of containers. Hazard communication is legally binding.

88. B: Layla needs to focus her report on the requested subject matter—how the organization is making a difference in the diversity relative to the hiring activity across the organization. She should ensure that her report identifies the employee demographics compared to other organizations in the area. Additionally, she can discuss how the department is working toward meeting the hiring goal. This may be one key performance indicator that she can address, Choice A, but she should stay focused on the subject matter and not delve into all of the HR metrics. Discussing recruitment concerns, Choice C, and a

campus recruitment initiative, Choice *D*, may be valid because they are related to the overall objective, and they will ensure transparency because they are part of the process to achieve the objective, but they should not be the main focus of the report.

89. D: A mission statement and vision statement help create a culture and reference for all employees and decision makers within the company. They can refer to what they do and what they are trying to do to create a shared purpose across different positions or locations. This also can influence customers, as they are looking at which companies share their values. It is not a required part of filing for a business license, making Choice *C* incorrect.

90. D: When a company furloughs employees, it expects them to return to work, whereas downsizing is a permanent reduction in the workforce. Choice *A* is incorrect; the volume for furloughs and downsizing is not necessarily different. Choice *B* is incorrect; employers can downsize or furlough their employees for multiple reasons, but the reason does not determine the choice of one over the other. Choice *D* is incorrect; companies should notify employees who are being downsized or furloughed.

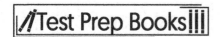

Practice Test #2

1. What does at-will employment mean?
   a. The employer can terminate anyone at any time for any reason, and the employee can leave at any time.
   b. The employer can terminate an employee for no cause, or for a legal reason, and the employee can leave at any time.
   c. The employer must provide a reason for termination, but the employee can resign at any time.
   d. The employer and the employee must agree to a mutual separation to end employment.

Read the following scenario and answer questions 2–3.

> HR at a rapidly growing tech company is in the process of selecting a new applicant tracking system (ATS) to help handle the projected increase in new hires in the next few years. There are also several hard-to-fill positions in the company that require highly specialized engineering qualifications.

2. When choosing an ATS, which of the following should HR consider a top priority?
   a. HR should evaluate the functionality of the new system from the perspective of stakeholders outside HR.
   b. As a department in an up-and-coming tech company, HR should take the lead on adopting state-of-the-art systems to hold a competitive edge over other companies.
   c. Because this is still a transition period, HR should select some functions that will remain paper-based.
   d. HR should forgo dealing with a vendor and simply have employees develop the ATS themselves, since they have a high level of technical knowledge.

3. In discussions with ATS software vendors, which of the following is the LEAST important for HR professionals to focus on?
   a. Integration
   b. User experience
   c. Reporting metrics
   d. Industry usage rates

4. In accordance with the guidance of the National Labor Relations Board (NLRB), which of the following is true of labor relations?
   a. The NLRB can facilitate settlements of labor disputes between employers and employees.
   b. Employees can achieve lawful recognition only by working through established labor unions.
   c. Employers may choose to set up a works council for their employees as a form of lawful representation.
   d. Employees must select one form of representation (for example, union, nonunion, legal, or governmental).

5. A requirement that all male employees must have short hair and be clean-shaven is an example of
_____.

6. Family counseling, grief counseling, and legal services are all types of _____ programs.

7. Nancy is preparing a budget for the training and development conference. The conference, which is held every year for all employees to attend, provides information related to the organization's success and accomplishments, future goals and objectives, and training sessions to teach key skills and techniques. Nancy has budgeted for the site location, food and beverages, employee salaries, materials, external facilitators' fees, giveaways, and emergency issues that may arise. These types of costs are which of the following?
   a. Training
   b. Indirect
   c. Direct
   d. Tax-deductible

8. Creative employees, such as writers, actors, and graphic artists, fall into the _____ category of exempt employee classification and are not covered by FLSA regulations.

9. When conducting a performance review, the company asks the supervisor, coworkers, customers, subordinates, and even suppliers for their input on working with the employee. What type of review would this be?
   a. 360 review
   b. Skill evaluation
   c. Leader assessment
   d. Team assessment

Read the following scenario and answer questions 10–11.

> Leaders at a mid-size organization that specializes in producing car batteries are working on developing a strategic plan for the next 10 years of the company. They are particularly interested in responding to the increased interest in hybrid and electric vehicles. Currently, the company's workforce is primarily concentrated in professionally licensed technicians working on the assembly floor.

10. Leadership has determined that more engineers with academic degrees will need to be added to the company. What is the first step that HR can take?
   a. Research and design meaningful job descriptions for desired new roles.
   b. Lay off enough factory technicians to offset the cost of new employees.
   c. Present a counter-strategy to maintain the current workforce as is.
   d. Canvass current employees who might be willing to change positions.

11. Part of the strategic plan involves building the company's battery research and development program capabilities. How can HR best assist with this part of the plan?
    a. Provide a budget plan for acquiring new research and development technologies.
    b. Organize a voluntary training session for employees who are interested in learning more about the projected research and development capabilities.
    c. Conduct a skills gap analysis to determine the capabilities of the current workforce and identify missing skills, and then develop a plan to fill the gap.
    d. Provide historical data about the battery research and development program's past performance.

12. An employee must file a complaint charge of discrimination with the Equal Employment Opportunity Commission (EEOC) within a period of how many days of the alleged incident?
    a. 180 days
    b. 90 days
    c. 120 days
    d. There is no time limit associated with filing a complaint charge of discrimination with the EEOC.

13. Martin and his wife have just had a baby and would like to change their medical benefit selections to include coverage for their new baby. As Martin is outside of the open enrollment period, he will need to make these changes based on a(n) _____ event.

14. An employer is closing a large facility with more than 50 employees and laying off all the employees that work there. What does the employer need to do before the job site closes?
    a. Give the employees a 60-calendar-day notice in writing.
    b. No notice is required if they are in an at-will state.
    c. Give the employees a two-week notice.
    d. There is no requirement, but it is a good business practice to give employees as much notice as possible.

15. Sophia is collecting data to complete a compensation analysis. This data will help the organization determine if salaries need to be increased or if they are appropriate and in alignment with the industry. Sophie has discovered a website that has information available on practically every job she needs to assess; however, she is hesitant to use the information. What factors should she rely on when determining whether to use this data?
    a. The data goes back several years.
    b. The data is recent and relevant.
    c. The data supports the recommendation of providing salary increases.
    d. The data supports the recommendation of not providing salary increases.

16. In addition to improving training for employees, HR would also like to update its own policies to better address issues of workplace misconduct. Which of the following would be a useful measure to enact?
    a. Developing the HR workforce to handle all aspects of reporting, investigating, and addressing complaints internally
    b. Contracting with a telecommunications group to set up a 24/7 harassment reporting phone hotline
    c. Prioritizing diversity when hiring new HR employees
    d. Maintaining close communication with senior-level leaders to streamline efforts

17. When conducting performance reviews, managers are asked to put their employees in order based on performance and assign bonuses accordingly. What is this type of review called?
   a. Forced rank
   b. Behaviorally anchored rating scales (BARS)
   c. Management by objectives (MBO)
   d. Critical incident appraisal

18. What are the primary pros and cons of using large job board websites?
   a. They reach many applicants, but they may end up being expensive in terms of price-per-click relative to click-to-hire ratios.
   b. They take over all HR recruiting functions but leave HR professionals out of work.
   c. They present a high-tech image to applicants but require too much training to implement.
   d. They establish the organization's online presence, but they open it up to cybersecurity threats from hackers and viruses.

19. Julian is working with the leadership team to ensure that the organization's employees have the skills and competencies needed to achieve the goals and objectives. He is conducting a skills gap analysis and discovers that many of the mid-level managers lack conflict resolution and team-building skills. What would be the best option for Julian to implement?
   a. Research training programs provided by external vendors, and provide information to the employees.
   b. Require these employees' managers to indicate this lack of skill in the upcoming performance evaluation.
   c. Conduct a specific training program for these employees that provides an opportunity to learn these skills.
   d. Conduct a recruitment to hire new mid-level managers who specifically have this skill set.

20. In which of the following elements of alternative dispute resolution are the parties required by law to follow the decision reached as a result of the arbitration process?
   a. Compulsory arbitration
   b. Binding decision
   c. Voluntary arbitration
   d. Constructive confrontation

21. What does "benchmarking" refer to in an HR context?
   a. Putting an employee "on the bench" or on the sidelines due to past performance
   b. Linking salary increases to performance metrics
   c. Identifying and setting goals relative to other organizations' performance
   d. Adhering to government regulations and other industry guidance

22. Which two of the following are examples of employee retirement plans?
   a. 401(k)
   b. 501(c)
   c. 457(b)
   d. 504(s)

Practice Test #2 | Error! No text of specified style in document.

23. _____ is a student-focused learning principle that involves an individual being self-directed in their learning.

24. Elise is preparing the annual performance reviews for her team. Each team member submitted recommendations of initiatives they would like to individually focus on. Michelle submitted four items she would like to focus on in the next calendar year. Which of the following is NOT a standard initiative for the HR team to focus on that should be replaced with a more appropriate initiative?
    a. Review, update, and implement a robust and flexible recruitment process.
    b. Audit the payroll processing to ensure that bills are being paid in a timely manner.
    c. Establish a new exit interview process with specific questions based on the employee's tenure.
    d. Conduct an annual salary survey to ensure salaries are aligned with the industry.

25. In order to promote an organization's benefits program, which of the following details should be included in a job posting?
    a. Salary range, including when increases will be considered during the calendar year
    b. Alternate work schedules, flexible spending accounts, and wellness programs
    c. Specific daily responsibilities and tasks of the position
    d. Supervisory responsibilities as well as who this position reports to

26. Which of the following is NOT a law or regulation that is administered by the Equal Employment Opportunity Commission (EEOC)?
    a. EPA
    b. ADEA
    c. Title VII of the Civil Rights Act
    d. FMLA

27. When is an employer allowed to deny Consolidated Omnibus Budget Reconciliation Act (COBRA) to an employee?
    a. If the employee stopped showing up to work without putting in a resignation
    b. If the employee passed away
    c. If the employee went from full-time, benefits-eligible status to part-time, benefits-ineligible status
    d. If the employee was fired for gross misconduct

28. Which of the following is more specific to the situation and is used to regulate and/or restrict an individual's behavior?
    a. Policy
    b. Rule
    c. Procedure
    d. Standard operating procedure (SOP)

Read the scenario and answer the following two questions.

Rosie is preparing a training class for all employees to attend to adequately prepare the organization in the case of a security issue. In addition to corporate espionage and theft, Rosie is also focusing on training employees on important security details that include security measures.

29. Which of the following items would not be addressed regarding security measures?
   a. Emergency communication systems
   b. First aid and AED locations and procedures
   c. Alarm locations, secure rooms, and security guard location
   d. Employee badges and facility security protocols

30. How often should Rosie train employees on the security plans and policies?
   a. Annually
   b. During new-hire orientation
   c. Every other year
   d. Every six months

31. Meeting, learning from, and socializing with colleagues within and outside of one's organization is known as which of the following practices?
   a. Networking
   b. Achieving work-life balance
   c. Formal education
   d. Fraternizing

Read the following scenario and answer questions 32 and 33.

Adam is a benefits specialist for his organization and is preparing his annual objectives for the upcoming year. One of his objectives is to have healthier employees across the organization. This objective is the overarching goal, with specific tasks identified as a wellness fair, a benefits expo, free flu shots, and a free smoking cessation program.

32. Adam's main objective to have healthier employees is a lofty goal to achieve. What could be problematic with this objective?
   a. It is vague with no measurable data points to indicate achievable success.
   b. It is unachievable because employee health is not the business of an organization.
   c. It is too specific, and there are too many defined tasks that will most likely not occur.
   d. It should be a departmental objective, not an individual objective.

33. What can Adam do to correct this objective?
   a. Eliminate the objective and replace it with the defined tasks he identified.
   b. Rewrite the objective to reflect the SMART principles.
   c. Keep the objective as written because it is a philosophical objective.
   d. Keep the objective and add more defined tasks to accomplish the goal.

34. Carol was tasked with researching, initiating, and implementing a new online training module for employees. The module would allow all employees, regardless of level and position, to complete mandatory training related to compliance, ethics, and regulatory topics. Unfortunately, the project did not meet the established goals regarding training offerings, budget, and timing. Certain regulatory training courses were not included, the final costs were over budget, and the rollout was more than three months late. Which of the following methods should Carol apply to this situation to determine why the objectives were not met?
   a. Process mapping
   b. Cause-and-effect diagram
   c. Value stream mapping
   d. SMART objectives

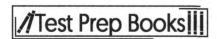

35. Albert is conducting interviews to fill two positions in a six-person workgroup. Which two of the following interview techniques would be the most effective for finding the best employees for the team?
    a. In-depth interviews
    b. Paired interviews
    c. Dyads or triads
    d. One-on-one interviews

36. A manager is questioning a union employee, and it may ultimately lead to a disciplinary action. Via the Weingarten rights, the employee is entitled to have which of the following present?
    a. A relative or close friend
    b. An attorney
    c. A representative from the union
    d. Another manager

37. Onboarding is the process for new hires to learn about the knowledge, skills, and behaviors needed to become valued and productive contributors to the company. This process is also known as which of the following?
    a. New-hire orientation
    b. Organizational socialization
    c. Pre-employment screening
    d. Organizational orientation

38. What is an advantage of hiring from external sources rather than internal sources?
    a. It is more time-effective and cost-effective.
    b. It adds to workforce diversity.
    c. It has a lower interview-to-hire ratio.
    d. It leads to more rapid promotions.

39. Who is the employer required to cover under the Consolidated Omnibus Budget Reconciliation Act (COBRA)?
    a. An employee who left a week before they reached their eligibility date for insurance
    b. A former employee AND that employee's spouse who were on the company's insurance
    c. An employee who declined benefits at work but now wants COBRA coverage
    d. A current employee is who eligible for benefits

Read the following scenario and answer questions 40–42.

> Marisa is evaluating her organization's total rewards plan to ensure that employees are earning a fair and competitive salary against the competition. Additionally, Marisa is interested in learning if employees are satisfied with the benefits package and non-compensatory programs, such as the alternative work schedule.

40. Which of the following should Marisa implement to begin her review of how employees view the current benefits package and non-compensatory programs?
    a. Classification review
    b. Compensation study
    c. Remuneration survey
    d. Employee satisfaction survey

41. Once Marisa has collected the data internally, she needs to compare the data to external data and information to determine comparability, equitability, and competitiveness. Which of the following should Marisa consult to make this determination?
    a. Classification review
    b. Compensation study
    c. Remuneration survey
    d. Employee satisfaction survey

42. Once Marisa has concluded her study of the internal data collected from employees and communicated the results to leadership, what should she do next?
    a. Formally report the results to executive leadership to see what they would like to do next in the process.
    b. File the results and refer to them only to compare to any remuneration surveys available.
    c. Coordinate with the Bureau of Labor Statistics to upload the data received and report the information.
    d. Communicate with employees to ensure they know their input is valued and important to the process.

43. What factors does a PESTLE analysis take into consideration?
    a. People, projects, and payments within an organization
    b. Political, economic, social, technological, legal, and environmental trends that influence the organization
    c. People, engagement, sustainability, time, limitations, and expectations in relation to a specific project
    d. The most proximal direct competitor

Read the following scenario and *answer questions 44–46.*

> Susan is responsible for administering the benefits program at her organization. Several employees have recently left the organization to take positions with other organizations or to retire. During their exit interview, she reviews the benefits coverage and ending date, retirement programs and options, and vacation leave payouts. Because the employees all indicated they would have health insurance with their new agencies or be covered under Medicare, Susan did not send out the applicable paperwork to select the option to continue the healthcare coverage at their own cost.

44. What ERISA amendment is Susan's organization in violation of by not sending former employees the paperwork with information on the options for continuing the group healthcare coverage?
    a. Family Medical Leave Act
    b. Uniform Services Employment and Reemployment Rights Act
    c. Consolidated Omnibus Budget Reconciliation Act
    d. Health Insurance Portability and Accountability Act

45. If a former employee decides to select the option to continue the healthcare coverage, how is the premium paid?
    a. The organization pays the full cost of coverage.
    b. The organization and former employee both pay 50%.
    c. The organization pays 25%, and the former employee pays 75%.
    d. The former employee pays the full cost of coverage.

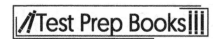

46. Because Susan's organization did not comply with the requirement of communicating with former employees their options to continue the group medical insurance coverage, what could the organization face?
   a. Civil and criminal penalties
   b. OSHA investigation and audit
   c. Civil penalties only
   d. FEHA investigation and audit

47. The National Labor Relations Board requires what percentage of eligible employees to sign authorization cards before it will order an election where employees can vote on whether to be represented by a union?
   a. At least 30%
   b. At least 50%
   c. 51%
   d. A majority of the employees who are eligible to vote

48. Which of the following activities is an example of downsizing?
   a. Implementing a hiring freeze
   b. Reducing the number of hierarchical levels
   c. Utilizing contingent workers to fill in
   d. Outsourcing work to an external service provider

49. What role should social media play in HR?
   a. HR can start an informational campaign warning employees that social media use is unprofessional.
   b. HR can use social media to promote its organization's brand as an employer.
   c. HR can create mandatory training sessions for all employees to incorporate social media communication into their job roles.
   d. HR can bring all social media functions in-house for greater consistency.

50. Which of the following employers is required to have an affirmative action plan in place?
   a. An employer who has 60 employees and $55,000 in federal contracts
   b. An employer with $40,000 in federal contracts
   c. An employer with 55 employees
   d. An employer who is part of the Department of Transportation

Read the scenario and answer questions 51.

Until recently, a company has allowed different business units to operate and organize themselves fairly autonomously. However, new corporate leadership would like to increase collaboration between departments and has come in with a "silo-busting" objective. The new leaders are also looking to create more standardization in job functions and organizational structure between departments. HR has been called on to aid with this objective.

51. In order to standardize job functions between departments, HR is conducting job analyses. Which of the following is LEAST likely to be included in the scope of these analyses?
    a. The type and frequency of tasks performed
    b. The industry standard for required competencies in this position
    c. The supervisory chain of who reports and who is reported to for the position
    d. The personal and professional qualifications needed

52. An organization's policies that govern employees' actions, describe acceptable and unacceptable behaviors, and guide employee behavior with specific details is referred to as which of the following?
    a. Code of conduct
    b. Values statement
    c. Ethical standards
    d. Employee handbook

53. What are two popular search tools to find peer-reviewed, evidence-based research?
    a. CNN and FOX
    b. Medline and Yahoo News
    c. Google Scholar and PubMed
    d. People Quest and People Soft

54. An organization is using a legacy HRIS because long-standing employees are comfortable with the software and feel it continues to meet their data management needs. However, several new employees are having difficulty using the outdated user interface and are pushing to adopt an entirely new platform. What is a good solution for this situation?
    a. Contract with a vendor that offers interface layer technology to develop a new user interface while maintaining the existing system.
    b. Get rid of the old system and invest in the latest HRIS before the current software becomes even more outdated than it already is.
    c. Reassign the new employees to positions that already have more cutting-edge software in place.
    d. Create an organization-wide site where employees can submit anonymous feedback about using the current HRIS.

55. Which is a true statement about the Americans with Disabilities Act (ADA)?
    a. The ADA is a federal law that prevents discrimination based on disability and requires employers to provide reasonable accommodations to disabled employees.
    b. The ADA applies only to full-time employees, not part-time or temporary employees.
    c. The ADA exempts private employers and only applies to municipal, state, and federal organizations.
    d. The ADA was included in the Civil Rights Act of 1964.

56. Bill filed a complaint with the Equal Employment Opportunity Commission (EEOC) alleging that the company he works for has engaged in unfair, unethical, and discriminatory practices related to internal promotions. He has been passed over for a promotion multiple times and believes he is being unfairly targeted due to his age. He submits his paperwork to the EEOC to be investigated. The EEOC investigates and finds there is no probable cause and dismisses the case. What can Bill do next?
    a. Nothing; Bill has exhausted his rights and has no further recourse.
    b. Bill can file a grievance with his union representative for a new investigation.
    c. Bill can request a right-to-sue letter and sue the employer in the court of law.
    d. Bill should quit because he will not be able to return to his position now that the employer is aware of his claims.

57. A _____ statement focuses on the day-to-day work of the organization.

58. Employer A is conducting interviews and skills assessments to fill a customer service position. The job involves active engagement with customers to help resolve problems in a timely manner. The employer is using the following four assessments to evaluate job candidates and will weigh the results according to their importance and relevance to the position. Order the following four skills assessments from the most important to the least important for this type of job.
    a. Reasoning
    b. Personality
    c. Cognitive ability
    d. General knowledge

59. Which of the following types of picketing is done by employees for the purpose of letting the public know that they are not represented by any one authority and thus plan to organize?
    a. Recognitional picketing
    b. Organizational picketing
    c. Consumer picketing
    d. Informational picketing

60. The Kirkpatrick Model of assessing a training program involves four levels, usually demonstrated in a pyramid structure. Beginning with the base of the pyramid, what is the order of the evaluation levels based on this model?
    a. Results
    b. Behavior
    c. Learning
    d. Reaction

61. Which two of the following are part of the key performance indicator (KPI) training metrics?
    a. Financial perspective
    b. Average training hours per employee
    c. Return on investment
    d. Internal business processes perspective

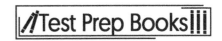

62. A Material Safety Data Sheet (MSDS) contains which of the following elements?
    a. Lockout and tagout signs
    b. Directions regarding emergency exit procedures
    c. Information about confined space entry
    d. Information about how to handle contact with a hazardous chemical

63. Edward has been tasked with preparing a proposal for a new benefits program. The proposal will be presented to the leadership team for final approval before moving to implementation. He has reviewed the employee demographics, current trends and analysis from the marketplace, current benefits usage, best practices, costs, and benefits. Additionally, he assembled several employee panels to ask questions, receive input, and gain insight into what is important to employees. All this information has been put together to make a final recommendation for a new benefits program. What will the likely result be from the leadership team?
    a. The leadership team will most likely approve the new benefits program because a decision needs to be made quickly and to ensure implementation begins immediately.
    b. The leadership team will most likely deny the new benefits program because the current program meets the needs of the employees and there have been no complaints.
    c. The leadership team will most likely not make a decision because they will need more data and information along with additional options to consider versus one recommendation.
    d. The leadership team will most likely approve the new benefits program because Edward prepared the recommendation on relevant and current data as well as employee feedback.

64. Which of the following is one of the best guidelines for employee handbooks?
    a. Include a disclaimer that states the handbook is not intended to be any type of contractual agreement between the company and employee.
    b. Require employees to sign off on revised versions of the handbook.
    c. Include policies that prevent the employee from leaving the company.
    d. Distribute printed copies of the handbook to new staff members during new employee orientation.

65. Frederico Balzo's CEO wants an idea of the effort required to staff the new stores. Which of the following would be the most useful metric for HR to provide?
    a. Time-to-hire
    b. Annual attrition rate
    c. Diversity ratio
    d. Productivity rate

Answer the following three questions based on this scenario:

Antoine is working on a big new HR initiative for his organization. The project is going to take many months to complete, and Antoine knows there are many things to consider,

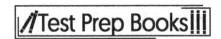

such as the goals of the project, the timeline and milestones, the necessary budget and resources, and how any obstacles will be addressed.

66. What is the best way for Antoine to establish the smaller project goals and milestones that will make up the stepping stones toward total project completion?
   a. Determine the budget for each milestone.
   b. Predict obstacles and how they might be overcome.
   c. Establish milestones that are specific, measurable, and timely.
   d. Allocate sufficient resources to meet the goal.

67. Antoine must create a budget for the initiative, including both direct costs and indirect costs. Which of the following is considered indirect costs?
   a. Labor and materials
   b. Temporary personnel
   c. Market studies
   d. Office furniture

68. Antoine has finished the initial plan for the HR initiative. Upon review, his supervisor has asked him to include a project adaptability section to address any possible changes that might affect the project's completion. Which of the following is NOT something that Antoine needs to include in this new section?
   a. Continuing education plans for each team member
   b. Plans for cross-training team members
   c. Notes on the professional strengths and weaknesses of each team member
   d. Budget options that account for changes in funding

69. The time length for eligible COBRA coverage varies depending on the type of qualifying event. Order the following qualifying events based on their coverage eligibility, from longest to shortest.
   a. Disablement of the employee
   b. Death of a spouse
   c. Divorce
   d. Termination

70. Why is succession planning important for an organization?
   a. It assigns a quantitative value to a company's future goals.
   b. It takes a proactive approach to preserving continuity in the face of worker attrition.
   c. It boosts morale by reducing interdepartmental competition.
   d. It creates clear lines of responsibility for effective communication.

71. During a job interview, asking an applicant about their childcare arrangements might be construed as discriminatory against working parents, especially working mothers. Which of the following would be a more appropriate question to ask?
   a. Which is a higher priority for you: workplace or family obligations?
   b. Do you have any commitments that will conflict with your work?
   c. Are you married or single?
   d. How old are your children?

72. How long should onboarding programs typically last?
    a. The employee's first week
    b. The employee's first day
    c. The employee's first year
    d. Ongoing throughout employment

Read the following scenario and *answer questions 73–74.*

Several employees at a battery factory are concerned about their level of exposure to chemicals used on the assembly floor. One employee has read an article about how certain chemical fumes have been linked with eye disease and even blindness. This employee has been circulating the information to other workers.

73. Which agency or department is responsible for the standards that guide HR's response in this type of situation?
    a. NLRB
    b. EEOC
    c. OSHA
    d. EBSA

74. What is an appropriate HR response?
    a. HR should caution the employee about spreading rumors without first talking to their supervisor.
    b. As a preventative measure, all employees should be required to buy stronger, more advanced safety goggles if they are assigned to positions on the assembly floor.
    c. HR should combat the rumors by circulating a more detailed scientific analysis of the batteries' chemical properties.
    d. After investigating the validity of the report, HR should determine whether it is possible to work with less hazardous materials or develop improved safety measures in collaboration with factory managers.

75. Which of the following is the major element of an affirmative action plan that examines the internal and external population of women and minorities to determine their theoretical opportunity for employment?
    a. Utilization analysis
    b. Availability analysis
    c. Job group analysis
    d. Organizational profile

76. Put the following steps of the collective bargaining process in order.
    a. Propose resolutions.
    b. Bargain for concessions.
    c. Hold discussions between the opposing sides to present information and ideas.
    d. Determine changes, updates, and additions to the agreement.

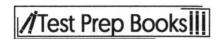

Practice Test #2 | Error! No text of specified style in document.

77. While conducting job interviews, many hiring managers evaluate candidates based on whether they are a "good fit" with the company's culture. What is an appropriate policy to have regarding "good fit"?
    a. Hiring managers should not consider it as a hiring factor because candidates always lie about their personalities during interviews anyway.
    b. Hiring managers should ensure that they are not relying on unconscious biases and determining fit based on shared age, race, socioeconomic status, or other demographics.
    c. Hiring managers should make it a top priority because fitting in is the highest predictor of success.
    d. Hiring managers should allow all applicants to work in the desired job for at least a day to test how well they fit into the work environment.

78. Which of the following communication strategies is used to establish a relationship where employees feel comfortable speaking directly with management about problems and suggestions?
    a. Town hall meetings
    b. Management by Walking Around (MBWA)
    c. Open-door policy
    d. Department meetings

79. An organization with a commitment to diversity would like to conduct a gap analysis. What is this analysis likely to focus on?
    a. The pay gap between salaries for men and women in comparable positions
    b. How the organization has progressed in its hiring practices over the past decade
    c. The organization's current status of employee diversity in comparison to its stated diversity hiring goals
    d. How the organization's diversity statement and policies differ from those of other organizations in its field

80. What part of a SWOT analysis evaluates internal factors that affect an organization's performance?
    a. Strengths and weaknesses
    b. Sources and ways
    c. Output and take-in
    d. Opportunities and threats

81. What was the principal intent of the Sarbanes-Oxley Act of 2002 (SOX)?
    a. SOX deregulated accounting standards for senior executives of accounting firms.
    b. SOX established high levels of transparency and accountability for senior executives in accounting and recordkeeping.
    c. SOX encouraged companies to increase transparency for shareholders by offering subsidies for compliance.
    d. SOX decreased protections for shareholders that were defrauded by institutions.

82. Which of the following communication strategies is used to allow management to check on employee progress, inquire about potential issues, and gain other feedback without relying on employees to "make the first move"?
    a. Open-door policy
    b. Brown bag lunch program
    c. Town hall meetings
    d. Management by Walking Around (MBWA)

83. _____ refers to the overall brand that an organization provides to its workforce, including compensation and benefits as well as employee culture.

84. Which of the following is the major element of an affirmative action plan that compares the availability of women and minorities to their current representation within each job group at the company?
   a. Availability analysis
   b. Job group analysis
   c. Utilization analysis
   d. Organizational profile

85. ADDIE is the most commonly used framework organizations use to enhance human resource development programs. What are the phases of the ADDIE model?
   a. Analysis, Development, Distribution, Implementation, Engagement
   b. Administration, Design, Delivery, Innovation, Evaluation
   c. Analysis, Design, Development, Implementation, Evaluation
   d. Administration, Development, Design, Instrumentation, Engagement

86. Which of the following is an illegal subject that cannot be discussed during a collective bargaining negotiation?
   a. Voluntary subjects
   b. Worker safety conditions
   c. Working conditions and terms
   d. Security clauses

87. An employer is reviewing their advantages and disadvantages in the marketplace internally and externally. Of the following, which analysis would you recommend?
   a. Scrum analysis
   b. Kanban analysis
   c. SWOT analysis
   d. Six Sigma analysis

88. Heather is an HR director who holds biweekly one-on-one meetings, monthly team meetings, and biannual recognition lunches with all her employees. During these meetings, she provides organizational updates, industry news, issues and concerns, and project statuses. She also goes around the room to ensure that all employees have an opportunity to discuss any issues, ask questions, or offer feedback. What is Heather displaying to her team during these sessions?
   a. Transparency and innovation
   b. Leadership and team-oriented culture
   c. Leadership and innovation
   d. Transparency and team-oriented culture

89. What term refers to employees becoming 100 percent vested in their retirement program after a specific number of years of service?
   a. Cliff vesting
   b. Graded vesting
   c. Immediate vesting
   d. Eligibility vesting

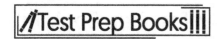

90. In an organization with a progressive discipline policy, an employee has received a verbal warning for a performance issue. The same employee is later found to be in violation of a different company policy. How should this infraction be handled?
   a. The employee should be immediately terminated.
   b. The employee should receive coaching from their manager.
   c. The employee should receive a second warning, followed by a formal written warning.
   d. The employee should receive another verbal warning since this is for a different violation.

Answer Explanations #2

1. B: An at-will employer can terminate an employee at any time, but still needs to follow all laws around discrimination and retaliation. An employee can also leave an employer at any time for any reason. Choice *A* is correct, but does not mention legal consequences, which are important even in an at-will state. Choices *C* and *D* both require the employer to provide a reason, which is not required in at-will employment.

2. A: Whenever HR is considering adopting new processes, such as selecting a new ATS, it must consider the needs of all stakeholders, including those outside HR. The purpose of ATS software is to help recruit the best employees to work throughout the organization, so HR needs to communicate with relevant stakeholders to determine which software functionalities will improve their experience. HR can also consider the ATS from the perspective of stakeholders outside the organization (i.e., applicants). Choice *B* is not the best choice because each organization may have unique needs for its ATS; serving the needs of the organization is more important than trying to outpace others. Choice *C* is also not a good choice because it will create confusion to maintain two systems at the same time. Choice *D* can also be eliminated because, while employees may have technical capabilities, they are not necessarily HR specialists, and this could detract from the overall goals of the organization.

3. D: It is most important for HR to choose a product that fits their organization's and stakeholders' needs, rather than seeking a "one-size-fits-all" solution based on others in the industry. Choice *A* is important because any new software will have to integrate well with other systems already in use. Choice *B* is also important because any system is only as effective as the people who use it; if it is too difficult for stakeholders to use the ATS, it will not be effective. Vendors should also be able to devise a plan for user support after the software purchase. Finally, Choice *C* is also essential in selecting an ATS. The advantage of using a digital applicant management system is that it can easily generate reports and metrics to inform HR and organizational decision-making.

4. A: Although disputes can often be settled within an organization, some situational factors may require external assistance. (Factors like the level of the complaint, the number of people involved, the size of the liability, etc., can influence whether an organization chooses to seek external settlement or mediation.) Choice *B* is not correct because there are various forms of nonunion representation for employees. Choice *C* is also incorrect because, in order to be recognized as lawful, works councils must be elected by employees without employer interference. Choice *D* is incorrect because employees may choose different forms of representation for different situations. For example, union representation can aid with collective bargaining for employees across many different organizations with an industry. However, nonunion representation like a works council can help employees handle situations specific to their workplace. Unions sometimes help with the election of works council representatives.

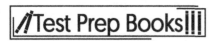

Answer Explanations #2 | Error! No text of specified style in document.

5. Disparate or adverse impact: Having specific grooming requirements, especially for one sex but not another, can create disparate or adverse impact, limiting potential employees who can apply for a job. For example, some religions dictate that men should grow a full beard or have long hair, and such requirements would unfairly remove these candidates from consideration for employment.

6. Employee assistance: Employee assistance programs (EAPs) are nonfinancial benefits offered to employees. These programs offer additional services to employees, such as legal advice, counseling, and ways to reduce stress and conflict.

7. C: Costs related to a single project or program, such as an event put on by the organization, are considered direct costs and should be budgeted accordingly. Regardless of the different costs associated with an event, such as materials, labor, salaries, and locations, they are direct costs because they are all related to one event.

8. Professional: There are three classifications of exempt employees with regard to the FLSA. Executive employees are management focused. Professional employees are learned or creative professionals, such as doctors or writers. Administrative employees are responsible for exercising discretion and judgement in matters directly related to general business management and/or customer dealings.

9. A: A 360 review is a type of review that evaluates the employee from all angles and directions, which is why so many people are contacted for the review. It is very informative but takes significantly longer than many other types of review. Choice *B*, skill evaluation, is looking at the employee's knowledge, skills, and ability (KSA) to do the job. Choice *C*, leader assessment, is a broad category of assessment for leaders of an organization, and Choice *D*, team assessment, is looking at a team's effectiveness and how it can improve.

10. A: HR should start by researching and designing meaningful job descriptions for desired new roles. Whenever new job positions are added to an organization, HR is responsible for creating the job descriptions for them. The job descriptions serve as a blueprint for hiring and organizing the expanded workforce. Particularly because these positions play an innovative and cutting-edge role in the organization, HR may need to conduct research by looking at similar jobs in other organizations to determine what to include in the scope of the job description. Choice *B* is not a good choice because laying off experienced employees to make way for unfilled positions is premature and will lead to staffing instability. Choice *C* is also not a good choice because HR should present workable solutions to help achieve future goals, and changing management is part of that. Finally, Choice *D* is not the best answer because, while some internal transfers may be possible, there is a difference between technical and academic skills. And again, the job descriptions must be in place before filling any roles.

11. C: HR should conduct a skills gap analysis to determine the capabilities of the current workforce, identify missing skills, and develop a plan to fill the gap. Strategic planning involves determining where an organization currently stands, where it wants to be, and the steps it needs to take to move from the present to the future. The same is also true of its workforce—HR needs to know the current capabilities of employees and plan how to fill any gaps that impede future performance. Choice *A* is something that would be handled by staff in the new department, not by HR. Choice *B* might be a good idea, letting employees know about the future of the organization, but it does not present actionable solutions for achieving the strategic plan. Finally, Choice *D* is not the best answer because it focuses on past trends rather than future goals.

12. A: An employee must file a complaint charge of discrimination with the EEOC within a period of 180 days of the alleged incident.

13. Qualifying: Changes to medical benefits can only be made during open enrollment periods unless the employee has experienced a qualifying event, such as marriage, divorce, the birth or adoption of a child, or the gain or loss of a spouse's employment.

14. A: The Worker Adjustment and Retraining Notification Act (WARN) requires employers to provide a 60-calendar-day notice if a facility with 50 or more workers is closing. There are exceptions in the cases of natural disasters or unforeseeable business circumstances, but it is required when possible.

15. B: Data should be recent and relevant for answering questions the organization may have regarding the analysis. If when or how the data was collected cannot be confirmed, it should not be used, making Choice A incorrect. Furthermore, data should not be used simply because it supports or does not support a particular recommendation because this creates bias, making Choices C and D incorrect.

16. C: Particularly in cases of workplace harassment based on sex, race, religion, or other factors, employees need to know that their concerns are taken seriously by HR and that their needs are reflected in the makeup of the HR department. Ensuring that HR follows the same D&I hiring standards as the rest of the organization can set the stage for building rapport with employees and help them feel represented. Choice A is not the best choice because there are situations in which HR should seek external help, especially in cases of a conflict of interest or high legal liability. Choice B is not the best choice either because many employees are unaware of hotline numbers, and the reporting may go through outside channels before returning to HR. Moreover, there could be significant lag time between the incident, the reporting, and the HR response. As for Choice D, while it is important for HR to keep an organization's leaders on the same page with regard to workplace conduct, it is also important that HR maintain a level of objectivity when case complaints are lodged against senior leaders themselves.

17. A: Forced rank is when managers are forced to rank their employees from best performance to worst performance. Choice B, behaviorally anchored rating scales (BARS), is rating an individual employee using statements about performance, with managers picking the statement that most closely resembles that employee's behavior. Choice C, management by objectives (MBO), are tangible objectives that an employee needs to meet. Choice D, critical incident appraisal, requires the manager to make a list of incidents they have witnessed from the employee, whether good or bad, and review it with them.

18. A: Large job sites like Monster, Indeed, CareerBuilder, and others help HR to reach a far larger applicant pool than other face-to-face recruiting strategies. However, the larger applicant pool also means that many more people click on job ads than will apply, and more will apply for jobs than will be hired. When devising a recruiting strategy, HR should consider the price of advertising on these sites (for example, some sites charge for job postings based on the number of visitors to the ad).

19. C: The best option for Julian is to conduct a specific training program for the mid-level managers who lack the identified skills. He should ensure that the employees have an opportunity to learn these skills prior to taking any further actions. Julian may want to research external training programs, Choice A; however, it is his responsibility to roll out this training to the employees, not to simply make them aware of the training. Although indicating the need for this skill in performance evaluations, Choice B, may be necessary in the future, it is important to ensure that employees have the opportunity to

increase their knowledge and skills in these areas first. The same is true regarding recruiting new employees with this skill set (Choice *D*).

20. B: In a binding decision, Choice *B*, the parties are required by law to follow the decision reached as a result of the arbitration process. In compulsory arbitration, Choice *A*, the disputing parties are required by law to go through the arbitration process. In voluntary arbitration, Choice *C*, the disputing parties choose to undergo the arbitration process. Finally, constructive confrontation, Choice *D*, is a type of mediation used in some extremely complicated or contentious disputes, particularly ones where neither party can agree to a compromise.

21. C: Benchmarking involves doing environmental scanning, locating leaders in the field, and determining what those organizations have done to achieve success. Through benchmarking, an organization can learn from others' success in setting and reaching performance goals.

22. A, C: 401(k) and 457(b) plans are both deferred compensation plans. 401(k) plans are for private sector employees, and 457(b) plans are for nonprofit employees. A 501(c), Choice *B*, is the tax code for a nonprofit, and Choice *D* is a made-up answer.

23. Connectivism: This is one of the five standard learning theories. It focuses on individuals being self-directed in their learning. This type of learning requires students to be proactive, outgoing, and inquisitive in educating themselves.

24. B: Appropriate HR initiatives generally focus on the recruitment process, Choice *A*, interview processes, Choice *C*, and annual salary surveys, Choice *D*. Although auditing the payroll processes to ensure timely payment is an ambitious initiative, it is not usually assigned to the HR function.

25. B: Benefits programs, such as alternate work schedules, flexible spending accounts, and wellness programs, are all excellent examples to highlight in job postings. Candidates should have a clear understanding of the programs available to employees.

26. D: FMLA stands for the Family Medical Leave Act, which outlines standards by which employees are granted unpaid time off for family or medical leave without being terminated from their jobs. All the other choices refer to things covered by the EEOC: EPA (Equal Pay Act, which prohibits salary discrimination based on sex), ADEA (Age Discrimination in Employment Act, which prohibits age discrimination for workers who are 40 and older), and Title VII of the Civil Rights Act (which prohibits discrimination based on race, color, sex, religion, or national origin).

27. D: COBRA has a caveat that if there was willful misconduct by an employee, the employer does not have to offer COBRA. This is the only allowance for an employee who was covered and ended employment where the employer does not need to offer COBRA. Choice *A* and Choice *C* are both situations where an employee had coverage and lost it, so they would need to be offered coverage. Choice *B* is incorrect since that employee could have family members covered. COBRA should still be offered to those family members.

28. B: A rule is more specific to the situation and is used to regulate and/or restrict an individual's behavior. A policy, Choice *A*, is a guideline that focuses on organizational actions. A procedure, Choice *C*, is a detailed description that answers when, what, who, and where. Finally, a standard operating procedure (SOP), Choice *D*, is a written set of instructions that documents how to perform a routine activity.

29. B: First aid and AED locations and procedures should be addressed during safety training and new-employee orientation. Although it may be prudent to review this information within the security plan training, it is vital to address specific items related to security measures during this training. These include emergency communication systems, Choice A; alarm locations, secure rooms, and security guard location, Choice C; and employee badges and facility security protocols, Choice D.

30. A: Employees should be trained annually to review the security plans, their importance, and the roles and responsibilities each employee has in the plan. Although it is a best practice to also provide this training during new-hire orientation, the best answer is annually.

31. A: Networking refers to interacting with others who have knowledge and expertise that can provide personal and professional growth. This action does not relate to work-life balance and is not a type of formal education. It is also a positive experience, whereas fraternizing normally has a negative connotation.

32. A: Adam's objective of having healthier employees is vague and ambiguous with no measurable data points to successfully achieve this goal. Healthy employees are most definitely the business of an organization and can be achieved if done properly, making Choice B incorrect. The objective is not specific, and the defined tasks are all achievable, making Choice C incorrect. Finally, the objective should be defined further with specific measurements and data points before moving forward as either a departmental or individual objective, making Choice D incorrect.

33. B: To correct the objective, Adam should rewrite it using the SMART principles. The objective should be smart, measurable, achievable, relevant, and time-based. The SMART principles allow for measured success, as opposed to not knowing if an objective has been achieved. Choice A is incorrect because each of the tasks would still need to be written in a SMART manner; otherwise, the same issue exists. Choice C is incorrect because objectives should not be written as philosophical objectives but rather as tangible and achievable goals. Choice D is inaccurate because by keeping the original objective, the same problem of not being able to measure success exists regardless of how many tasks are identified to support the goal.

34. B: Carol should initiate a cause-and-effect diagram to determine why her project did not meet the established objectives. She can also use a gap analysis or root cause analysis to pinpoint where the process deviated from the plan.

35. B, C: Paired interviews are consecutive interviews with two employees who will work with the new employee. This is a great way for the workgroup members to meet with and have some say in who will become their new team members. Similarly, dyad and triad interviews are in-depth interviews conducted by two or three people with whom the new employee will be working. Choice A is usually conducted by one person and does not give the group members any chance to meet or give feedback on their potential new team members. The same applies to Choice D.

36. C: Via the Weingarten rights, a union employee is entitled to have a union representative present if they are being questioned by a manager in a discussion that may ultimately lead to a disciplinary action.

37. B: Onboarding, also known as organizational socialization, is the process for new hires to learn about the knowledge, skills, and behaviors needed to be valued and productive members of the team and organization. New-hire orientation, Choice A, refers to the administrative process of reviewing benefits, creating a security badge, and training on payroll processing, time-card management, and other important processes that all employees participate in. Pre-employment screening, Choice C, is

conducted prior to the actual hiring of a candidate, and organizational orientation, Choice *D*, is a term that combines several of these concepts.

38. B: One benefit of hiring from external sources is that it adds to workforce diversity. Internally sourced hires, such as internal transfers, can lead to employees who are already familiar and comfortable with workplace culture, but external hires are more likely to add diversity in terms of demographics, backgrounds, personalities, and working styles. Choice *A* is not correct because far less time and money are needed to recruit internally sourced hires. Also, internal hires have a lower interview-to-hire ratio (that is, far more interviews are needed to lead to a hire from an external source compared to an internal source), so Choice *C* is also incorrect. Choice *D* is also not an advantage of external hires.

39. B: An employer is required to offer COBRA to all qualifying former employees, including their dependents and spouses, that were covered under the employer's medical, dental, vision, and specialty medical plans. Choice *A* and Choice *C* are incorrect since you must have medical insurance through your employer before leaving to be eligible for COBRA. Choice *D* is incorrect, since COBRA is for the continuation of benefits after employment and would not impact current employees.

40. D: An employee satisfaction survey is an excellent tool to establish how employees feel about internal programs, such as benefits and flexible work schedules.

41. C: In order to establish how the organization aligns with competitors, a remuneration survey can be consulted to determine if the current salaries, benefits, and programs are in alignment with other organizations. Remuneration surveys are excellent sources to use as benchmarks.

42. D: It is vital to communicate with employees after requesting their participation in a survey. This ensures they know they are important to the process and that their feedback is vital to ensuring that proper programs are implemented.

43. B: The acronym PESTLE stands for political, economic, social, technological, legal, and environmental. This refers to categorized trends that influence the organization and can be used to anticipate potential opportunities and risks in a variety of areas.

44. C: The Consolidated Omnibus Budget Reconciliation Act, commonly known as COBRA, is the amendment to the ERISA law that requires an organization employing 20 or more employees to allow for the continuation of healthcare coverage after separating from employment. Regardless of an individual communicating that they will not take advantage of the continuation of coverage option, this does not alleviate the organization from their responsibility to send out the paperwork to allow the individual to have the information to make this choice.

45. D: If a former employee decides to continue the group medical insurance coverage with their previous employer, the individual is responsible for paying the entire cost of the coverage. Organizations may also impose an administrative fee of 2% to cover the costs of keeping the former employee on the roster.

46. A: Because the organization did not comply with the COBRA requirements, they could face both civil and criminal penalties. Choice *C* is incorrect because the choice of criminal penalties is left out. Although there may be audits and investigations conducted to determine policy, procedure, and protocols, Choices *B* and *D*, these would most likely be conducted by the Department of Labor, not OSHA or FEHA.

47. A: The National Labor Relations Board requires at least 30% of eligible employees to sign authorization cards before it will order an election where employees can vote on whether to be represented by a union.

48. A: Implementing a hiring freeze, Choice *A*, is an example of downsizing. Reducing the number of hierarchical levels, Choice *B*, is an example of corporate restructuring. Utilizing contingent workers to fill in, Choice *C*, and outsourcing work to an external service provider, Choice *D*, are examples of workforce expansion.

49. B: Today, there are countless ways organizations and HR can use social media. Branding is an important way to communicate with customers, applicants, and other stakeholders, and social media is an appropriate platform for reaching them. Choice *A* is not a good choice because social media is incredibly widespread already and there are appropriate, professional ways to use it, depending on each industry. Choice *C* is also not necessary because not all job functions require social media posting on behalf of the organization. Finally, Choice *D* depends on the needs of the organization and isn't a requirement of social media use.

50. A: Employers with 50 or more employees and $50,000 in federal contracts are required to have affirmative action plans in place, as well as employers who are members of the federal banking system and employers who issue, sell, or redeem U.S. savings bonds.

51. B: It is unlikely that the industry standard for required competencies in a position would be included in the scope of a job analysis. Because this effort is intended to standardize positions within different departments of the same organization, HR is less likely to consider outside evaluation criteria. Looking at industry standards for job positions is relevant when crafting new job descriptions, which is not the objective in this case. All the other choices refer to important criteria about the qualifications, type of work, and organizational structure essential to the function of the position.

52. A: An organization's policies that govern employees' actions, describe acceptable and unacceptable behaviors, and guide employee behavior with specific details is referred to as the code of conduct.

53. C: Google Scholar pulls all scholarly research through Google's search engine, and PubMed provides access to a wide range of legitimate medical, health, and life (including HR topics) research.

54. A: The best solution would be contracting with a vendor that offers interface layer technology to develop a new user interface while maintaining the existing system. Because the main issue is the user interface—that is, the part of the software that employees use to access and manage the data—interface layer technology can help to extend the usefulness of the system. Although it is important to stay on top of technology developments, it is impractical and costly to make major system changes that may not be necessary.

55. A: The ADA is a federal law that prevents discrimination based on disability and requires employers to provide reasonable accommodations to disabled employees. The ADA also stipulates that public entities be accessible for disabled persons. The law applies to all types of work (part-time, full-time, or work during a temporary period) in organizations with 15 or more employees. The ADA became a law in 1990.

56. C: Bill's next steps can be to request a right-to-sue letter and sue the employer in court. Although Bill does not have to proceed with these steps, he does have this option available to him. Choice *A* is inaccurate because he does have further options. Choice *B* is also inaccurate because filing a grievance

Answer Explanations #2 | Error! No text of specified style in document.

should have been done prior to filing the complaint with the EEOC; however, Bill could have immediately filed with the EEOC and skipped filing a grievance. Choice *D* is also inaccurate because, based on Bill's claims and allegations, he is protected from retaliation from his employer or fellow employees.

57. Mission: A mission statement answers the "what" and "why" of an organization's work as well as what makes the company different from others in the same field. A mission statement should not be confused with a vision statement, which focuses on the future goals of the organization.

58. B, C, A, D: In a customer service-focused job, it would be very important that the representative be personable and able to positively engage with the customer, even when the customer is facing a problem or has a complaint about the company. The representative must also be able to clearly understand the customer's problem and then use reasoning to determine the best solution to the problem. General knowledge is also important, but it would be the least essential of these four because training can be provided to ensure that the employee fully understands how to do the job.

59. D: Informational picketing, Choice *D*, is done by employees for the purpose of letting the public know that they are not represented by any one authority and thus plan to organize. Recognitional picketing, Choice *A*, is done by employees for the purpose of encouraging their employer to recognize their union as their representative. Organizational picketing, Choice *B*, is done by employees for the purpose of convincing other employees to join their union. Finally, consumer picketing, Choice *C*, takes place when employees picket to discourage the public from doing business with the employer in question.

60. D, C, B, A: The base of the pyramid is the reaction, which measures learners' responses to the training. The next level up is learning, which evaluates how learners improve their knowledge, skills, and abilities through the training. Behavior measures whether and how much learners change their behavior based on their training. The top of the pyramid is results, which analyzes how the organization as a whole benefits from the training program.

61. B, C: KPIs are used to evaluate the effectiveness of a training department. KPIs include things like average training costs and hours per employee, the budget spent on training, and the company's return on its training investment. The financial perspective, Choice *A*, and internal business processes perspective, Choice *D*, are both part of the balanced scorecard, a method that measures a variety of training successes, including both financial and nonfinancial metrics.

62. D: A Material Safety Data Sheet (MSDS) identifies all hazardous substances in the workplace and describes procedures for handling these substances. These sheets state what should be done if someone has inappropriate contact with a hazardous substance.

63. D: The leadership team will most likely approve the new benefits program being recommended. Edward has based his recommendation on current data, both internally and externally, as well as input from current employees, and therefore the leadership team can have confidence in the analysis. The first step that should be taken when a decision needs to be made is to examine relevant data and research. Edward has done this and gone further in his analysis by conducting the sessions with employees.

64. A: To guarantee that employment-at-will remains in effect, one of the best guidelines for employee handbooks is to include a disclaimer that states the handbook is not intended to be any type of contractual agreement between the company and employee.

65. A: Time-to-hire is the key performance indicator (KPI) most closely related to filling the positions at the expanded locations. Knowing the current time-to-hire helps the company budget for how long it will take to recruit and onboard new employees based on the number of vacancies and available HR staff. The other choices do not refer to KPIs that measure things related to hiring.

66. C: Goals and milestones should be set using the SMART system; they should be specific, measurable, achievable, relevant, and time-targeted. This ensures that each milestone can be reached within a reasonable time frame and that there are clear, measurable aspects to indicate when and how well the goal was reached. Establishing the budget, Choice *A*, predicting obstacles, Choice *B*, and allocating resources, Choice *D*, are all aspects of planning the project as a whole, but the SMART system is the best way to set up those stepping stones to overall project completion.

67. D: Things like office furniture and leadership salaries are considered indirect costs, meaning that they affect the project but also serve the organization as a whole. Direct costs, such as in Choices *A*, *B*, and *C*, are costs specifically associated with the project.

68. A: While continuing education is important on a general basis, it is not usually something that is specific to the adaptability of a project. Cross-training team members, being aware of everyone's strengths and weaknesses, and having room in the budget for fluctuations in funding—Choices *B*, *C*, and *D*—are all important aspects of project adaptability.

69. C and/or B, A, D: Divorce and the death of an employed spouse, Choices *C* and *B*, have a 36-month eligibility period. An employee who becomes disabled has a 29-month period of eligibility, and termination of employment has an 18-month eligibility period.

70. B: Succession planning refers to the process of planning for future leadership in an organization to ensure that key knowledge, relationships, and other valuable assets are not lost when leaders resign or retire.

71. B: Employers are prohibited from asking applicants any questions that may lead to hiring discrimination based on things like age, gender, nationality, and religion. Questions about family, children, and marital status are particularly likely to target women. Interviewers must ensure that they are asking the same or similar questions to all applicants and that the questions remain relevant to the job function. In this case, Choice *B* is the best because it approaches the important issue for the employer—how much availability does the applicant have? —without introducing needlessly personal or discriminatory factors. All the other choices include topics that would be inappropriate to ask about during an interview.

72. C: Typical onboarding programs should last for the employee's first year to ensure there is ample time and opportunity for full orientation to the organization. Although there are some specific items, such as payroll processes or timekeeping management, that should be delivered on the first day or during the first week, the organization should make a concerted effort throughout the employee's first year of employment to ensure full orientation to the culture.

73. C: OSHA refers to the Occupational Health and Safety Administration, which administers workplace safety standards. The other choices are incorrect: NLRB stands for the National Labor Relations Board,

which provides standards for unions and other employee relations. EEOC stands for Equal Employment Opportunity Commission, which oversees cases of workplace discrimination. EBSA stands for Employee Benefits Security Administration, which administers and enforces standards for employee benefits like retirement and health plans.

74. D: HR should conduct due diligence into any employee's claims of workplace hazards. If the concerns are valid, OSHA guidance indicates that employers should look for ways to eliminate hazards completely before enacting other measures like improved safety practices or protective equipment. Choice *A* is not the best answer because employees should not feel punished or silenced for raising safety concerns. Choice *B* is also not a good choice because OSHA standards prohibit employers from requiring employees to buy necessary safety equipment; this should be provided by the employer. Finally, Choice *C* is not the best choice because health and safety information should be presented in a way that can be easily understood by employees. Not all factory workers can be expected to understand a highly technical report about chemicals.

75. B: An availability analysis, Choice *B*, examines the internal and external population of women and minorities to determine their theoretical opportunity for employment. A utilization analysis, Choice *A*, compares the availability of women and minorities to their current representation within each job group at the company. A job group analysis, Choice *C*, is a list of all titles that make up each job group. Jobs are grouped according to those with similar content, responsibilities, compensation, and opportunities for advancement. Choice *D*, an organizational profile, is a snapshot of an organization and organizes the key components and competitions within that organization.

76. D, C, A, B: The five steps to the collective bargaining process are prepare, discuss, propose, bargain, and settle. Preparation involves determining what needs to be changed, added, removed, or updated in the current agreement. Next, the sides should come together to discuss proposals and ideas for reconciliation. Resolutions should be proposed and considered by both sides, followed by bargaining for concessions. Finally, a settlement is reached, and each side reviews and signs the final documents.

77. B: Although fit is always an important factor for ensuring a positive workplace dynamic, hiring managers should be conscious of how they determine fit, balancing it with an organization's diversity and inclusion (D&I) policies.

78. C: An open-door policy, Choice *C*, is used to establish a relationship where employees feel comfortable speaking directly with management about problems and suggestions. Town hall meetings, Choice *A*—formal gatherings for the entire company that are commonly referred to as "all-hands meetings"—tend to focus on sharing information "from the top down" concerning the overall organization. These meetings are not usually designed to allow feedback from employees about smaller-detail issues. Management by Walking Around (MBWA), Choice *B*, as the name suggests, involves having managers and supervisors physically get out of their offices and interact with employees in person. MBWA allows management to check on employee progress, inquire about potential issues, and gain other feedback without relying on employees to "make the first move." Finally, department meetings, Choice *D*, are formal gatherings of employees and management in a given department that typically take place on a set day and time, allowing everyone involved to share ideas and offer solutions to company challenges.

79. C: A gap analysis is a method of studying a current state in order to determine how to move to a desired state. In this case, the organization is trying to meet its stated diversity goals, and it must first understand its current diversity status.

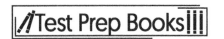

80. A: The acronym SWOT stands for strengths, weaknesses, opportunities, and threats. The strengths and weaknesses a SWOT analysis reveals are internal factors that put the organization at an advantage or disadvantage compared to other organizations in the industry. Opportunities and threats are external factors that can positively or negatively influence an organization's performance.

81. B: Passed in the wake of global corporate accounting scandals, SOX provides greater protection to shareholders and investors by emphasizing transparency and accountability. The legislation mandates that senior executives report financial information to shareholders and the Securities and Exchange Committee (SEC). Furthermore, SOX imposes harsher penalties for white-collar crime and requires detailed reporting to the SEC whenever there is a significant fluctuation in a company's finances.

82. D: Management by Walking Around (MBWA), as the name suggests, involves having managers and supervisors physically get out of their offices and interact with employees in person. MBWA allows management to check on employee progress, inquire about potential issues, and gain other feedback without relying on employees to "make the first move." An open-door policy, Choice *A*, is used to establish a relationship where employees feel comfortable speaking directly with management about problems and suggestions. A brown bag lunch program, Choice *B*, is an informal meeting (usually including employees and management) that is used to discuss company problems over a "brown bag" lunch. The lunch setting and company-provided meal can help create a relaxed setting for exchanging ideas. Finally, town hall meetings, Choice *C*, tend to focus on sharing information "from the top down" concerning the overall organization. These meetings are not usually designed to allow feedback from employees about smaller-detail issues.

83. Employee value proposition: The employee value proposition (EVP) refers to the overall benefits and value an employer provides to its employees. The EVP is the answer to the "what's in it for me" question for the employee. The five primary components of the EVP are compensation, benefits, career, work environment, and culture.

84. C: A utilization analysis, Choice *C*, compares the availability of women and minorities to their current representation within each job group at the company. An availability analysis, Choice *A*, examines the internal and external population of women and minorities to determine their theoretical opportunity for employment. A job group analysis, Choice *B*, is a list of all titles that make up each job group. Jobs are grouped according to those with similar content, responsibilities, wage rates, and opportunities for advancement. Finally, an organizational profile, Choice *D*, depicts the organization's staffing patterns to determine if any barriers exist to equal opportunity employment.

85. C: The ADDIE model has five phases: Analysis, Design, Development, Implementation, Evaluation. It is vital to follow these steps in sequence. ADDIE is highly effective, can be applied to any project or program, and is extremely flexible.

86. D: Security clauses are an illegal subject that cannot be discussed during a collective bargaining negotiation. Voluntary subjects, worker safety conditions, and working conditions and terms are all legal subjects that can be discussed during a collective bargaining negotiation.

87. C: A SWOT analysis is an organization looking at their strengths, weaknesses, opportunities, and threats. Strengths are internal, while opportunities look at the marketplace and how your strengths can set you apart going forward. Weaknesses are also looking internally, and threats are looking at what is upcoming that could be detrimental to your business. Choices *A*, *B*, and *D* are project management techniques which can help, but are not analyses in themselves.

88. D: By engaging the team via meetings and recognition, providing information, and encouraging a dialogue, the HR director is exhibiting characteristics of transparency and team-oriented culture. Employees who have this type of leadership often feel more valued, are more productive, and have greater satisfaction with their job and organization.

89. A: Cliff vesting has one eligibility point related to years of service, and once that is met, the employee is fully vested in the benefit. Graded vesting, Choice *B*, refers to a set schedule in which employees become vested at a certain percentage for each year of service. A typical graded vesting schedule would be 20 percent for each year, up to five years of service, at which time the employee would be 100 percent vested. Immediate vesting, Choice *C*, refers to being automatically vested in 100 percent of the benefit—this would always apply to an employee's contributions regardless of a cliff vesting or graded vesting schedule. Eligibility vesting, Choice *D*, is not a real type of retirement vesting.

90. C: In a progressive discipline policy, a verbal warning is typically followed with a second warning that is paired with a formal written warning. This is true even if the warning is for a different type of employee violation.

Practice Test #3

1. A company with an open-door policy is trying to facilitate what type of communication?
   a. Downward communication
   b. Upward communication
   c. Diagonal communication
   d. Horizontal communication

2. Jacobi is a human resources manager who wants to invest in more employee retention initiatives. He is looking to outsource the employee rewards program to an experienced vendor. What should Jacobi look for when evaluating vendors?
   a. The vendor offers the least expensive rewards.
   b. The vendor learns about the organization's business goals.
   c. The vendor accommodates advance orders.
   d. The vendor has a strong company culture.

3. Which of the following is not a method of internal sourcing?
   a. Employee referrals
   b. Promotions and transfers
   c. Walk-in applicants
   d. Recruiter-sourced hires

Answer the following three questions based on this scenario:

A long-time employee has recently resigned, and Janice has been tasked with determining the needs of the company and filling the position accordingly. Because the employee was with the company for more than 20 years, a great deal has changed both in the workforce and in the company's needs and direction. Janice knows she will have to conduct a thorough assessment to determine the best course of action. Her boss wants her to complete a job analysis of the position, determine what skills the new employee will need to have, and develop a plan for screening, interviewing, and hiring the right person for the job.

4. When completing the job analysis, Janice knows she must assess the scope of the work, including the assignments and responsibilities of the position as well as the skills and qualifications needed to do the job. What else must she consider?
   a. A critical skills gap analysis
   b. A job description
   c. Internal and external relationships
   d. Social media presence

5. The company has made some major advancements in its use of technology in the last several years, and the job that Janice is trying to fill now has a more involved technical component. Which skills assessment test would be helpful in determining if a potential candidate would be able to handle this new aspect of the job?
   a. Technical or mechanical proficiency test
   b. Physical ability test
   c. English proficiency test
   d. General intelligence test

6. When Janice is ready to interview applicants, she plans to conduct in-depth interviews with her top three candidates. As part of the interview, she plans to have the applicants use the STAR technique to structure their responses to some of the interview questions. What does the STAR technique involve?
   a. Summary, Task, Assessment, Results
   b. Situation, Task, Action, Results
   c. Situation, Traits, Assessment, Response
   d. Summary, Traits, Alignments, Roles

Read the following scenario and answer questions 7–9.

> Amelia is conducting a recruitment for a new position within the organization. The new position requires a specific certification, undergraduate degree, and one year of experience. When Amelia reviews the applications submitted, she identifies those with these specific requirements and schedules an initial round of interviews. She prepares the questions to focus on the work the organization will need done to ensure the best candidates are selected to move to the second round of interviews with the hiring managers. At the conclusion of the initial interviews, she is disappointed in the results. Although most of the candidates provided answers to the questions, none of the answers were in-depth, and the candidates lacked real-world experience.

7. What should Amelia do immediately following the initial interviews?
   a. Notify the candidates that the organization will not be proceeding with this recruitment.
   b. Prepare a new plan for the recruitment and present it to the HR team for feedback.
   c. Communicate the results and concerns regarding the candidates with the hiring manager.
   d. Repost the recruitment to engage a new group of candidates and conduct interviews.

8. What should Amelia consider changing in the required qualifications to ensure candidates with the right background and job experience apply?
   a. Nothing; the qualifications are appropriate for the position.
   b. Eliminate the years of experience necessary and only require the degree and certification.
   c. Increase the years of experience and allow for experience to substitute for the degree.
   d. Add supervisory experience to the qualifications to attract candidates who have more experience.

9. If Amelia and the hiring manager decide to move forward with the highest-ranking applicants from the initial recruitment, which of the following would be an appropriate step to add to the recruitment process?
   a. No additional steps
   b. Written exercise similar to the work performed
   c. Additional interview with the entire team
   d. Longer interview with specific and difficult questions

10. What information should be included in a written disciplinary warning? Select all that apply.
   a. Notice of the suspension term being implemented
   b. Any witnesses to the incident
   c. Date and time of the incident
   d. Which policy was violated

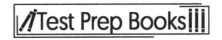

11. What is an employer with more than 50 employees required to do for a nursing mother employee under the Fair Labor Standards Act (FLSA)?
   a. Provide a private bathroom for a mother when it is their normal break time.
   b. Provide a private non-bathroom space for the mother during their normal break time.
   c. Provide a private non-bathroom space for the mother as frequently as needed.
   d. There is no space requirement for accommodation if the mother has a car in the parking lot and breaks are provided when necessary.

Read the following scenario and answer questions 12–14.

> Joseph is working on a recruitment for his marketing team. The team comprises employees who have been with the organization for at least five years, with the most tenured employee having more than 20 years of experience. The department manager has made it a priority to promote internally to ensure that employees are provided opportunities to grow and develop within the organization. The organization also has a robust employee referral program that many employees, including the marketing team, have taken advantage of. The open position is now vacant due to an employee retirement.

12. When proposing a recruitment plan to the department manager, which sourcing method should Joseph suggest as the most appropriate method for this position?
   a. Internal sourcing first and then external sourcing
   b. External sourcing first and then internal sourcing
   c. Internal sourcing only
   d. External sourcing only

13. After Joseph posts the position, he receives complaints from current employees that they should have been considered first for the position instead of external candidates. What should Joseph do to mediate this situation?
   a. Follow up with the individuals who complained, and communicate the sourcing strategy for this position and the importance of sourcing externally to the entire team.
   b. Discuss the situation with the department manager and consider allowing internal candidates to be considered along with external candidates.
   c. Close the posting and initiate an internal promotion-only recruitment for the position to appease the current employees.
   d. There are no actions Joseph should take regarding this situation because the recruitment is appropriate for the organization and the manager should handle the complaints.

14. Joseph is concerned about the new team member fitting within the current workgroup dynamic. The team has been together several years and works extremely well together. What could Joseph add to the recruitment process to address the chemistry and fit of the potential new hire?
   a. Written exam and sample work assignment
   b. Myers-Briggs personality assessment
   c. Workgroup interview with the entire team
   d. One-on-one interview with the most senior team member

15. Which one of the following statements is true regarding developing jobs within an organization?
    a. Jobs are developed based on an individual's particular skill set and background.
    b. Jobs are developed based on goals and objectives established by the leadership to ensure that qualified employees perform duties that contribute to the overall interests of the organization.
    c. Jobs are developed based on the budget and what level of job responsibilities that budget can afford.
    d. Jobs are developed based on the supervisor's discretion and the responsibilities that the supervisor wants performed.

16. What is an example of the qualitative impact of a well-managed corporate social responsibility (CSR) program?
    a. It improves feelings of employee satisfaction.
    b. It generates revenue by developing new customers and contacts.
    c. It reduces an organization's legal liabilities.
    d. It involves many activities that are tax-deductible.

17. Which of the following is an example of a wrongful discharge?
    a. An employee who shared company information with a competitor
    b. An employee who takes home office supplies to help with an in-home consulting business
    c. An employee who accepts a gift in excess of $50 from a single client
    d. An employee who took time off from work to serve on a jury

18. When a strategic plan calls for changes in employee skills, knowledge, behaviors, and/or work deliverables, what is the role of HR?
    a. HR holds multiple meetings and initiates various types of communication to reach out to managers, ensuring they are on the same page and personally training their employees.
    b. HR works with the legal team to ensure that the organization has the authority and management right to make the changes requested to the strategic plan.
    c. HR prepares exit strategies and severance packages for employees who do not meet the new requirements necessary to accomplish the plan.
    d. HR facilitates these changes by implementing updated policies, procedures, training, and other appropriate plans to ensure employees have the necessary skills to deliver the plan.

19. In working on her analysis of the open positions, Amanda has decided to conduct a market analysis. She wants to do a detailed comparison of the job factors and decides to group those factors and then assign a dollar amount to each. Which market analysis method is she using?
    a. Factor comparison method
    b. Ranking method
    c. Classification/grading method
    d. Competitive market analysis method

20. The following are considered paid time according to Fair Labor Standards Act (FLSA) EXCEPT:
    a. Short rest periods during the workday
    b. Travel time during a workday commuting from job site to job site
    c. A voluntary lecture the employee attends that is outside normal working hours and is not job-related
    d. Travel time to a special one-day location, much further than the normal job site, for the employee

21. Amanda also reviews the salary structure for each position. She has determined that two comparable positions have a minimum salary of $50,000, but one position has a range of 30 percent, while the other one has a range of 40 percent—thus giving one position greater opportunity for growth, and ultimately a higher salary, than the other. What is the maximum salary for each job?
    a. $80,000 and $90,000
    b. $15,000 and $20,000
    c. $35,000 and $30,000
    d. $65,000 and $70,000

22. Which of the following communication types, while making it easy to distribute information to a large group of individuals very quickly, may also lead to "information overload"?
    a. Intranet
    b. Email
    c. Newsletter
    d. Word-of-mouth

Read the following scenario and answer questions 23–24.

> Evelyn is new to the HR team at a software company. One of her primary job responsibilities is to manage the performance management process for the organization. Annual performance reviews are due for all employees, and she is working with the management and supervisory staff to ensure that all employees receive an annual review. Evelyn is struggling to get participation from staff, and many managers and supervisors are not aware of the forms, process, or time frame to complete the performance evaluations.

23. Evelyn has been tasked with reversing a recent trend of late and incomplete performance reviews. What should she immediately do to engage the management and supervisory staff in the performance management process?
    a. Provide training, forms, required timeline (including due dates), and coaching on delivering employee evaluations.
    b. Implement a new policy that requires evaluations be conducted by the annual due date or disciplinary actions will be taken.
    c. Discuss the situation with the HR director and CEO and request their immediate attention to the issue.
    d. Continue to send out emails and communications requesting the documents within the time frame needed.

24. A newly promoted supervisor asks Evelyn what the purpose of performance management and evaluation is so that he can complete the documents thoroughly and accurately. What should Evelyn tell him?
    a. The purpose is to coach and counsel employees in areas of improvement.
    b. The purpose is to rate employees' performance and identify areas of growth.
    c. The purpose is to offer encouragement and recognition of performance.
    d. The purpose is to foster a culture of constant improvement and development.

25. What is one way an organization can provide benefits that cater to a diverse talent pool?
    a. Provide higher salaries to underrepresented groups.
    b. Provide progressive options like benefits for same-sex partners or paternity leave.
    c. Provide different benefit options based on employee background and interests.
    d. Ignore benefits that deal with the employee's personal life, such as family benefits.

26. What types of taxes comprise the Federal Insurance Contributions Act (FICA)?
    a. Federal, Social Security, and Medicare
    b. Federal, Social Security, Medicare, and Additional Medicare
    c. Federal, State, Local, Social Security, and Medicare
    d. Social Security, Medicare, and Additional Medicare

27. What is a benefit of long-term disability insurance?
    a. Long-term disability insurance pays a portion of an employee's salary for five years after a work-related injury.
    b. Long-term disability insurance pays a portion of an employee's salary until they can return to work after being out on short-term disability.
    c. Long-term disability insurance pays a portion of an employee's salary for up to 26 weeks after a non-work-related injury.
    d. Long-term disability insurance pays a portion of an employee's salary for an indefinite number of years after a non-work-related injury.

28. Which of the following positions falls under the Fair Labor Standards Act (FLSA) regulations?
    a. Non-exempt positions
    b. Exempt positions
    c. Professional positions
    d. Administrative positions

Answer the next three questions based on the following scenario:

Hector has been tasked with developing a company-wide training program. He knows that there is a lot to consider with such a large-scale undertaking, including the fact that adult learners often have a variety of different learning styles that work best for them. He needs to make sure that his training program will be thorough and effective. It's going to take a lot of work and planning on his part to ensure a successful program.

29. There are five elements to effective training classes. Which of the following is the first step Hector must address in creating his program?
    a. Motivation
    b. Transference
    c. Orientation
    d. Retention

30. When creating the training program, there are several things Hector must consider from the outset. His boss has asked him to write a plan that assesses the goals of the organization and his department, current job descriptions, performance measures, and legal and compliance requirements. These are all part of what kind of assessment?
    a. IDPs
    b. Needs analysis
    c. Learning theory
    d. Delivery assessment

31. Hector plans to incorporate both primary teaching styles, passive and participatory, as a way to keep his training program interesting and to avoid repetitiveness and boredom. He knows that participatory teaching usually has the highest retention rate, so he wants to make sure that he includes a lot of this style. Which of the following activities will likely have the highest retention rate?
    a. Having the participants teach the information to others
    b. Allowing time for the participants to practice what they are learning in the training course
    c. Conducting group discussions around key aspects of the information
    d. Having the instructor conduct demonstrations that apply the information covered in the training

32. Which of the following statements regarding the Family Medical Leave Act is accurate?
    a. Employers are required to maintain employees' group health insurance coverage while they are out on FMLA leave.
    b. Spouses who work for the same employer each receive 12 weeks of FMLA time for the birth of their child.
    c. Employers cannot require employees to take their paid leave, such as vacation or sick leave, when using FMLA.
    d. FMLA only covers leave for the birth or adoption of a child or a serious health condition of the employee or child.

33. An employer setting a policy that employees receive a verbal warning and then a written warning before being terminated is creating what type of policy?
    a. Termination policy
    b. Progressive discipline policy
    c. Offboarding
    d. Documentation process

34. Michelle is working with the sales department to initiate a recruitment for a new sales representative. She is new to the organization and industry and wants to ensure that she conducts an effective and successful recruitment. Michelle meets with the hiring manager and other employees in this position to gain insight and a full understanding of the position before initiating the recruitment. Is it important for Michelle to have this information? Why or why not?
    a. It is not important to the recruitment because Michelle should proceed with the most recent job description for the recruitment process.
    b. It is important so that Michelle can provide correct details about the position in the recruitment brochure and hire a candidate with the right skill set.
    c. It is not important to the recruitment because Michelle should conduct the process with complete subjectivity, which will allow for an unbiased process.
    d. It is important so that Michelle can have a good working relationship with the hiring manager and employees beyond the recruitment for this position.

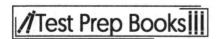

35. Which of the following is NOT a type of leave covered by the FMLA?
    a. Qualifying exigency
    b. Professional sabbatical
    c. Foster-care placement
    d. Military caregiver

36. Human Resources and Payroll will be implementing a new timekeeping and payroll system. This new system will require employees to enter their time worked and leave time directly into the system versus writing out a paper timesheet. Supervisors will therefore need to approve the timesheets of their direct reports within the system for Payroll to process paychecks. What can HR and Payroll do to encourage support and engagement with the new system?
    a. Provide in-person training complete with demonstrations on how to use the system, pointing out the efficiencies and available information.
    b. Create a train-the-trainer program and require these individuals to meet with employees and provide training as needed.
    c. Prepare an in-depth communication and training guide to send out to all employees and supervisors.
    d. Provide employees with the customer service contact information of the provider and direct them to the provider.

37. The CEO wants to cut costs by eliminating a popular employee program that subsidizes public transportation commutes. HR is concerned about the effect this proposal will have on workers. What is an appropriate response?
    a. HR does not have the authority to overrule the CEO and should avoid giving negative feedback unless it is specifically solicited by the CEO.
    b. HR should engage in environmental scanning and research ways that other companies have enacted cost-cutting measures.
    c. HR should eliminate the program and create a feedback survey where employees can share their feelings if they don't like the CEO's decision.
    d. HR should inform the CEO of the value of the program by presenting metrics related to the ROI of the current plan, such as the ability to reach more productive and qualified workers thanks to the transportation program.

38. Which of the following would be considered an inappropriate pre-employment screening?
    a. Marital and parental history
    b. Criminal background check
    c. Medical and drug screenings
    d. Financial and credit history checks

39. There is a new employee in Janelle's department. On the new employee's first day, Janelle sets up a team lunch at a nearby restaurant and asks the new employee to attend. During lunch, Janelle asks the new employee about his past work experiences and personal interests. She also lets him know that she can help him with any questions he might have during his first week. What skill is Janelle practicing?
    a. Relationship building
    b. Continuing education
    c. Empathy
    d. Critical thinking

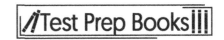

40. Why should employers train employees to use social media effectively?
    a. Employers generally do not like to train employees to use social media because it can be a distraction from their work.
    b. An employee with social media skills provides an organization with an advantage in the fields of marketing and advertising.
    c. Employees using social media are friendlier in the work environment.
    d. If employees can use social media, they are more likely to be up to date on current news.

41. Which of the following laws establishes the minimum standards for benefits plans of private, for-profit employers?
    a. Pension Protection Act
    b. Employee Retirement Income Security Act
    c. Equal Pay Act
    d. Health Insurance Portability and Accountability Act

42. Lori has recently worked with her HR team and the organization to recruit and hire many new employees. With production increases and the customer needs changing, the organization set a strategic goal to increase the workforce by 50 percent. With such a dramatic increase in newly hired employees, the workforce culture has changed substantially. Lori wants to ensure that the newly hired employees, as well as the tenured employees, are engaged, involved, and have a positive and inclusive work environment. What should Lori establish to make sure all employees are provided with these opportunities?
    a. Employee satisfaction survey
    b. Employee business resource groups
    c. Department and organization meetings
    d. Performance evaluation meetings

43. Which of the following is true regarding severance pay?
    a. Severance pay is not required by law.
    b. Receipt of severance pay guarantees a former employee will not file a lawsuit against the employer.
    c. Severance pay increases an employer's contributions to unemployment tax.
    d. Severance pay guarantees that an employee will receive other benefits such as the continuation of healthcare coverage or outplacement services.

44. Amanda begins by making a comparison of salaries among the positions within the organization. Some positions have higher qualifications and may require more education and training. Additionally, some positions are more crucial to the company and thus have greater impact than others. Still, Amanda wants to make sure that the salaries for the different positions are fair compared to other employees and positions. What type of analysis is Amanda conducting?
    a. External equity
    b. Internal equity
    c. Equal pay
    d. Job pricing

45. Melissa is an HR specialist at a financial services corporation. A manager in the accounting department recently approached her with some concerns about a high-performing employee who seems more disengaged and pessimistic than usual. The accounting manager says the employee's change in attitude has started to negatively affect the quality of their work. Which type of benefit program might Melissa suggest as a support for the employee?
    a. Defined contribution plan
    b. Employee assistance program
    c. Managed care plan
    d. Corporate wellness program

46. When using the empirical-rational strategy to initiate change, what is the best way to accomplish the change successfully?
    a. Provide an employee lunch when communicating the change.
    b. Educate employees with new information on the change.
    c. Incentivize the change to relay the benefit employees will experience.
    d. Have the leader of the organization communicate the change.

47. What is the purpose of a pilot program?
    a. The purpose of a pilot program is to assign leadership and decision-making roles to a program, designating leaders as "pilots."
    b. The purpose of a pilot program is to function as a test program, in which leadership conducts analyses to assess the program's feasibility and revenue-wielding potential.
    c. The purpose of a pilot program is to rescue a pre-existing project from certain failure.
    d. The purpose of a pilot program is to validate the success of a project by awarding higher salaries and bonuses to leadership.

48. What tasks are associated with offboarding an employee?
    a. Returning any company equipment and keys
    b. An exit interview
    c. A tour of the job site and new hire orientation
    d. Both A and B

49. Which of the following would detract from work-life balance?
    a. Increased overtime
    b. Telecommuting options
    c. Onsite childcare
    d. Flexible schedules

50. What is a catch-up contribution?
    a. A type of annual retirement contribution program for older employees in which the company matches any savings over the elective deferral
    b. A type of annual retirement contribution to help older investors compensate for missed opportunities to save for retirement earlier in their careers
    c. A type of retirement contribution that allows employees with at least 10 years of service to invest more than the elective deferral limit
    d. A type of retirement contribution that allows employees with at least 15 years of service to invest in all types of retirement accounts the company offers

51. Which of the following is a characteristic of an ineffective salary and benefits survey?
    a. Includes multiple positions
    b. Reflects comparable industries
    c. Avoids controversial topics
    d. Ignores inaccurate information

52. An employee files a grievance. After the employee discusses the grievance with the union steward and the supervisor (who are both in agreement), what is typically the next step in the formal grievance process?
    a. A committee of union officers will discuss the grievance with the appropriate managers in the company.
    b. The national union representative will discuss the grievance with designated company executives.
    c. The grievance will go to arbitration.
    d. The union steward will discuss the grievance with the supervisor's manager and/or the HR manager.

53. Under the Uniformed Services Employment and Reemployment Rights Act (USERRA), what are an employer's responsibilities to an applicant that has past, present, or planned future military service?
    a. The employer is not allowed to discriminate against any military service and must work with applicants to understand comparable skills from previous service.
    b. The employer can choose to not hire someone based on future military service if they know that person will be deployed soon.
    c. The employer does not have to consider any previous military experience towards job experience since it is difficult to compare.
    d. USERRA is focused only on current employees and does not have rules for job applicants.

54. According to the Equal Pay Act, what aspects of a job must be equivalent to merit equal wages?
    a. Working conditions, responsibility, gender, seniority
    b. Effort, production quantity, responsibility, merit
    c. Skill, responsibility, production quantity, merit
    d. Skill, working conditions, effort, responsibility

55. Which statement is most reflective of the Pareto analysis system?
    a. 20 percent of output is generated by 80 percent of input.
    b. 80 percent of output is generated by 20 percent of input.
    c. Decisions should be made democratically rather than statistically.
    d. Resources need to be allocated according to need rather than according to productivity.

56. Which of the following is a reason HR might outsource the payroll function?
    a. To eliminate human resources costs
    b. To do away with payroll direct deposit
    c. To avoid taxes associated with improper IRS filings
    d. To free up human resources for other strategic goals

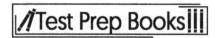

57. A company is laying off 20 percent of its workforce. Which of the following must be afforded to the individuals whose positions are being eliminated and who are presented with a document known as a separation agreement and general release?
   a. They must sign and return the agreement during the meeting where they are presented with it.
   b. They must be given severance pay in return for signing the agreement.
   c. They must be given a period of 45 days to sign and return the agreement, with a seven-day revocation period.
   d. They must be given the advantage of having a lawyer review the agreement, for which they will be reimbursed by the company.

58. George is recruiting for several positions and is working on updating the job descriptions. In addition to the specific roles and responsibilities of the open positions, he wants to add information specific to the organization's mission, values, vision, culture, and working environment. What is George describing to prospective employees?
   a. Employer brand
   b. Corporate culture
   c. Work-life balance
   d. Total rewards

59. Which of the following federal laws established employee classification and regulated minimum wage, overtime pay, on-call pay, recordkeeping, and child labor?
   a. Family Medical Leave Act
   b. Fair Labor Standards Act
   c. Davis-Bacon Act
   d. Walsh-Healy Act

60. Which of the following accurately represents the fishbone diagram?
   a. The fishbone diagram is centered on the analysis of management and does not consult the entire organization.
   b. The fishbone diagram identifies the effects and works to determine causes.
   c. The fishbone diagram investigates the causes of problems. It is crafted after comprehensive brainstorming, determines positive and negative consequences, and isolates various components.
   d. The fishbone diagram is a way to provide a visual representation of a distribution of data.

61. Michael contacts HR to assist with a question regarding how to code a timecard. His employee, Jack, attended a training session for four hours outside of his normal workday. The training was conducted after hours and was provided to increase knowledge related to new tools and reports available in the payroll system. How should HR instruct Michael to report this time?
   a. Because the training was after hours and did not alter his usual work schedule, the timecard should reflect the training but with no pay.
   b. The training should be reported similar to standby pay and paid out at this same rate for the time he attended.
   c. The training was voluntary and not required as part of his job or assignment, so this time is not payable.
   d. The training should be reported per the standard process regarding payable hours and, if necessary, the overtime policy.

Read the following scenario and answer question 62.

The manager of the IT department currently conducts biannual employee evaluations. The evaluation is filled out on a single sheet of paper. On the front of the paper, employees are scored as "meets/does not meet expectations" on 15 core skills and competencies. On the back of the paper, the manager writes more detailed feedback about areas in need of improvement. The paper is returned to employees within two weeks of the evaluation period.

62. The IT manager would like HR's feedback about how to improve this evaluation. What would be the most helpful recommendation?
   a. IT employees are used to working with cutting-edge technology, so the paper form should be replaced by an electronic one.
   b. Biannual evaluations are not frequent enough; employees should get official managerial feedback every one to two months.
   c. There should be additional evaluation standards beyond "meets expectations" to recognize and encourage employee achievement.
   d. The front page of the evaluation is too formulaic and should be eliminated; the manager can just relay the back page of feedback.

63. Which of the following is an example of a performance-based pay plan?
   a. Commission pay
   b. Base pay
   c. Shift pay
   d. Reporting pay

64. Tommy is reviewing the milestones of the HR department to determine if the new recruitment process is effective and provides departments with quicker turnaround to fill open positions. Which of the following metrics should Tommy review to assess the success of the new process?
   a. Percentage of open positions compared to total headcount, or attrition rate
   b. Direct feedback from supervisors on the quality of the candidate pools for open positions
   c. Comparison of the current number of days needed to fill positions with the former process
   d. Number of open positions per department across the organization prior to the new process

65. OSHA requires that organizations adhere with specific regulations regarding hazardous chemicals, including providing training, labeling hazardous chemical containers, and providing access to MSDS information. What does MSDS stand for?
   a. Mandatory Substance Data Sheets
   b. Measurable Safety Detailed Slips
   c. Material Safety Data Sheets
   d. Menacing Safety Data Slips

66. Which of the following is not a standard function of the Occupational Safety and Health Act?
   a. Develop standards for employee personal protective equipment.
   b. Provide fixed payments to injured employees and their dependents.
   c. Establish guidelines to assist employees in the event of a pandemic disease outbreak.
   d. Ensure safe working conditions for employees, and establish safety management standards.

Practice Test #3 | Error! No text of specified style in document.

Use the following scenario to answer the next two questions:

Abigail has been tasked with investigating reports of misconduct by one of her organization's employees. This individual has already received verbal and written warnings and, according to reports, has not corrected the behavior.

67. Abigail's company uses a multilevel, progressive discipline schedule. What might be the next step to address this employee's behavior?
    a. A second written warning
    b. A meeting with the employee and the witnesses to the incident
    c. A suspension
    d. Termination

68. Should the company decide to terminate the employee, what actions must be taken? Select all that apply.
    a. Conduct the termination quickly in a face-to-face meeting.
    b. Provide the employee with a written request for a termination meeting.
    c. Gather coworkers into a conference room during the termination.
    d. Deactivate the employee's building and systems access.

69. A company may decide to outsource which of the following functions to free up staff time, reduce costs, improve compliance, and avoid fines related to Internal Revenue Service (IRS) filings or incorrect payments?
    a. Payroll
    b. HR
    c. Information technology
    d. Marketing

70. Which of the following is a law that applies to employers with 15 or more employees and prohibits discrimination based on race, color, religion, sex, or national origin?
    a. Age Discrimination in Employment Act of 1967
    b. Fair Labor Standards Act
    c. Title VII of the Civil Rights Act of 1964
    d. Equal Employment Opportunity Commission

71. Which of the following focuses on creating opportunities for employees to learn about, engage in, and benefit from diverse ideas?
    a. Group assessments
    b. Mentoring program
    c. Cross-cultural training
    d. Diversity and inclusion

72. What is a lean way of communicating HR programs, policies, and practices, including real-time updates?
    a. An employee handbook that is reprinted and redistributed with each new version
    b. In-person conferences that regularly review protocols
    c. An online employee handbook that is accessible to every employee and is updated online
    d. Social media

Use the following scenario to answer the next two questions:

> An employee has filed a lawsuit against ABC Corporation citing wrongful termination of a whistleblower. The employee has made claims that the company has been requiring employees to work unpaid overtime as well as paying female employees less than their male counterparts. The employee has also claimed that the company hires many more white male gender than it does women or people of color.

73. If it is found that the company did require employees to work unpaid overtime, which federal law did this violate?
    a. EEOC
    b. FLSA
    c. SCA
    d. Title VII

74. Which of the company's purported actions is a violation of the Equal Employment Opportunity Commission?
    a. The company did not violate the EEOC.
    b. Hiring more white male gender than women and people of color
    c. Lower wages for women
    d. Unpaid overtime

75. What are non-discretionary benefits?
    a. Benefits that utilize group discounts to save the company money
    b. Benefits that employers choose to provide to retain their workforce
    c. Benefits that employers must provide based on legal statutes
    d. Benefits that are offered to employees on a pre-tax basis

76. Which of the following is an example of an employee recognition program?
    a. An end-of-year bonus
    b. A plaque given for 15 years of service to the organization
    c. A thank-you note and a gift card for a job well done
    d. A merit given during annual review time

Use the following scenario to answer the next two questions:

> Jose has been tasked with reviewing all of the employee records in his organization. His company is a federal contractor with nearly 100 employees and is subject to the Internet Applicant Rule. Reviewing the files is a daunting task, but his supervisor has given him plenty of time to conduct his reviews and make recommendations for correcting errors, obtaining missing documents, and any other remediations that might be needed.

77. All of the organization's employees have completed I-9 forms on file. Which I-9 forms can be removed from the files and destroyed according to federal guidelines?
    a. Forms older than three years
    b. Forms older than five years
    c. Forms older than eight years
    d. I-9 forms cannot be removed or destroyed.

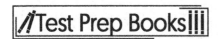

78. Jose has discovered that some of the employee medical files with regard to family medical leave may be incomplete. Which of the following is NOT information that should be included in these records?
    a. Dates of leave taken
    b. Copies of employee notices
    c. Employee and dependent information for COBRA
    d. Records of premium payments

Read the following scenario and answer questions 79–82.

> Liz is working on hiring a large group of individuals under the age of 18 for a youth employment pilot program. Several departments are interested in participating to bring in a group of young individuals to assist with certain jobs that will support the full-time staff. The departments have all identified a specific need and job that will be assigned to the new employees. After the first six months, Liz will evaluate the program to determine if it should continue, be expanded, be altered, or conclude.

79. Liz has received many applications for the youth employment program. She wants to sort the applications into groups by age. What are the age groups she should use?
    a. Ages 14 and under, age 15, age 16, ages 17 and 18
    b. Under 14, age 14, age 15, age 16, age 17, age 18 and over
    c. Under 14, ages 14 and 15, ages 16 and 17, age 18 and over
    d. Ages 14 and under, ages 15 and 16, ages 17 and 18

80. Liz required departments to submit a requisition for the number of youth employees required along with the specific work that would be performed and the hours scheduled to work. If the work and hours aligned with the FLSA standards, Liz approved the request; however, if the work and hours were outside of the scope of the FLSA requirements, the requisition was denied and returned to the department to update for reconsideration. Once the request was approved, Liz determined which age group would be most appropriate for the request to match up the candidates with a position. Which of the following positions would NOT be suitable for an employee who is 15 years of age?
    a. Cashier representative—tallying sales and collecting payments via cash or credit
    b. Food server—taking and delivering food orders to customers as well as collecting payments
    c. Maintenance crew—cleaning office space, including vacuuming, dusting, or other cleaning
    d. Warehouse dock worker—loading and unloading products to or from the conveyor line

81. Liz received several applications from individuals who are 18 years of age. How do the FLSA child labor laws apply to this group of candidates in the youth employment program?
    a. Youths who are 18 years of age may not drive on the job or operate a company vehicle.
    b. The FLSA child labor laws do not apply to youths once they reach 18 years of age.
    c. The FLSA child labor law of specific hours and times of day standards apply.
    d. Youths who are 18 years of age may perform cashiering, shelf stocking, and bagging.

82. When evaluating the youth employment program, Liz realized there were numerous candidates aged 18 and over. What should she consider adding to the program details to deter this and ensure that only candidates aged 17 and under apply?
    a. Nothing, as Liz can use the pool of candidates over the age of 18 for other full-time positions with the company.
    b. Hire those over the age of 18 to ensure that the organization has increased flexibility regarding scheduling.
    c. Only accept applications from internal employees' children to ensure the candidates are under the age of 18.
    d. Update the applicant requirements to indicate that only individuals under the age of 18 will be considered.

83. What is the strongest advantage of external sourcing?
    a. Encouraging connections with job seekers
    b. Cost-effectiveness, as the costs are generally low
    c. Candidate familiarity with the organization and culture
    d. Support of building diversity and bringing fresh perspectives

84. During a performance review, Jordan's manager shares some concerns that Jordan does not seem to have friends at work, show interest in others, or get along well with her team members. Jordan knows that she is a shy person but would like to use this opportunity for personal improvement. How can she proactively address this opportunity?
    a. Throw a weekend party for everyone at work and force herself to socialize.
    b. Schedule 10-minute intervals during her workday where she actively and positively engages with her coworkers.
    c. Send a flowery apology email to her coworkers.
    d. Ask her best friend to apply for a job at her company so that she can prove her manager wrong.

85. What is the primary goal of a business continuity plan?
    a. A business continuity plan is a strategy that is implemented in a time of an organization's prosperity to sustain growth.
    b. A business continuity plan is a portion of the hiring process where employers ask job candidates how they specifically plan to contribute to the organization.
    c. A business continuity plan is the maintenance of productivity during and after a disruption.
    d. A business continuity plan is when an organization uses a disruption to fire workers in order to increase productivity.

86. Which of the following statements is NOT accurate regarding the Americans with Disabilities Act?
    a. The ADA only protects employees who have physical medical conditions.
    b. The ADA protections apply to every aspect of job application procedures.
    c. The ADA requires employers to provide reasonable accommodations to employees.
    d. The ADA is a federal law that prevents discrimination based on disability.

 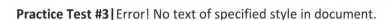

Practice Test #3 | Error! No text of specified style in document.

87. In _____ arbitration, the disputing parties are required by law to go through the arbitration process.

88. Amelia is responsible for sending out Consolidated Omnibus Budget Reconciliation Act (COBRA) notifications when an employee exits the organization. Regardless of the reason for separation, she must adhere to the notification requirements to ensure compliance. When is Amelia required to send out the initial COBRA notice regarding continuation of coverage options?
    a. On the day the separation notice is received
    b. Within 90 days of separation
    c. Within two weeks of separation
    d. On the day of separation

89. When an organization assigns employees to foreign countries, what is the legal and moral obligation HR assumes responsibility of for these employees and their families?
    a. Tax accountants
    b. Housekeeping
    c. Duty of care
    d. HR advocates

90. Which of the following is a law that prohibits discrimination against any individuals who are over the age of 40 related to hiring, firing, promotions, changes in wages or benefits, or other employment-related decisions?
    a. Age Discrimination in Employment Act of 1967
    b. Fair Labor Standards Act
    c. Title VII of the Civil Rights Act of 1964
    d. Equal Employment Opportunity Commission

Answer Explanations #3

1. B: Upward communication is when employees communicate to their supervisors and the leadership within the company, and that is what this company is trying to promote. Choice *A*, downward communication, is when leadership is trying to communicate with their employees. Choice *C,* diagonal communication, is when employees communicate with a supervisor in another department. Lastly, Choice *D*, horizontal or lateral communication, would be communication across company lines at the same level, such as line workers speaking to line workers in different departments, or supervisor to supervisor in different departments.

2. B: Jacobi should look for a vendor that learns about the organization's business goals so that the rewards program is tailored to the company's strategic initiatives. Choice *A* is incorrect because the right rewards program vendor may not be the least expensive. Choice *C* is incorrect because accommodating advance orders should be a given for any vendor, and it is more important to work with a vendor who can handle rush orders. Choice *D* is incorrect because the strength of the vendor's company culture does not necessarily indicate a good fit with the organization.

3. C: Walk-in applicants are considered a method of external sourcing. Employee referrals, Choice *A*, promotions and transfers, Choice *B*, and recruiter-sourced hires, Choice *D*, are all methods of internal sourcing. All methods have pros and cons regarding timeliness, cost, and quality of candidates.

4. C: A full job analysis must include an examination of the relationships required for the job. These relationships include who the employee will be working with within the company, such as coworkers, supervisors, and team members, as well as external relationships with vendors, customers, and others. The employee must be able to maintain effective working relationships. A critical skills gap analysis, Choice *A*, is used to determine the employment needs of a company; this is not necessary in this scenario, as Janice already knows what position must be filled. Analyzing the duties, assignments, and responsibilities as part of a job analysis for the position already constitutes creating a job description, Choice *B*, and Choice *D*, the company's social media presence, does not come into play until Janice is ready to recruit a new employee—it is not part of the job analysis.

5. D: A general intelligence test shows how quickly an applicant can process information, gather new information, and solve complex problems. A candidate who does well on this type of test will likely be able to quickly learn how to use the technology and how to implement it in the best way for the job. A technical or mechanical proficiency test, Choice *A*, tests the applicant's ability to handle tools, machinery, and other types of equipment, such as in construction, carpentry, and other specialized fields. It does not test the applicant's ability to use technology. Choice *B* tests an applicant's physical abilities, such as their running speed or ability to complete pushups. This test is often used in physically demanding jobs, such as firefighting and law enforcement. Choice *C* tests an applicant's ability to understand and use the English language.

6. B: With the STAR technique, the applicant explains the situation as context for the issue. They then describe the task, problem, or challenge they encountered. The applicant then discusses the action they took to resolve the issue and the results of that action. Choices *A, C,* and *D* are not actual terms associated with this technique.

7. C: Amelia should immediately meet with the hiring manager and discuss the results from the interviews. This meeting should include ideas for a new plan for recruitment, options for moving

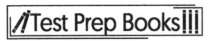

forward with the current applicant pool, and other ideas to ensure the best candidate is identified and selected for the position.

8. C: Many organizations will substitute two years of additional experience for a degree so that candidates with different backgrounds and career paths still qualify for the position. Eliminating the experience, Choice *B*, would most likely not yield more qualified candidates and may result in fewer candidates with the ability to perform the job functions. Similarly, adding supervisory experience, Choice *D*, may not yield more qualified candidates but could deter qualified candidates. Some positions prioritize work experience over a degree, and Amelia should consider this when preparing job descriptions and minimum requirements.

9. B: Many organizations test applicants' abilities in typing, report writing, presentation delivery, or other areas to determine the most qualified candidate. Although adding another interview to the process, Choice *C*, with the entire team may provide more information, it may not provide the most appropriate and applicable information necessary to select the best candidate. The same could be said about adding more questions that are difficult to answer, Choice *D*.

10. B, C, D: Written warnings should include the specific behavior and details of the incident in question, along with any witnesses to the incident, the date and time of the incident, and which policy was violated. Written warnings are issued prior to escalating to any suspension action, Choice *A*, and thus would not include suspension terms.

11. C: Under the Patient Protection and Affordable Care Act (PPACA) in the FLSA, employers that have 50 or more employees are required to take extra precautions for their employees. This requirement mandates that employers provide a non-bathroom private location for expressing milk and provide breaks as much as needed. Compensation for breaks occurs the same as it would for other employees, but the breaks must be provided when needed. Choices *A*, *B*, and *D* fail to meet this criterion.

12. D: Based on the current demographics of the team, the most appropriate sourcing method would be external sourcing. By sourcing candidates externally, the team will be provided with a new employee who will bring new experiences and ideas to the group, which could produce better team and individual results, including new perspectives and ways to work. Although it may be prudent to also include an internal sourcing method at some point in the process, an external sourcing method would be the best approach.

13. B: Although Joseph could follow up with employees to communicate the sourcing strategy and its importance, Choice *A*, the complaints were specific to not being allowed to apply for the position, and therefore this action will not address the main issues. Joseph should work with the department manager and consider allowing internal candidates to be considered along with external candidates, Choice *B*. HR should own any communications to employees regarding a recruitment strategy, making Choices *C* and *D* incorrect.

14. B: A Myers-Briggs personality assessment or an equivalent personality test may be a great option for Joseph to add to the process. This test will show personality differences, as well as communication styles, leadership styles, and other important pieces of information that could help Joseph and the department manager make the best candidate selection. Although written exams, sample work assignments, and additional interviews could provide important information, they generally will not allow for specific personality traits to be displayed.

Answer Explanations #3 | Error! No text of specified style in document.

15. B: Establishing jobs with the criterion described in Choice *B* helps to establish a robust candidate selection pool as well as ensuring that the selected individual is performing tasks and duties that align with the organizational, departmental, and divisional goals.

16. A: Employee satisfaction is closely linked to feelings of contributing to meaningful work. Particularly for the younger generation of workers, employees want to feel that they are making a positive impact on society. CSR is one way that an organization can allow employees to feel that they are helping others, the environment, and/or their community. The other choices refer to things with a monetary benefit, which would be quantitative rather than qualitative.

17. D: Wrongful discharge can occur when an employee is terminated after they refuse to do something unsafe, unethical, or illegal, such as a pharmacist refusing to sign off on a prescription to be dispensed that does not have a date. This type of termination is wrongful because it violates public policy. Additionally, wrongful discharge can occur when an employee is terminated after an employer promised them job security, thus violating an implied employment agreement. In this example, an employee should not be fired for taking time off work to serve on a jury, which falls under the category of violating public policy.

18. D: HR is responsible for facilitating the changes needed by implementing new training programs, updating policies and procedures, and ensuring the workforce has the needed knowledge, skills, and behaviors to accomplish the goals outlined in the new strategic plan. Additionally, HR may need to recruit new employees if the strategic plan calls for specific expertise or additional workload.

19. A: The factor comparison method identifies job factors and then groups those factors while assigning a dollar amount to each group. It is a systematic and analytical way to determine the value of each job, though it can be a complex method. The ranking method, Choice *A*, simply ranks jobs based on their values. The classification/grading method, Choice *C*, groups jobs based on skill level, and the competitive market analysis method, Choice *D*, uses external data to compare jobs to like positions at other companies.

20. C: If a lecture the employee attends is genuinely voluntary, outside of working hours, not job-related, and no work activities take place, the employee does not need to be compensated for that time. Choice *A* is compensable since short rest periods, not including meal breaks, are typically paid. The time varies by state, but these are normally shorter than 20 minutes. Choice *B* and Choice *D* are both considered compensable working time, as they are traveling during normal working hours.

21. D: Range refers to the difference between the minimum and maximum salaries for a position. A position that begins at $50,000 with a range of 30 percent has a maximum salary of $65,000. A 40 percent range means that the maximum salary is $70,000. Choice *A* adds $30,000 and $40,000 rather than using the percentages. Choice *B* shows the dollar amounts of the maximum salary increases rather than the total salaries, and Choice *C* subtracts the percentage from the base salary rather than adding it to the base salary.

22. B: Email, Choice *B*, makes it easy to distribute information to a large group of individuals very quickly but may also lead to "information overload." The intranet, Choice *A*, has the benefit of eliminated risk of important information being accessed by someone outside the organization. Intranets can be effective at communicating important ongoing information about the company, such as policies and procedures. Newsletters, Choice *C*, can provide a variety of information and have the potential to do so in an engaging and welcoming manner. However, newsletters can be labor-intensive. Finally, word-of-mouth,

Choice D, can quickly spread information throughout a group of people. However, information can become muddled, misinterpreted, and unrecognizable as it is passed from person to person.

23. A: Although all these actions may be appropriate at times to address the issue, the first thing Evelyn should do is to provide training for the managers and supervisors. This training should include information on the process, forms, and timeline, as well as coaching on how to deliver an effective evaluation. Evelyn should respond to questions and provide real-life examples to situations that may arise during the process.

24. D: The overall purpose of a performance management and evaluation process is to foster a culture of constant improvement and development. Although the evaluation may include coaching, counseling, recognition, and encouragement, the sole purpose is to enhance the organizational culture by consistently growing and developing employees.

25. B: Organizations that consistently rank high in diverse and inclusive business practices often base business decisions on personal needs of employees, such as offering spouse and dependent benefits to same-sex partners and offering paternity leave in addition to maternity leave.

26. D: The Federal Insurance Contributions Act, known as FICA, includes Social Security, Medicare, and Additional Medicare taxes. Choice A, B, and C are incorrect because federal, state, and local taxes are designated as their own tax categories.

27. B: Long-term disability insurance is a type of disability insurance that takes over when an employee cannot return to work after being out on short-term disability. It pays an employee a percentage of their salary until they can return to work or for the number of years listed in the employer's policy. Choice A and Choice D are both incorrect because the number of years an employer pays for long-term disability insurance is discretionary. Choice C is incorrect because it is short-term disability insurance that pays a portion of the employee's salary for shorter durations, typically between 10 and 26 weeks.

28. A: Non-exempt positions fall directly under the regulations of the FLSA. Non-exempt positions do not involve the supervision of other employees, require specialized education or training, or use independent judgment for decision-making. Positions that are exempt, which include professional and administrative positions, do not fall under the regulations of the FLSA, so Choices B, C, and D are incorrect.

29. C: The first step of a training class should be orientation, which involves introducing the training class to adult learners and explaining what they will learn and how it applies to their current work. Choice A, motivation, is the second step. It involves encouraging learners to actively participate in the training for their own benefit. Choice D, retention, refers to helping learners retain what they have learned in the training program, and Choice B, transference, is helping learners apply what they have learned to their work.

30. B: A needs analysis can help narrow the focus on what kinds of training are needed within an organization. Conducting a needs analysis can include reviewing the goals of the organization and each department, performance measures and results, employee attrition, complaints, and legal and compliance requirements. IDPs, Choice A, are individual development plans. These are more employee-specific rather than company-wide. Learning theory, Choice C, refers to the different ways that people learn information. This is helpful in creating the course materials but is not a determining factor in deciding what type of training is needed. Choice D is a made-up answer.

31. A: Studies have shown that the best way to retain material is to teach it to others. Practice and group discussions, Choices *B* and *C*, have the second and third highest retention rates, respectively. Demonstration, Choice *D*, is a passive teaching method.

32. A: Employers are required to maintain group health insurance coverage for an employee who is out on FMLA leave. The coverage must be the same as prior to the FMLA leave. Spouses who work for the same employer receive a TOTAL of 12 weeks of FMLA time for the birth of their child, making Choice *B* incorrect. Employers can require employees to take their paid leave, such as vacation or sick leave, when using FMLA; additionally, this requirement must be stated in the company policies, making Choice *C* incorrect. FMLA covers leave for the birth or adoption of a child, placement of a foster child, the serious health condition of the employee, spouse, child, or parent, and additional needs related to military service members and caregivers, making Choice *D* incorrect.

33. B: A progressive disciplinary policy is one with progressively higher discipline for repeated infractions. This type of policy helps create consistent employment practices, which can limit bias in termination, as well as help employees succeed by working with them to understand policies before termination. Choice *A*, termination policy, would vary by company but would likely only involve the termination; any write-ups beforehand would not apply. Choice *C*, offboarding, is the term for all the processes and decisions after an employee resigns or is terminated, but this process doesn't take place beforehand. Lastly Choice *D*, documentation, should be taken and maintained for all performance conversations, but the question referred to discipline specifically.

34. B: Choice *B* is correct because it is important for Michelle to provide accurate details about the position in the recruitment brochure and to hire a candidate with the right skill set. Choice *A* is not the best choice because without gaining the insight from the department manager, Michelle may be working with an outdated job description that does not fully describe the work or reflect new work. Choice *C* is incorrect because although subjectivity can be important to a recruitment process, it should align with the importance of understanding the needs of the department and position. Choice *D* is incorrect because although having a good working relationship with the hiring manager beyond the recruitment is important, it should not be the primary reason for discussing the current recruitment needs.

35. B: Professional sabbaticals are not covered by the FMLA. Choice *A*, qualifying exigency leave, Choice *C*, leave for foster-care placement, and Choice *D*, military caregiver leave, are all covered by the FMLA.

36. A: The best response to rolling out a new system, regardless of the function, is to provide in-person training that demonstrates the new system, uses, and functions. Additionally, pointing out the efficiencies and how the new system will positively impact the employee can increase engagement with the new system. Although a train-the-trainer program can be useful, Choice *B*, it is best to have one consistent training program to ensure the message and delivery are consistent. Additionally, an in-depth communication and training guide, Choice *C*, may work to ensure that all employees have information available to them in an easy-to-use guide, but it is not the best response out of the choices. This training guide could include the customer service contact information, Choice *D*, but if questions arise as to the functionality of the new system, an internal contact should be provided to employees. Choice *D* is not the best response to the new system.

37. D: HR wants to demonstrate the importance of the program; however, the CEO is mostly interested in its cost. In this case, HR should translate the program's value into monetary terms by analyzing its ROI. Choice *A* is not a good choice because HR has a responsibility to provide input regarding changes

that affect workers. Choice *B* is also not the best choice because, while it can be part of an overall fact-finding strategy, it does not present actionable results for decision-making now. Also, Choice *C* is not a good strategy because it seeks worker feedback after the decision has already been made.

38. A: Pre-employment screenings generally include criminal background checks, medical and drug screenings, financial and credit history checks, and other background information reviews. An inappropriate screening would be checking the marital and parental history of a candidate, which would include asking questions regarding these subjects during the interview process.

39. A: Janelle is being friendly, providing support, showing kindness, and creating a positive work environment for the new employee. These are all aspects of building a relationship which promotes better teamwork and a positive work environment.

40. B: Employees who possess an aptitude for social media skills provide an additional asset to the company in the areas of marketing and advertising.

41. B: The Employee Retirement Income Security Act (ERISA) establishes the minimum standards for benefits plans of private, for-profit employers. ERISA also established the Pension Benefit Guaranty Corporation, which guarantees payment of vested benefits. The Pension Protection Act, Choice *A*, is an amendment to ERISA that strengthened the pension system by increasing minimum funding requirements. The Equal Pay Act, Choice *C*, is a law that requires employers to pay equal wages to both men and women who perform equal jobs in the same organization. The Health Insurance Portability and Accountability Act (HIPAA), Choice *D*, is an amendment to ERISA that improves the continuity and portability of healthcare coverage and addresses preexisting conditions.

42. B: Employee business resource groups are an excellent tool that can increase employee engagement by connecting employees to others outside of their usual working environment. These groups allow for new connections to be made between employees and opportunities for them to be more diverse and inclusive in their daily work and interactions.

43. A: Severance pay is not required by law. A receipt of severance pay does not guarantee that a former employee will not file a lawsuit against the employer (Choice *B*). Severance pay does not increase an employer's contribution to unemployment tax (Choice *C*). Finally, severance pay does not guarantee an employee will receive other benefits (Choice *D*).

44. B: Internal equity refers to the comparison of salaries within the organization. External equity, Choice *A*, is a market pricing comparison, reviewing salaries offered by different companies for similar positions. Job pricing, Choice *D*, refers to all of the different elements of determining the salaries for various positions. Job pricing includes external and internal equity, market information, and job descriptions and analysis. Choice *C* is a made-up answer.

45. B: An employee assistance program helps employees identify mental health, relationship, legal, or financial concerns and find short-term interventions. Choice *A*, defined contribution plan, refers to a retirement plan in which employees or employers can contribute a specific amount, so this wouldn't help a demoralized employee. Choice *C*, managed care plan, is a type of healthcare plan. While the employee's personal issues may have to do with healthcare, suggesting a managed care plan without first understanding the employee's situation would be unsupportive. Choice *D*, corporate wellness program, is a wellness program that encourages employees to maintain and improve their health. While

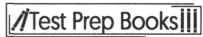

the employee may benefit from participating in a corporate wellness program, they may need attention or assistance with an issue not addressed by the program.

46. C: In order to effectively manage change with the empirical-rational strategy, it is important to incentivize the change. If employees undergo a change but understand how it can positively impact them, they are more likely to accept it and agree with it.

47. B: Also known as an experimental trial or feasibility study, a pilot program is designed to be small-scale. A pilot program's purpose is to enable an organization to test new methods, new products, or engineer new methods or techniques without incurring significant cost. Tremendously important to research, pilot programs can be considered laboratories of innovation and experimentation because they allow logistical considerations, structural efficiencies and deficiencies, and profitability to be evaluated and determined. Pilot programs are widely used in application by many companies, notably Microsoft Corporation, Pfizer Inc., The Dow Chemical Company, and Xerox Corporation.

48. D: Offboarding an employee is an important part of Human Resources' duties to ensure that the employee leaves with a good perception of the company. The offboarding process can include an exit interview, turning in equipment, changing login information for computer systems, and even the temporary transference of job duties. Choice *C* is describing two processes that would be associated with a new employee, not one that is leaving.

49. A: Increased overtime would detract from work-life balance since it would take more time away from the employee's personal life. Choice *B*, telecommuting options, Choice *C*, onsite childcare, and Choice *D*, flexible schedules, are all ways a company can improve its employees' work-life balance.

50. B: A catch-up contribution is a type of annual retirement contribution that helps older investors compensate for missed opportunities to save for retirement earlier in their careers. Choice *A* is incorrect because companies do not need to match the invested funds for the contribution to be designated as "catch-up." Choice *C* is incorrect because, in some cases, employees with at least *15* years of service at a single organization can invest more than the elective deferral limit. Choice *D* is incorrect because catch-up contributions do not expand the number of retirement accounts available to employees with at least 15 years of service.

51. C: Avoiding controversial topics would render a salary and benefits survey ineffective because employees could not freely share their opinions. An effective salary and benefits survey should be representative of the market and region, Choice *B*, inclusive of multiple positions at various levels, Choice *A*, low cost, convenient and easy to navigate, and precise and accurate, Choice *D*.

52. D: The union steward will discuss the grievance with the supervisor's manager and/or the HR manager. After this, a committee of union officers should discuss the grievance with the appropriate managers in the company. The national union representative would then discuss the grievance with designated company executives. If, after this process, the grievance is still not settled, it would then go to arbitration.

53. A: An employer cannot discriminate against employees that have served or plan to serve in the military. There is also an obligation to review candidates and consider skills from their military experience that are comparable to the job they are applying for. Choice *B* is incorrect because not hiring based on future service would be discrimination. Choice *C* is incorrect since previous military experience

should be considered. Choice *D* is incorrect since USERRA has rules for applicants as well as current employees.

54. D: According to the Equal Pay Act, skill, working conditions, effort, and responsibility must be equivalent to merit equal wages. Choices *A*, *B*, and *C* are incorrect because the act does allow for pay differentials for seniority, merit, production quantity or quality, and geographic work differentials.

55. B: The Pareto analysis system is a statistical model that postulates that 80 percent of output is generated by 20 percent of input. Management can use this rule to identify where to invest scarce resources. Other names for this rule are the "80-20 rule" and "law of the vital few." Remembering these other names can be helpful because they highlight the essential functionality of the rule. By constantly searching for the most productive members of an organization or the resources that yield the most revenue, management personnel can prioritize employees or investments over others. This analysis can be useful when restructuring an organization, rating employee performance, making capital investment, and much more.

56. D: A human resources department might outsource the payroll function so employees can focus on the organization's other strategic initiatives. Choice *A*, eliminating human resources costs, would be impossible, even if the department chose to outsource payroll. Choice *B*, getting rid of direct deposit, is not a reason to outsource the payroll function because outsourcing typically adds or improves direct deposit services. Choice *C*, avoiding taxes associated with improper IRS filings, is incorrect because outsourcing payroll can only help companies avoid fines for improper filings, not taxes.

57. C: During a larger group reduction in force (RIF), the affected employees who are being laid off and given a document to sign, known as a separation agreement and general release, must be given 45 days to sign and return the agreement, along with a seven-day revocation period. This allows them time to consider the terms of the agreement and to review the agreement with a lawyer if they choose to do so.

58. A: George is specifically describing the organization's employer brand when discussing the mission, values, vision, culture, and working environment. Choices *B*, *C*, and *D* are incorrect because these elements—culture, work-life balance, and total rewards—are all incorporated in the employer brand.

59. B: The Fair Labor Standards Act (FLSA) is also known as the Wage and Hour Law. The FLSA established employee classification and regulated issues related to wages and child labor. The Family Medical Leave Act, Choice *A*, allows eligible employees in an organization unpaid leave time to care for themselves and family while protecting their jobs. The Davis-Bacon Act, Choice *C*, applies to contractors working on federally funded contracts over $2,000. The Walsh-Healy Act, Choice *D*, applies to contractors working on federally funded contracts over $10,000.

60. C: The Fishbone Diagram is a tool that seeks to analyze the primary causes of a problem. Ultimately, the diagram engages problems and investigates remedial efforts for improvement. In a group formation, a consensus is gathered to identify possible causes, such as employee performance, outdated technology, inefficient methods of production, or environmental implications. By isolating each factor, the diagram details organizational procedure to scientifically diagnose potential inefficiencies.

61. D: The training should be reported as time worked because this is considered a postliminary task per the Portal-to-Portal Act, which is an amendment to the Fair Labor Standards Act (FLSA). Because the training is job-related and was recommended by the supervisor, this time should be paid at the employee's normal rate of pay and, if necessary, the overtime rate.

Answer Explanations #3 | Error! No text of specified style in document.

62. C: The purpose of an employee evaluation is to give meaningful feedback that leads employees to set and achieve new goals. If employees are simply scored on whether they meet expectations, they may not be given the impetus they need to set and achieve high performance objectives. Choice *A* is not the best answer because, while HR should work to incorporate new technologies where appropriate, this is not the most meaningful change that the process needs. Choice *B* is not the best answer because evaluations that are too frequent can be just as harmful as evaluations that are too infrequent; they might increase employee stress, feelings of micromanagement, or feelings that evaluations are not very meaningful. Finally, Choice *D* is not the best answer because the back page of the evaluation only focuses on areas of improvement and doesn't recognize any positive areas of performance.

63. A: Commission pay is an example of a performance-based pay plan because it is used to motivate employees to perform at a higher level. Commissions incentivize sales by giving a percentage of each sale to the employee responsible for it. Choice *B*, base pay, is the basic pay the employee receives for performing their role. Choice *C*, shift pay, and Choice *D*, reporting pay, are both types of differential pay, which reward employees for performing work that is less than desirable.

64. C: Tommy should review the current number of days needed to fill a position with the new process against the number of days needed to fill a position with the previous process. In doing so, he is comparing the metrics between the current and baseline data to show if there has been an improvement in filling positions faster with the new process. Choices *A* and *D* are important pieces of information but are specific pieces of data at a particular point in time. The attrition rate and number of openings do not show a trend or the effectiveness of a process. Choice *B* is an excellent source of information because it is always important to gauge the satisfaction of employees regarding specific processes and programs; however, this data would not provide a reliable measurement of the turnaround time for filling new positions.

65. C: The acronym MSDS stands for Material Safety Data Sheets. These sheets are required to include any potential hazards of the product and how to work with the product safely. Material Safety Data Sheets are vital to having a complete and effective health and safety program.

66. B: OSHA is not responsible for providing fixed payments to employees who have suffered from an injury in the workplace. This function is provided by workers' compensation programs administered by organizations and their risk management departments.

67. C: Once an employee has received a verbal and then a written warning, the next step in a multilevel, progressive discipline schedule is usually a suspension, anywhere from one day to one month, depending on the company's policies. A second written warning, Choice *A*, is not usually effective after both a verbal and a written warning have already been issued. Making witnesses present their accusations face-to-face, Choice *B*, could make employees unwilling to come forward to report behavioral issues. Termination, Choice *D*, is usually a last resort when all other options have been exhausted.

68. A, C, D: Terminations should be conducted swiftly and face-to-face. The employee's coworkers should be gathered in a conference room to allow the employee privacy while cleaning out their personal belongings, and the employee's building and systems access should be deactivated during this process. There is no need to request a termination meeting, Choice *B*, though written separate agreements are sometimes provided during the termination.

69. A: Payroll functions are vital to the success of an organization and can be costly to maintain in-house. Organizations may make the decision to outsource this function to reduce costs and improve compliance and resource allocation.

70. C: Title VII of the Civil Rights Act of 1964 prohibits discrimination based on race, color, religion, sex, or national origin. The EEOC administers and oversees this law, along with the Age Discrimination in Employment Act of 1967.

71. C: Cross-cultural training allows employees to engage in opportunities that broaden their experience. This training allows for hearing about others' experiences so they can benefit from these ideas. Group assessments, Choice *A*, are a way to evaluate candidates in a group setting with exercises and sample issues to gauge how individuals respond to and resolve issues. Mentoring programs, Choice *B*, match two individuals for learning and growth opportunities. Cross-cultural training is a component of diversity and inclusion programs, Choice *D*.

72. C: An online employee handbook is a paperless method with an immediate notification system that minimizes waste yet keeps all employees informed.

73. B: The Fair Labor Standards Act of 1938 (FLSA) established standards for minimum wage and overtime pay, among other things. EEOC, Choice *A*, is the Equal Employment Opportunity Act, which prohibits workforce discrimination. Choice *C* is the McNamara-O'Hara Service Contract Act (SCA), which governs contractors and subcontractors. Choice *D* is part of the EEOC and applies to employers with 15 or more employees.

74. C: Paying female employees less than their male counterparts for the same work is a violation of EEOC rules, Choice *A*, that prohibit discrimination based on sex. Hiring a disparate number of people from one demographic, Choice *B*, is a violation of the Uniform Guidelines on Employee Selection Procedures (UGESP), and not paying for overtime, Choice *D*, violates the FLSA.

75. C: Non-discretionary benefits are benefits employers are legally mandated to provide, such as social security, Medicare, workers' compensation, unemployment insurance, unpaid family medical leave, and continuation of healthcare coverage. Choice *A* is incorrect because non-discretionary benefits are not related to group discounts that save money for the organization. Choice *B* is incorrect because non-discretionary benefits are not optional for companies; rather, they are mandated by law. Choice *D* is incorrect because non-discretionary benefits are not pre-tax benefits.

76. C: A thank-you note and a gift card for a job well done is an example of an employee recognition program. An end-of-year bonus, Choice *A*, is an example of additional compensation an employee receives as a one-time payment that does not become part of their base pay. A plaque given for 15 years of service to the organization, Choice *B*, is an example of a service award. Finally, a merit given during annual review time, Choice *D*, is an example of incentive pay given to employees for good performance.

77. A: I-9 forms must be kept on file for three years after the date of hire or for one year after the termination date, whichever is later. Choices *B*, *C*, and *D* are made-up terms.

78. C: There are no retention requirements with regard to COBRA records associated with family medical leave. However, there are Employment Retirement Income Security Act (ERISA) record retention requirements that must be considered. Choices *A*, *B*, and *D* should all be included in records associated with family medical leave.

Answer Explanations #3 | Error! No text of specified style in document.

79. C: Liz should categorize the applications by age and use the same categories as FLSA to ensure accuracy and compliance when assigning work tasks and scheduling hours. These age categories are under 14, ages 14 and 15, ages 16 and 17, and age 18 and over.

80. D: Employees hired at the age of 15 are not allowed to perform any work related to loading or unloading products to or from a conveyor line or a truck. Additionally, there are other limitations regarding the work employees aged 15 can perform. They may not operate power-driven lawn mowers, work with any hazardous materials, work with freezers or meat coolers, or conduct any work with a power-driven machine.

81. B: Once youths reach 18 years of age, they are now legal adults, and the FLSA child labor laws no longer apply. Work, hours, and wages would now be regulated by the standard FLSA regulations, not the child labor law regulations.

82. D: When evaluating the program, if Liz sees that there is a higher number of candidates who are over 18, she should consider updating the applicant requirements to specifically indicate that only individuals under the age of 18 will be considered. If an applicant is over the age of 18 at the time of application, the application will not be considered.

83. D: One of the strongest advantages of external sourcing for recruitment is that it supports building a diverse workforce and brings fresh perspectives to an organization. Although any recruitment should encourage connections with job seekers, external sourcing can be more costly than internal sourcing, making Choices *A* and *B* incorrect. Additionally, candidates who are sourced externally with no connection to an internal source will most likely not have familiarity with the organization and culture, making Choice *C* incorrect. This is a strength of internal sourcing.

84. B: Creating pockets of time during the day to cultivate positive interactions with colleagues is an effective way to work on interpersonal skills. The other options listed would be inappropriate and socially unacceptable responses to a performance review.

85. C: Business continuity plans are tools used to identify potential threats and their associated impacts. These plans establish procedures to handle interruptions, disruptions, and/or loss of business functions. Business continuity plans respond to a variety of crisis scenarios, such as loss of administrative capacities, a hack into the operating system, and threat of workplace violence. These plans must be observed by all staff to ensure the plan's effectiveness. If an employee does not comply, disciplinary measures should be enforced by the organization.

86. A: The ADA not only protects employees who have a physical medical condition but also applies protections to those with a mental medical condition. The ADA protections apply to every aspect of the job application procedure, employment, and promotions.

87. Compulsory: Compulsory arbitration is when the disputing parties are required by law to go through the arbitration process. Voluntary arbitration is when the disputing parties choose to undergo arbitration as a means to resolve the dispute.

88. B: Although the length of time an individual can be eligible for COBRA coverage will differ based on the circumstances, to comply, employers are required to provide an initial COBRA notice within 90 days of the individual's separation.

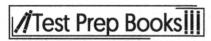

89. C: Duty of care is the term used to describe the legal and moral obligation HR is responsible for when employees are assigned to foreign countries. This duty of care extends to the families of the employee as well and can include safe housing, healthcare access, translation service, emergency care, and education.

90. A: The Age Discrimination in Employment Act of 1967 prohibits discrimination against anyone 40 years of age or older regarding hiring, promotions, wages, benefits, termination, and other actions. The Equal Employment Opportunity Commission administers and oversees this law, along with Title VII of the Civil Rights Act of 1964.

Answer Explanations #3 | Error! No text of specified style in document.

*/i*Test Prep Books|||

aPHR Practice Tests #4-#11

To keep the size of this book manageable, save paper, and provide a digital test-taking experience, the following tests can be found online:

- Practice Test #4
- Practice Test #5
- Practice Test #6
- Practice Test #7
- Practice Test #8
- Practice Test #9
- Practice Test #10
- Practice Test #11

Scan the QR code or go to this link to access it:

testprepbooks.com/bonus/aphr

The first time you access the tests, you will need to register as a "new user" and verify your email address.

If you have any issues, please email support@testprepbooks.com.

Dear aPHR Test Taker,

We would like to start by thanking you for purchasing this study guide for your aPHR exam. We hope that we exceeded your expectations.

Our goal in creating this study guide was to cover all of the topics that you will see on the test. We also strove to make our practice questions as similar as possible to what you will encounter on test day. With that being said, if you found something that you feel was not up to your standards, please send us an email and let us know.

We would also like to let you know about other books in our catalog that may interest you.

PHR

This can be found on Amazon: amazon.com/dp/1637757514

SHRM-CP

amazon.com/dp/1637758820

We have study guides in a wide variety of fields. If the one you are looking for isn't listed above, then try searching for it on Amazon or send us an email.

Thanks Again and Happy Testing!
Product Development Team
info@studyguideteam.com

FREE Test Taking Tips Video/DVD Offer

To better serve you, we created videos covering test taking tips that we want to give you for FREE. **These videos cover world-class tips that will help you succeed on your test.**

We just ask that you send us feedback about this product. Please let us know what you thought about it—whether good, bad, or indifferent.

To get your **FREE videos**, you can use the QR code below or email freevideos@studyguideteam.com with "Free Videos" in the subject line and the following information in the body of the email:

- • a. The title of your product
- • b. Your product rating on a scale of 1-5, with 5 being the highest
- • c. Your feedback about the product

If you have any questions or concerns, please don't hesitate to contact us at info@studyguideteam.com.

Thank you!

Made in United States
Orlando, FL
07 December 2024